N.L.

15

380

1/11/06

10.

Vagrant Writing

THEORY/CULTURE

General editors: Linda Hutcheon and Paul Perron

Vagrant Writing

Social and Semiotic Disorders in the English Renaissance

Barry Taylor

Staffordshire Polytechnic

University of Toronto Press
Toronto   Buffalo

First published in Canada and the United States by
University of Toronto Press 1991
Toronto and Buffalo

ISBN 0–8020–5885–X

© 1991 Barry Taylor

All rights reserved. No part of this publication may be
reproduced, stored in a retrieval system, or transmitted, in any
form, or by any means, electronic, mechanical, photocopying,
recording or otherwise, without the prior permission, in writing,
from the publisher.

Canadian Cataloging in Publication Data

Taylor, Barry
Vagrant writing: social and semiotic disorders
in the English Renaissance

(Theory/culture; 9)
Includes bibliographical references and index.
ISBN 0–8020–5885–X

1. English literature – Early modern, 1500–1700 –
History and criticism.   2. Literature and society –
England – History – 16th century.   3. Literature
and society – England – History – 17th century.
4. Semiotics and literature.   5. Renaissance –
England.   1. Title.

PR418.S64T38   1991   820.9′003   C91–094434–2

Printed and bound in Great Britain by
Billing and Sons Ltd, Worcester

To Bill and Kathleen Taylor

Contents

Acknowledgements

I owe a great deal to the following people who have contributed in various ways to the development of this book over a number of years: the participants – students and staff – in the MA programmes in Renaissance Studies and English Renaissance Literature at the University of Sussex (1981–2), in particular Chris Baxter, Jonathan Dollimore, Alan Sinfield and Lizzie Thynne; Alan Fair, Alison Light, Eric Woods, and fellow members of the Sussex Graduate Critical Theory Workshop (1981–5), my Ph.D. supervisor, Peter Stallybrass, always generous and supportive, both personally and intellectually, and Geoff Hemstedt, who took over that role at a late stage and was his usual involved and critically stimulating self; Peter Baldwin and Elaine Lyons, Liam Greenslade, Yvonne Tasker, David Cairns and Roger Lowman and Marion Read of the English Department at King Alfred's College, Winchester, all of whom have been extraordinarily generous in making word-processing facilities (and their time and patience) available to me.

At Sussex, much of the groundwork for the book was laid in conversation with Paul Brown, and despite the subsequent divergence of our paths, it is still in a sense to him that *Vagrant Writing* is argumentatively and affectionately addressed. More recently, I am particularly indebted to Malcolm Evans and Duncan Webster for their critical and sympathetic engagement, and to my brother, Steve Taylor, who has known when I have needed encouragement. Jackie Jones at Harvester Wheatsheaf has been a patient and consistently supportive editorial presence.

I, and the book, owe more than can be stated here to Christine Bridgwood; it is for her that I want it to be good enough. My parents have worked hard over the years to assure my, and my brothers', education; in that sense this book is also the fruit of their labours, and I dedicate it to them, with gratitude and love.

And therefore the Psalmist sayeth, of the reprobate and unthankful sort: I have let them loose even according to the desires of their hartes, and they shall wander in their own inventions.

George Gascoigne, *The Needles Eye*

... then one realises that what was chased off limits, the wandering outcast of linguistics, has indeed never ceased to haunt language as its primary and most intimate possibility. Then something which was never spoken and which is nothing other than writing itself as the origin of language writes itself ...

Jacques Derrida, *Of Grammatology*

Looke not, generous Reader (for such I write to) for more in the few following lines then a plaine and simple verity, unadorned at all with eloqution or Rhetoricall phrase, glosses fitter perhaps to be set upon silken and thynne paradoxicall semblances than appertaining to the care of who desires to lay downe a naked and unmasked Trueth.

Henry Reynolds, *Mythomystes*

Introduction: Vagrancy as Writing/Vagrant Writing

'Going back from the Lord, they are written and registered in the earth.'

St Jerome

For the very end of myths is to immobilise the world; they must suggest and mimic a universal order which has fixated once and for all the hierarchy of possessions.

Roland Barthes[1]

The discourse of the vagrant

Thomas Harman's *A Caveat for Common Cursitors* (1566) is an early example of the Elizabethan pamphlet campaign dedicated to rooting out and exposing to justice 'all vagrants and sturdy vagabonds, as passeth through and by all parts of this famous isle, most idly and wickedly' (p. 81).[2] The vagrant or sturdy vagabond presents a number of interrelated challenges to the stable social order – real or imagined – of Commonwealth, in whose name Harman and his fellow pamphleteers write. Harman provides us with a synechdocic representation of that order – of 'naturally' fixed hierarchical relations structured around local manorial centres – in his eulogy of his dedicatee the Countess of Shrewsbury's charitable practices:

I well, by good experience understanding and considering your most tender, pitiful, gentle and noble nature – not only having a vigilant and merciful eye to your poor, indigent and feeble parishioners; yea, not only in the parish where your honour most happily doth dwell, but also in others environing or near adjoining to the same; as also abundantly pouring out daily your

ardent and bountiful charity upon all such as cometh for relief
into your luckly gates. (p. 81)

The legitimate social order is what falls within the panoptical sweep of
the aristocrat's 'vigilant and merciful eye'. The vigilant eye questions
and judges the subjects within its range, sifting the deserving from the
undeserving, the feeble from the idle, the local from the interloper,
constituting the parish as a space of definition and discipline. The
merciful eye revises the disciplinary structure into one of benevolence
– the proximity and familiarity which allow the supervisory gaze
to function are also the conditions in which social relations may
appear as a natural order of affective bonds. The supervisory gaze
is recast as one of parental concern, and the economic power of the
aristocrat figures as the spontaneous overflow – beyond any economy
of calculation – of a natural source: a spring 'abundantly pouring out
daily its ardent and bountiful charity'. The topographical 'frame' of
the parish allows a disciplinary structure of fixed and closely regulated
social relations to be represented as an unmediated expression of
natural laws and affinities.

For Harman, the vagrant's primary violation of this order is his or
her assumption of a false identity, by presenting the appearance of a
member of the indigent or helpless poor:

> ... the abominable, wicked and detestable behaviour of all
> these rowsey, ragged rabblement of rakehells that – under
> the pretence of great misery, diseases, and other innumerable
> calamities which they feign – through great hypocrisy do win
> and gain great alms in all places where they wil[il]y wander, to
> the utter deluding of the good givers. (p. 81)

The vagrant's deliberate confusion of categories – erasing the
distinction between the sturdy and the deserving poor – initiates
a process in which the wandering of the vagabond entails a vagrancy
of the signifier – or the surface appearances of social being – from
its ground in the signified – the 'natural' hierarchical ordering of
rank and status. For commentators such as Harman, the result is
a pervasive semiotic destabilisation, an uncoupling of appearances
from reality:

> I have of late years gathered a great suspicion that all should
> not be well, and, as the proverb saith: 'Something lurk and lay
> hid that did not plainly appear'. (p. 82)

The vagrant inhabits a counter-order of 'dissimulation and ... scelerous secrets' (p. 82) which she maintains and protects, according to Harman, by three principal modes of semiotic larceny: disguise, or the wearing of false apparel; the carrying of forged letters and patents; and the use of an impenetrable criminal dialect, or, in Harman's phrase, an 'unlawful language'.

As we have seen, Harman places disguise at the root of the vagrant's transgressions. A powerful example of this false reproduction of the signs of illness and disability which mark the deserving poor is offered in Harman's encounter with a 'counterfeit crank':

> So coming out at a sudden, and beholding his ugly and irksome attire, his loathsome and horrible countenance, it made me in a marvellous perplexity what to think of him, whether it were feigned or truth. (p. 111)

The undoing of the fundamental category distinction between the true and the feigned produces a crisis of thinking, a disjunction between the world's appearance and the established categorical system through which the subject orders it into perceptual coherence, and into meaning. The disguising of the vagrant tips the world towards illegibility.

In its more sophisticated forms – those of the cony-catcher or itinerant con man – the disguising and other ruses of the vagrant begin to assume the status of a self-conscious art form, and the satisfactions of the practitioner appear, correspondingly, to be as much aesthetic as pecuniary. As one of the cony-catchers in Robert Greene's first pamphlet states, reflecting on some of his colleagues' recent 'drifts':

> In faith, masters, these things are prettily done – common sleights, expressing no deep reach of wit. And I wonder men are so simple to be so beguiled. I would fain see some rare artificial feat indeed, that some admiration and fame might ensue the doing thereof ... ye shall hear, my boys, within a day or two, that I will accomplish a rare strategem indeed, of more value than forty of yours, and when it is done it shall carry some credit with it! (p. 236)

In his 'wit' and inventiveness, his cultivation of the 'rare artificial feat', and his expectations of 'admiration and fame', the cony-catcher represents dissimulation as a transgressive art – a corruption of the inventive and mimetic faculties which inform the 'legitimate' arts. More specifically, as an itinerant, a mimic, an illusionistic manipulator of apparel and plausible words, the cony-catcher is the criminal *alter ego* of the 'true' actor. The cony-catcher as actor, expert in the orchestration of significant details into a telling representation of social types, is sharply portrayed by the author of *The Defence of Cony-Catchers*:

> Is there not here resident about London, a crew of terrible hacksters in the habit of gentlemen, well apparelled, and yet some wear boots for want of stockings, with a lock worn of their left ear for their mistress's favour, his rapier *à la revolto*, his poynado pendant ready for the stab, and cavalierst like a warlike magnifico? (p. 361)

The hackster operates in a mimetic mode which offers the reader (or the informed witness) the same pleasures of amused recognition which are aroused by the satirical impersonations of the boy's acting companies or of Jonsonian comedy. Indeed, this passage in *The Defence* succeeds one in which the author turns the charge of cony-catching against Robert Greene, playwright and anti-vagrant pamphleteer. In doing so, the writer explictly associates the social being and morality of the cony-catcher with that of the 'legitimate' actor:

> But now sir by your leave a little, what if I should prove you a coney-catcher, Master R.G. .... . Ask the Queen's Players, if you sold them not Orlando Furioso for twenty nobles, and when they were in the country sold the same play to the Lord Admiral's Men, for as much more .... . But I hear when this was objected, that you made this excuse: that there was no more faith to be held with players, than with them that valued faith at the price of a feather: for as they were comedians to act, so the actions of their lives were chameleon-like, that they were uncertain, variable, time-pleasers, men that measured honesty by profit, and that regarded their authors not by desert, but by necessity of time. (pp. 360–1)

Greene's excuse, as reported, is that if he has acted like a vagabond con-man, then his victims are con-men themselves. Whether we ascribe it to Greene or his accuser, the description of the actors here duplicates precisely the terms of the discourse on vagrant criminality: faithlessness, a chameleon-like instability of identity, a submission of will and conscience to the flux of contingencies, a subordination of honesty to profit. The author of the *Defence* has his own polemical reasons for collapsing the categorical distinctions between the vagrant and a variety of 'legitimate' social and professional groups, but the association of vagrancy with acting develops the parallel in greater point-by-point detail than other instances, and also dovetails with a more generalised discourse against acting and theatricality which is not determined by this specific polemical context:

> It ys nowe publyshed . . . and set foorth . . . that . . . all Fencers Bearewardes Comon Players in Enterludes & Minstrels, not belonging to any Baron of this Realme or towardes any other honorable Personage of greater Degree . . . whiche . . . shal wander abroade and have not Lycense of two Justices of the Peace at the leaste . . . wher and in what Shier they shall happen to wander . . . shalbee taken adjudged and deemed Roges Vacaboundes and Sturdy Beggars, intended of by this present Act. (Act 16 Eliz., c.5 s.5)[3]

As this shows, the itinerant actor falls within the purview of the Elizabethan Vagrancy Acts, and is subject to a licensing procedure which, as we will see shortly, is closely allied to the issuing of passports and certificates by the authorities to other categories of 'legitimate' vagrant. The wandering of the actor is allowable, in other words, as long as he carries with him written evidence that he is still located within the topography of subordination, despite his geographical dislocation.

Antitheatrical discourses of the period suggest, however, that even when the actor is licensed there is another, more fundamental association between acting and vagrancy, which derives from a causal relation between stage-plays and *idleness*: idleness being identified as the enabling precondition of vagrancy:

> They [stage-plays] are the ordinary places for vagrant persons, masterless men, thieves . . . coney-catchers, contrivers of treason and other idle and dangerous persons to meet together and to make their matches to the great displeasure of Almighty God and the hurt and annoyance of her Majesty's people . . . .
> They maintain idleness in such persons as have no vocation,

and draw apprentices and other servants from their ordinary
works and all sorts of people from the resort unto sermons
and other Christian exercises to the great hindrance of trades
and profanation of religion established by her Highness within
this realm.[4]

In this complaint to the Privy Council, the Lord Mayor and Aldermen
of the City accuse the theatre of both creating and maintaining
idleness: creating it by seducing the impressionable subject from
the disciplinary 'theatres' of work and religious observance into
a disorderly, heterogeneous anti-community of inveterate idlers;
maintaining it by generating an order of representation which is
not regulated by or anchored to any prescriptive moral discourse:

> . . . neither in polity nor in religion are they to be suffered in
> a Christian commonwealth, specially being of that frame and
> matter as usually they are, containing nothing but profane
> fables, lascivious matters, cozening devices, and scurrilous
> behaviours, which are so set forth as that they move wholly
> to imitation and not to the avoiding of those faults and vices
> which they represent.[5]

What is significant here is the distinction suggested between the
'matter' of the representation and the way it is 'framed' or 'set forth'.
The distinction suggests that however dangerous the matter, there
exists the possibility – which stage-plays evade – of framing it in a
way that would make the whole representation – matter plus frame –
acceptable to authority. That representation would be one which set
forth the matter so as to move the spectator 'to the avoiding of those
faults and vices which they represent'. The acceptable representation,
in other words, would be one which enclosed the dubious matter
within the terms of an orthodox moral/theological discourse; which
submitted the economy of mimesis to a disciplinary economy of
exemplarity.

For the City authorities, the stage-play involves a threefold
evasion of the order and discipline which compose a 'Christian
commonwealth': into the suburban 'Liberties' where the theatres
have deliberately established themselves outside the jurisdiction of
the City; into the chaos of idleness, outside the disciplinary regimes
of vocation and the master; and into a space of representation – of
'imitation' – which refuses the disciplinary closure of the *exemplum*.
Imitation without discipline appears from the viewpoint of authority as

a process in which the lawlessness of the unregulated representation reproduces itself contagiously in the lawless behaviour of the imitative spectator – 'they [the plays] impress the very quality and corruption of manners which they represent'. This fear of a constitutional indiscipline of theatrical mimesis – the fear of a vagrancy of the signifier from the disciplinary enclosure of the signified – will be the subject of my discussion of Jonson's *Cynthia's Revels* in the final chapter of this book.

Another of the principal charges laid against actors in the period is that their occupation allows them to assume illicitly the appearance of their social superiors. In the moral play *Histriomastix*, written at an unknown date in Elizabeth's reign, a group of tradesmen led by the shakily self-educated Posthaste decide to abandon their vocations and form a company of actors:

> Belch   I pray sir, what titles have travelling players?
> Posthaste Why, *proper fellows*, they play lords and kings.[6]

Here, the mimetic domain of the play is an imaginary space in which fantasies of self-advancement, of an overturning of the fixed social order of proper identities and entitlements, may be granted. The humour at this point in the play, as Philip Edwards suggests,[7] depends upon the contrast between this compensatory fantasy, safely projected into the special arena of dramatic imitation, and the ragged reality of the tradesmen's actual social condition. This same effect reappears in Posthaste's enjoyment of Lord Mavortius's hospitality on the engagement of the company to perform in the nobleman's house: 'We have caroused like kings . . . . A gentleman's a gentleman that hath a clean shirt on, with some learning, and so have I.'[8] In one sense, this is merely a playful assumption and exposure of the semiotic constitution of social rank, its significance safely enclosed by the intoxication and euphoria of the moment. However, this moment is also that when the tradesmen are about to secure a new status as Lord Mavortius's licensed players, and so embark upon a process of social advancement in the 'real' world beyond the fantasies of the play-space and the taproom.

The next act of the play shows the actors consolidating their position as Lord Mavortius's liveried men, but it also reveals how their social elevation is part of a wider and more fundamental social process – the erosion of customary structures of social authority, rank and dependency by the curtailing of feudal hospitality. One of

Lord Mavortius's old servants, who has been dismissed with most of his fellows, complains:

> For service this is savage recompense.
> Your fathers bought lands and maintained men.
> You sell your lands, and scarce keep rascal
> boys,
> Who ape-like jet in guarded coats.

Lord Mavortius replies:

> I keep a tailor, coachman and a cook.
> The rest for their board-wages may go look.
> A thousand pound a year will so be saved
> For revelling, and banquetting and plays.[9]

Within the terms of the play's own moral discourse, the break-up of the feudal household results from the arbitrary whim of the aristocrat, and his dedication to self-gratification over social duty. It is this dislocation, at the anchoring point of the social order, between personal desire and the obligations of 'degree' which thrusts the traditional servant from the protection of his customary position into the uncertainties of wage-labour ('board-wages'), and confirms the actors in their 'illegitimate' displacement from their natural vocations into a degree which is not properly theirs.[10] As the university writer Philomusus complains of professional players in the Second Part of *The Return from Parnassus*:

> Vile world, that lifts them up to high degree
> And treads us down in grovelling misery.
> England affords these glorious vagabonds,
> That carried erst their fardels on their backs,
> Coursers to ride on through the gazing streets,
> Sooping it in their glaring satin suits
> And pages to attend their masterships.
> With mouthing words that better wits have framed
> They purchase lands, and now Esquires are
> named. (ll.1, 916–28)[11]

The nobleman of *Histriomastix* sells his lands in order to support the low-born player, who returns here to purchase land and confirm his new gentlemanly status. The complaint against the decline in feudal 'hospitality' mounted in *Histriomastix* represents the point at which the discourse against actorly imitation intersects with discourses on a general collapse of the customary hierarchy of social degree, where the dramatic enactment of social mobility becomes an achieved social fact. At the beginning of *Histriomastix* the appropriation of the signifiers of high degree – titles and apparel – was a fantasy contained within the illusionary space of the drama. In the *Parnassus* play the social world of London in the 1590s has itself become a theatrical space – 'the gazing streets' – where the supremacy of the signifier is staged, where the signs of status are no longer anchored to the natural determinations of blood and birth, and the vagabond lords it over the gentleman writer.

Both the vagrant and the actor embody a double principle of evasion: a physical wandering from the places (the parish, the social rank) where identity and relationship are constituted and fixed; and an uncoupling of the 'natural' relationship between signifier and signified, the appearance and the reality of social position and status. The physical wandering makes possible the vagrancy of the signifier, because the geography of hundred and parish is also a topography of supervision, a classificatory grid within which the true identity of the subject may be 'read' by reference to the origin of the birthplace. By wandering from the locality where the inherited 'degree' of the subject is recorded and publicly recognised, the vagrant and the actor open out a domain of *imitatio* or fictionality in which the 'natural' ligatures of social and semiotic order are wilfully decomposed.

* * *

This relationship between a decomposition of established social relations and the dissolution of the sign's internal economy is reiterated in Harman's other examples of the vagrant's 'scelerous secrets'. Harman's Rogues

> will carry a certificate or passport about them from some Justice of the Peace, with his hand and seal unto the same, how he hath been whipped and punished for a vagabond according to the laws of this realm, and that he must return to T—, where

he was born or last dwelt, by a certain day limited in the same, which shall be a good long day. And all this feigned, because without fear they would wickedly wander, and will renew the same where or when it pleaseth them; for they have of their affinity that can write and read. (p. 97)

The certificate or passport is a piece of writing which stands in for the 'natural' relation between subject and place of birth which the vagrant has broken, an artificial means of resealing the relation of person to origin. Such official written documents, throughout Harman's account, supplement the law of fixed 'natural' relations – of place and hierarchy – administered by the local power of the Justices. As a form of writing, however, the passport, warrant or patent is open to the force of reiteration and therefore to falsification. For Harman the unmediated supervisory gaze of the Justice and other officials over the local topography of 'places' is the original form of the law, authenticated by its emergence from the natural law of degree. The vagrant's forged papers, therefore, represent a subversion of this natural order of identities, relations and communication through a departure into the domain of the supplementary, the artificial, of writing. In this and its other contrivances, vagrancy opens up a dangerous topography of writing – in its broader Derridean sense – in which the supposedly natural economy of the sign is replaced by an ungrounded, 'unlawful' vagrancy of the signifier.

As actor, as forger, as con-man, the vagrant in his wandering threatens the associated orders of the Commonwealth and stable signification. The notorious 'canting' or professional language of the cony-catcher and other vagrants is, then, only one particularly notable element in this wider counter-order of writing. In fact, the 'unlawful language' (Harman) of the vagrant is perhaps the most readily recuperable of his semiotic transgressions. While the pamphleteer Harrison can describe it as a language 'without all order and reason', canting is in effect little more than an alternative nomenclature which substitutes its own terms in a directly decodable fashion for those of the dominant language, and supplies its own new terms for the taxonomical categories of the criminal subculture. The commentators confront this sub-language not as a crisis of signification, but as a challenge of translation which is operable within the terms of the orthodox economy of the sign. Harman offers such a translation in the following dialogue:

The upright cove canteth to the rogue: The
upright man speaketh to the rogue.

UPRIGHT MAN. Bene lightmans to thy quarroms! In
what libken hast thou libbed in this darkmans,
whether in a libbege or in the strummel?

Good-morrow to thy body! In what house hast
thou lain in all night, whether in a bed or in
the straw?

ROGUE. I couched a hogshead in a skipper this
darkmans.

I laid me down to sleep in a barn this
night. (p. 148)

Harman's evident pleasure in decoding the 'pelting speech' of the
vagrants reveals that this is one area of semiotic disorder where
a reassertion of mastery by the users of the dominant language
is possible. The radical challenge of the vagrant to the conceptual
order of the sign is to be located somewhere other than in this
simple enciphering of the terms and categories of 'ordinary' language:
namely in the unfixing of the 'natural' relation between signifier
and signified in the vagrant's delinquent arts of impersonation and
forgery.

It is this disarticulation of the sign – and the disintegration of fixed
social identities which attends it – which is countered by the actions
of the authorities after the discovery and apprehension of a vagrant.
Harman recounts the arrest by a printer of a 'counterfeit crank' who
has run through a series of false identities:

The printer . . . rebuked him for his beastly behaviour, and told
him of his false feigning, willed him to confess it, and ask
forgiveness. He perceived him to know his deep dissimulation,
relented and confessed all his deceit; and so remaining in the
Counter three days, was removed to Bridewell, where he was
stripped stark naked, and his ugly attire put upon him before
the masters thereof, who wondered greatly at his dissimulation.
For which offence he stood upon the pillory in Cheapside, both
in his ugly and handsome attire, and after that went in the mill
while his ugly picture was a-drawing; and then was whipped at
a cart's tail through London, and his displayed banner carried
before him unto his own door, and so back to Bridewell again,

and there remained for a time and at length let at liberty, on
that condition he would prove an honest man, and labour truly
to get his living. And his picture remaineth in Bridewell for a
monument. (pp. 117–18)[12]

The pillory and the procession are the stages of a juridical theatre
which counteracts the semiotic larcenies of the vagrant-actor. In
this theatre of authority, the deceptive significations of the vagrant
are disarticulated and laid bare to the gaze of supervision, a process
which is then fixed and published in the 'demystified' representations
of the banner and the portrait. The procession from the pillory to the
vagrant's 'own door' and on to Bridewell is an exemplary reassertion
of the official topographical relation between the subject's dwelling- or
birthplace and the *loci* of authority: the geography of order which the
vagrant has escaped in his wanderings. The whole judicial process
restores the vagrant to his proper place within the official regimes
of visibility and exemplarity – an *arrest* of the mobility and duplicity
which, as Robert Greene complains, render the vagrant invisible:

> If I should spend many sheets in deciphering their shifts, it were
> frivolous, in that they be many, and full of variety, for every day
> they invent new tricks and such quaint devices as are secret, yet
> passing dangerous, that if a man had Argus' eyes, he could scant
> pry into the bottom of their practices. (p. 174)

The pillory is a scene both of punishment and deciphering, where
the vagrant is at once demobilised and translated from the semiotic
register of the cipher to that of the *exemplum*:

> This counterfeit crank, now view and behold,
> Placed in pillory, as all may well see,
> This was he, as you heard the tale told,
> Before recorded with great subtlety,
> Abused many with his impiety,
> His loathsome attire, in most ugly manner,
> Was through London carried with displayed
> banner. (p. 153)

With this ballad, Harman's book concludes by marking its own
contribution – as a demystifying 'glass' – to the process of judicial
deciphering. As such it joins those other glasses or mirrors which
we will encounter in the following pages whose function is to reflect

the true order of hierarchically disposed Being beneath the illusory play of appearances:

> Thus I conclude my bold beggars' book,
> That all estates most plainly may see,
> As in a glass well polished to look,
> Their double demeanour in each degree;
> Their lives, their language, their names as
> they be,
> That with their warning their minds may be
> warmed
> To amend their misdeeds, and so live
> unharmed. (p. 153)

The restoration of a clear vision which sees things 'as they be' is made possible by the rediscovery of the 'true' ground of social being in the hierarchical field of 'estates' and 'degree'. The exemplary representations of the pillory and the pamphlet bring the vagrant back within a regime of the sign whose transparency is predicated on the social regime of the Commonwealth.

* * *

As we have seen, for sixteenth-century commentators the rise of the professional actor epitomises a process of social transformation which is seen as converting the natural order of Commonwealth into one where identities and relationships have been subjected to a metamorphic agency which is found in its quintessential form in the imitative process of theatrical representation:

> ... there is such a confuse mingle mangle of apparell in Ailgna
> [England], and such preposterous excesse therof, as every one
> is permitted to flaunt it out, in what apparell he lust himselfe,
> or can get by anie kind of meanes. So that it is verie hard to
> knowe, who is noble, who is worshipfull, who is a gentleman,
> who is not.[13]

What Philip Stubbes laments here, in pursuing the relationship between the disorderliness of the theatre and social disorder in general, is a collapse of the order of Commonwealth into a state of illegibility, in which the relationship between the essence and the accidents (the signified and signifiers) of social rank is no longer naturally determined, and where in consequence the knowledge of social agents and relations is no longer a spontaneous act of recognition, but involves a hazardous labour of *interpretation*. As Jean E. Howard comments on this passage:

> To counter such dramatistic play, Stubbes evokes an essentially feudal notion of identity as determined by the estate or social position to which one had been born. People may be seen as actors, certainly, but as actors in a play scripted by God, in which individual parts are pre-ordained and fixed.[14]

A play scripted by God: that play, as the Book of Nature adapted to the theatre of society, as the temporal enactment of the Word, is the Commonwealth. The conflict between that prescriptive ideal social order and the illegibility of social transformation is dramatised by sixteenth-century writers as a struggle between Word and anti-Word, between the stability of the natural sign and the 'mingle mangle' of a vagrant semiosis. As the antitheatrical discourses suggest in their dual attack against the actor's vagrancy and against the vagrancy of theatrical mimesis, within the terms of the Commonwealth imaginary it is not possible to disentangle the semiotic force of social disorder from the social force of a disorderly semiotics.

It is at this chiasmic intersection that *Vagrant Writing* pitches its enquiry. In doing so, its aim is not to celebrate a putative oppositional politics of the signifier, with the vagrant, the cony-catcher, the gipsy, the harlot and the itinerant actor as its transgressive activists. The demonising of transgressive individuals within the discourses of Commonwealth is precisely a strategy of displacement which seeks to contain an anxiety – at once volubly expressed and forcefully disavowed – that the sources of disorder are to be located systemically, in an internal dislocation and divagation of order and authority themselves. In short, what the ideologists of Commonwealth confront is not so much a transgressive mobilisation of the signifier as a structurally motivated crisis of the sign *in toto*: a release of the energies of differentiation and dissemination which threatens to expose as imaginary both the immutable Signified of the Word, and the order of Commonwealth which it underwrites. We can watch a version of this process being played out on a reduced scale if we return to Thomas Harman, and to the second edition of his *Caveat for Common Cursitors*.

The vagrancy of discourse

The writer against vagrancy claims for his own words a plainness and transparency which oppose and unmask the duplicitous significations of the vagrant:

> Let it suffice ye then in this, to read the simple true discourses of such as have by extraordinary cunning and treachery been deceived, and remembering their subtle means there, and sly practices here, be prepared against the reaches of any such companions. (p. 236)

As an aid to deciphering, the pamphlet's (here Robert Greene's) 'simple true discourses' are intended to represent a restoration of the 'natural' economy of the sign. Greene's short narratives of cony-catching are presented as episodes in a continuing battle between 'outward simplicity on the one side and cunning close treachery on the other' (p. 245), or in other words between those who act in the faith that the relationship between appearances and reality is stable and transparent, and those – like the following 'artificial coney-catcher' – who exploit this innocent reading of the world's surfaces by contriving to uncouple appearance from reality, signifier from signified:

> These kind words, delivered with such honest outward show, caused the young men, whose thoughts were ever free from any other opinion than to be as truly and plainly dealt withal as themselves meant, accepted his offer . . . (p. 247)

The pamphleteer's aim is prophylactically to enclose the deceptively 'kind words' of the con man with his own authentically kind warnings, which work to restore the univocal discourse of 'true and plain' dealing.

However, despite this necessary commitment to the idea of stable and transparent language, a pamphleteer such as Harman may find that his own work is subject to a constitutional vagrancy of the word which renders even the central term of his own discourse unstable:

> Although, good reader, I write in plain terms – and not so plainly as truly – concerning the matter, meaning honestly to all men, and wish them as much good as to mine own heart, yet, as there hath been, so there is now, and hereafter will be curious

heads to find faults. Wherefore I thought it necessary, now at this second impression to acquaint thee with a great fault, as some taketh it (but none as I mean it) calling these vagabonds *cursitors* in the entitling of my book, as runners or rangers about the country, derived of this Latin word *curro* . . . Who is so ignorant by these days as knoweth not the meaning of a *vagabond*? . . . Yet this plain name *vagabond* is derived, as others be, of Latin words, and now use makes it common to all men. But let us look back four hundred years sithence, and let us see whether this plain word *vagabond* was used or no. I believe not: and why? Because I read of no such name in the old statutes of this realm, unless it be in the margin of the book, or in the table, which in the collecting and printing was set in. But these were then the common names of these lewd loiterers: *faitours, Roberdsmen, draw-latches,* and *valiant-beggars.* If I should have used such words, or the same order of writing as this realm used in King Henry the Third or Edward the First's time – Oh, what a gross barbarous fellow have we here! His writing is both homely and dark, that we had need to have an interpreter. Yet then it was very well, and in short season a great change we see. (p. 87)

Harman begins this epistle to the second edition of his pamphlet with the conventional avowal of the plainness of his words and the honesty of his meaning – a claimed integrity of discourse which allows the simplicity of the heart's intentions to speak without distortion through the clarity of a plain style.[15] Despite this intention, however, Harman has been accused by some readers of the first edition of wilfully wandering from the sure ground of vernacular plainness and clarity – where a vagabond is a vagabond – into the obscure regions of linguistic innovation and Latinate artificiality where a vagabond, according to Harman, is a *cursitor*.

Harman's defence of this usage does not start – as it might have – from the acknowledgement that *cursitor* is required by his taste for alliteration, which here also has the functional justification of supplying a vivid and readily memorised title for his work. In other words, the use of *cursitor* is not determined by the 'natural' economy of plain sense and style, but by the demands of market visibility, served by an aptitude for the artifices of acoustic patterning. To admit in this way the alliterative force of *cursitor* would be to acknowledge a rhetorical dimension of discourse which has no place in Harman's ideology of plain style and transparent meaning – a dimension in which words exert a persuasive force through a variety of 'artificial' patternings and devices, rather than effacing themselves before the self-declarative immediacy of the truth.

Harman, of course, will not defend his contested usage by admitting his departure from the community of plain-speakers into the company of verbal contrivers and double-talkers, because this would be to erode the categorical distinction between his own discourse and that of the cony-catcher. Instead of defending *cursitor* as an allowable contrivance, Harman asserts that it is in fact a 'plain name'. In order to justify this claim, he embarks upon the historical and philological excursus I have just quoted, whose implications, despite his own intentions, are as damaging to the ideology of transparent language as the avowal of rhetoric would have been.

Harman's defence of *cursitor* rests in his assertion that 'the plain name *vagabond*' which his opponents favour was itself originally a new-fangled Latinate interloper into the community of established vernacular terms. If, he suggests, we look to the place where such terms are established, fixed and authorised – in 'the old statutes of this realm' – we will find that 'vagabond' (like those it names) has at its first emergence only a marginal and supererogatory status. Conversely, the authorised vernacular terms of that period – *'faitours, Roberdsmen, draw-latches,* and *valiant-beggars'* – have become by the sixteenth century so estranged from common usage that 'we . . . need to have an interpreter'.

This justification of Harman's rhetorical practice opens up a history of words and their meanings in which the categorical distinctions between the plain and the obscure, the customary and the new-fangled, the natural and the artificial, the vernacular and the alien tongue are dissolved.[16] History transforms the alien term into a plain and common one, while the 'homely' word becomes 'dark' and requires translation. From this perspective, the relationship between the verbal signifier and its signified is not essentially and transhistorically fixed, but migratory and metamorphic, determined within a grid of historical and cultural co-ordinates which is in a state of perpetual reconfiguration. The significance of this episode of linguistic debate for the wider argument of the present book is that it shows Harman being pushed by the exigencies of rhetorical practice towards an unwitting dissolution of the categorical distinction which founds the 'official' linguistic and social ideologies of his text – the distinction between the delinquent signifying practices of the vagrant and his own 'lawful' writing.

For Harman, an ideology of univocal discourse is an essential element in his defence of 'true and plain' dealing. His vision of social order and justice is grounded in a conception of the social domain in which identities and relationships are established and organised by natural law, and 'true and plain dealing' is the direct and undistorted reproduction of that divinely implanted paradigm of social relations within the particular actions and interactions of specific individuals and communities. The function of language – and of other semiotic systems such as apparel – within such a godly and lawful social order is to be a transparent medium through which that paradigm of identity and relationship is articulated within and between consciousnesses. By subordinating itself to the eternal order of the Truth, language renders itself continuous with the Word by which that order was created.

As I have already indicated, I shall refer to the ideal social order which I have just sketched by the name of Commonwealth. In the sixteenth century that term is used to legitimate both the policies of governments and the proposals of their critics, but in both cases, the vision of an ideal hierarchical order, stabilised by its continuity with natural law and the Word, is the mediating term between the domain of metaphysical certainties and that of worldly praxis. In both cases too, an ethic of plain dealing and plain speaking is an essential part of the ideology.

However, the crucial difference between the governmental and oppositional articulations of the discourse of Commonwealth is that governments have the legislative, juridical and institutional means to activate Commonwealth as the ideological basis of the mechanisms of social discipline and control. The Tudor and Elizabethan Vagrancy Acts are examples of legislation which attempt to enforce a social and economic discipline founded in the prescriptive paradigm of Commonwealth, a tendency which is visible throughout the period's social and economic legislation, most notably in the 1563 Statute of Artificers, with its attempt to reassert the principles of guild organisation, the local economy, and patriarchal discipline against the disintegrative forces of the developing capitalist organisation of production, the increasing power of credit within the economy, and of inflation and unemployment.

In claiming to regulate the socio-economic domain in conformity with the paradigm of Commonwealth, governments also claim a legitimating continuity between the Word (which underwrites the paradigm) and the discourses of orthodox knowledge and belief, of individual and social discipline, which are circulated through statutes and proclamations, homilies and legal judgments, school-book and prayer-book. The induction of the loyal subject into the disciplines of Commonwealth is consequently also a process of assimilation to a regime of orthodox knowledges – the order of officially endorsed and divinely sanctioned truths – and to the speech community of lawful discourse. We can see this interdependency of the disciplinary and the epistemological-discursive dimensions of the socialisation process laid out in its ideal form in the 1562 *Homily of the State of Marriage*:

> The word of Almighty God doth testify and declare whence the original beginning of matrimony cometh, and why it is ordained.
>
> It is instituted of God, to the intent that man and woman should live lawfully in a perpetual friendship, to bring forth fruit, and to avoid fornication. By which means a good conscience might be preserved on both parties, in bridling the corrupt inclinations of the flesh within the limits of honesty: for God hath strictly forbidden all whoredom and uncleanness, and hath from time to time taken grievous punishment of this inordinat lust, as all ages and stories have declared.
>
> Furthermore, it is also ordained, that the Church of God and his kingdom might by this kind of life be conserved and enlarged; not only in that God giveth children by his blessing, but also that they be brought up in the parents godly, in the knowledge of God's word; that thus the knowledge of God and true religion might be delivered by succession from one to another, that finally many might enjoy that everlasting immortality.[17]

Matrimony, as sanctioned by Church and State, establishes the family as the first station in the subject's induction into the ideological order of Commonwealth. In the first place, matrimony contains and regulates the sexual energies of the body, directing them beyond personal gratification to the uses of the social body, through the reproduction of the godly family. Even as the patriarchal structure of matrimony establishes and transmits the fundamental terms of social discipline – the subordination of the body, the socialisation of the child, the authority of man over woman – so, in the same movement, it conserves and reproduces the authoritative discourse of godly knowledge, or the Word.

The fruitfulness of marriage rests in this conservation of the Word within the relays of patriarchal succession; a perpetual rearticulation of truth which binds the subject within a Providential temporal order which links the 'original beginning' of Creation to the promised end of 'everlasting immortality'. In this, the transmission of the Word opens out the metaphysical reality of the providential time-scheme beneath or within the mere sequential succession of secular temporality, just as on the synchronic axis it makes available – to the godly subject – the eternal structures of Being which underpin the shadow-play of earthly appearances.

The godly citizen who assumes his or her ordained place within the hierarchy of social order also, then, orientates him- or herself in relation to the order of truth which persists beneath the epi-phenomenal order of worldly circumstance and appearance. Within such a system, the forms of subjection are also those of coherent subjectivity: they constitute the medium through which the fundamental terms of identity and relationship within which the self is grounded become known.

What this also implies is that the insubordination of ungodly subjects is not only a violation of social order, but an alienation from the truth. The delinquent short-circuits the process of disciplined, through-seeing perception by which the godly read the terms of their 'natural' subjection inscribed behind the screen of worldly circumstance. The delinquent's 'reading' is instead fixated upon the enticing but ontologically deficient forms of secular 'reality'. In these terms, social delinquency is conceived as a revolt of the body's senses and appetites against the higher faculty of the understanding, a wilful curtailment of the proper relation between the senses, the reason and the truth. The delinquent performs a reading of the world in which its forms are not referred to the metaphysical paradigm which structures them and defines them in their truth. Lawlessness and sin, in other words, are refusals of the Signified; an excision of the metaphysical dimension in which referentiality is properly grounded.

It is this ideological context which determines Harman's ethic of plain words and its struggle with the counter-principle of vagrant semiosis: on the one hand a social ethic of discourse in which semiotic activity cleaves faithfully to the transcendental signified of the Word, and on the other a delinquency of signs which have been wilfully detached from that metaphysical anchorage. Through the demonised figure of the vagrant, Harman and other commentators ascribe social and semiotic disorder to a willed evasion of the communal imperatives of social hierarchy and the Word. The disturbances which the vagrant embodies are firmly located within the domain of individual and social discipline.

However, the disturbance in the stability and transparency of Harman's own 'lawful' discourse whose epicentre is the word *cursitor* suggests another way of conceptualising the social and semiotic disruptions which occupy the writer against vagrancy.

The discourse on vagrancy is founded in an opposition between the stasis of eternal structures and the unlawful mobility of individual social agents. This is a conceptual structure which, among its other implications, involves a negation of history. Truth and order are eternally the same; any departure from the Same into difference or innovation is a diversion into illusion and disorder which – as it cannot arise from the eternal self-identical integrity of the cosmological system – can only be the product of the aberrant individual will, running wild from its systemic constraints. The possibility of change at the level of the *system* is not countenanced, and in the light of this, History as a secular process cannot be said to exist. Instead there is that eternal return of the Same which is represented in the repetitious temporal cycles of orthodox sixteenth-century historiography. As the exemplary instance of the *Mirror for Magistrates* suggests, secular history here is an illusory order of action and event, projected by acts of illicit self-determination; the arc of a doomed flight in defiance of the gravitational field of Providential inevitability.[18]

The ideology of Commonwealth which implies this negation of secular history is clearly best adapted to a society which can claim some plausible connection to the image of a placid, organically self-reproducing social order which the ideology enshrines. Tudor and Elizabethan England – despite the assertions of some twentieth-century literary and cultural historians – was not such a society, but one unsettled by rapid and fundamental socio-economic change. It is for that reason that the discourse of Commonwealth, whether it is used by governments as an instrument of ideological stabilisation, or by their opponents as an instrument of critique, is always characterised in this period by the retrospective invocation of an idealised medieval past. The rest of this book will be concerned with tracing the effects of this contradiction between ideology and historical process across a number of related sixteenth-century discursive fields. The disturbance I have noted in Harman's preface will serve as an introductory example of what happens when an ideology of stasis, immutable structure and metaphysically anchored truth is required to contain, interpret and regulate a social order in historical transition.

For Harman, if there is a disturbance in the order of things – a loosening of social cohesion, a confusion of social identities, an equivocality in the signs and meanings circulating through the community of speaking subjects – its source cannot be in the customary socio-economic system which appears in his work, sublimed into ideality, as the Commonwealth. Disruption can only be the result of anti-systemic behaviour, an assertion of delinquent individuality against the constraints of social and natural order. Similarly, in the sphere of communication, disorder must arise from a deliberate destabilisation of the order of 'lawful language' by the semiotic larcenies of the cony-catcher or counterfeit crank.

What Harman's preface reveals, however, is a process of semiotic dislocation and estrangement which is active – despite the writer's self-policing vigilance and his subordination of his discourse to the uses of the Commonwealth – within the fabric of his own plain and truthful words. The name of that process is history, which Harman's philological excursus reveals to be the medium within which *all* signs and meanings – not just those of the double-talker – are characterised by a metamorphic volatility which will not be contained by the transcendental fixities of the Commonwealth paradigm.

In the following chapters I shall discuss this contention between metaphysically anchored systems of social and discursive order and the deconstituting force of historical process, as it manifests itself in the textual disturbance which marks representative works from a range of sixteenth- and early seventeenth-century discourses. Chapter One discusses Hooker's *Laws of Ecclesiastical Polity* as an attempt to develop a conceptual framework which will preserve the metaphysical legitimation of the authority of the Elizabethan State Church, while accommodating the fact of its historical deviation from the continuity of Catholic tradition. In doing so, Hooker articulates a strategy of mediation which is designed to reconcile the competing claims of transcendental principle and secular praxis, stasis and historical process, conservation and innovation. The development of such strategies will be a persistent concern in my discussion of other discursive areas.

Chapter Two pursues the imprint of the ideology of Commonwealth on Tudor and Elizabethan discourses – governmental and oppositional – on social and economic regulation. In doing so it aims to show how the acknowledgement and disavowal of systemic crisis is discursively enacted around the demonised figures of Narcissus and the Usurer, a process which also creates a conceptual bridge between disruptions of the socio-economic order and disorders within the psychic and bodily 'economies' of the subject.

The next two chapters explore the connection between the semiotic dimension of social order/disorder and the interaction of authority and disruption within the literary text. My discussion of George Gascoigne takes his career as exemplifying an unresolved tension between the writer as dutiful servant of the Commonwealth and as semiotic delinquent, and considers the strategies by which he and other writers attempt to contain the energies of writing and render it conformable to the prescriptions of the Word. The following chapter on George Puttenham's *Arte of English Poesie* moves from the hazards of writerly praxis to consider the negotiation of this tension between the text and the Word at the level of rhetorical theory.

Chapter Five focuses on Hoby's translation of Castiglione's *The Book of the Courtier* in order to explore the connection between the equivocal position of the writer and that of the courtier, and how the case of the courtier exposes threats to the metaphysical legitimation of the Prince's secular authority which Castiglione will attempt to counter through the mediating strategies of courtship. The exploration of the arts of the courtier continues in my final chapter, where I discuss the drama of courtship in Jonson's masques and his play *Cynthia's Revels*. In the case of the masque I focus on Jonson's dramatic deployment of Neoplatonic philosophy as a means of subliming the extravagances of courtly image and accomplishments into a representation of the radiance of metaphysical authority. *Cynthia's Revels* is discussed as a play which enacts a troubled deconstruction of this process of legitimation by confronting the metaphysical strategies of the masque with the satirical empiricism of Jonsonian comedy. In the generic uncertainties and representational aporias of *Cynthia's Revels* the contention between the metaphysical and the worldly, and between a lawful and a vagrant semiosis, traces its effects at the very centre of secular authority, in the self-legitimating performances of courtly power.

Note: The spelling and punctuation in quotations are those of the editions cited. For full details of the editions used, readers are referred to the bibliography.

1

The Semiotics of Settlement: Hooker's *Laws of Ecclesiastical Polity*

> The way of religion is to lead the things which are lower to the things which are higher through the things which are intermediate. According to the laws of the universe all things are not reduced to order equally and immediately; but the lowest through the intermediate, the intermediate through the higher.
>
> Pope Boniface VIII, *Bull: Unam Sanctam*[1]

At the centre of the public contention which occasions Hooker's writing there is a dispute between two conceptions of time. As Hooker characterises it, the challenge of militant Puritanism resides primarily in its fundamentalism, its determination to return to the Word as the governing principle of secular practice. In this uncompromising referral of the contemporary moment to an extra-historical origin Hooker sees a negation of that human temporality in which historically specific formations, unprescribed by Scripture, are free to emerge: formations such as that which Hooker defends – the Anglican Church in its rupture from the Apostolic tradition enshrined at Rome.[2]

The opposition, in short, is between an apocalyptic mode which apprehends the transcendental as perpetually imminent and shaping each instant of worldly experience, and a vision of melioration, or re-formation, which locates transcendence at the end of an extended process of rational self-determination. An example of this antagonism is to be found in the opposed temporal structures of a militant Puritan work such as Foxe's *Acts and Monuments*, and of Hooker's *Laws*.

In the *Acts and Monuments* the linearity of historical time – the progress of the persecution of the Protestant martyrs through the years of Mary's reign – is constantly negated by an insistence upon the structural identity of each episode, a structure which reproduces in each episode that of the life and passion of Christ: Witness, Trial, Mortal Suffering, Glorification. What appears to be a temporal progression reveals itself in truth as the perpetual repetition of an archetypal moment, and in the book's apocalyptic movement through the witness of Edward's reign and the persecution of Mary's, to the final glorification under Elizabeth, historical time itself is arrested within the same structure.[3]

In contrast, Hooker's practice is, by his own account, linear and accumulative:

> For as much help whereof as may be in this case, I have endeavoured throughout the body of this whole discourse, that every former part might give strength unto all that follow, and every later bring some light unto all before. So that if the judgements of men do but hold themselves in suspense as touching these first more general meditations, till in order they have perused the rest that ensue; what may seem dark at the first will afterwards be found more plain, even as the later particular decisions will appear I doubt not more strong, when the other have been read before . . . . (I, p. 149)

According to this model, the metaphysical origin is not the point of the prior dissolution of human history but a causal principle which is known precisely through its gradual and partial manifestation in the progression of phenomena which it informs.

The difference between these two temporal modes is also one of epistemological perspective. The Puritan model takes as its own the perspective of the predestinating Deity Himself, for whom all human history is already known, as it is proleptically encompassed by His own originating act. Hooker's perspective, in contrast, is that of post-lapsarian humanity, for whom the price of the Fall is precisely an estrangement from the metaphysical order articulated by the originating Word. This clash of opposed perspectives is also present in Hooker's attacks on the Puritan shibboleth of *inspiration*. Here again, the dispute over time is central: inspiration, it is claimed, represents an immediate receptivity of the saint to the eternal order of the Word as it is revealed in Scripture, and so repeats certain paradigmatic moments of Apostolic insight. Hooker's objection is that such moments, in which the order of eternity intersects with human time, are to be seen as dependent upon the unrepeatable mediating presence of Christ in history:

But consider I beseech you first touching the Apostle, how that wherein he was so resolute and . . . peremptory, our Lord Jesus Christ made manifest unto him even by intuitive revelation, wherein there was no possibility of error. That which you are persuaded of, ye have it no otherwise than by your own probable collection, and therefore such bold asseverations as in him were admirable, should in your mouths but argue rashness . . . . (I, p. 267)

With the withdrawal of this unique mediator, such peremptoriness is, in Hooker's account, no longer possible; the approach to knowledge loses its immediacy and becomes an indefinitely protracted process:

The search of knowledge is a thing painful; and the painfulness of knowledge is that which maketh the Will so hardly inclinable thereunto. The root hereof, divine malediction; whereby the instruments being weakened wherewithal the soul (especially in reasoning) doth work, it preferreth rest in ignorance before wearisome labour to know . . . . (I, pp. 173–4)[4]

As this question of conviction and incontrovertible declaration suggests, the eternal moment of the Word is a moment of fully present and stable meaning: the Puritan claim, according to Hooker, is to have access, beyond the dubieties and approximations of human discourse, to that original language in which God, uniquely, speaks as He means. As the direct transcription of this divine speech, Scripture is accorded by the Puritans a self-declarative authenticity, a total adequation of meaning to signification, which places it beyond interpretation. Hooker's objection is again based on his commitment to the perspective of a post-lapsarian humanity for which the self-identical discourse of the Word is a lost origin. Accordingly Scripture is not exempted by Hooker from the general condition of human discourse, which is characterised by a radical dislocation of sign and meaning. As a consequence, the meanings of Scripture are only produced by a historical accumulation of interpretative decisions:

For whatsoever we believe concerning salvation by Christ, although the Scripture be therein the ground of our belief; yet the authority of man is, if we mark it, the key which openeth the door of entrance into the knowledge of Scripture. The Scripture could not teach us the things that are of God, unless we did credit men who have taught us that the words

of Scripture do signify those things. Some way therefore,
notwithstanding man's infirmity, yet his authority may enforce
assent . . . . (I, p. 267)

As this suggests, Hooker's historicist approach to language derives
from the principles of Humanist philology, principles which open
a space of deferral within the generation of meaning which is also
potentially a political space within which the negotiation between
transcendental principle and pragmatic necessities may be attempted.
We will meet another instance of this relation between philology and
politics in Chapter Two's discussion of usury.[5]

The certainties of the Puritan's model of intuitive revelation are
replaced in Hooker's practice by approximation, probability and the
rational interrogation of appearances:

> . . . it shall clearly appear unto any man of judgement that
> the most which can be inferred upon such plenty of divine
> testimonies is only this. That some things which they maintain,
> as far as some men can probably conjecture, do seem to have
> been out of Scripture, not absurdly gathered . . . . (II, p. 275)

From this position the Puritan insistence on the primacy of personal
revelation appears as the threat of an anarchic subjectivism:

> . . . if in so great variety of ways as the wit of man is easily
> able to find out towards any purpose, and in so great liking as
> all men have especially unto those inventions whereby someone
> shall seem to have been more enlightened from above than
> many thousands, the Church did give every man license to
> follow what himself imagineth that 'God's spirit doth reveal'
> unto him . . . what other effect could hereupon ensue, but the
> utter confusion of his church under pretence of being taught,
> led and guided by his Spirit . . . ? (I, p. 281)

This contention over the nature of Scripture is at once the question
which originates the encyclopaedic project of the *Laws* , and the point
at which the possibility of its self-cancellation manifests itself. In
seeking to open a space for human action and decision – the
space, for example, in which the work of measured innovation
which constitutes Anglicanism is undertaken – Hooker is obliged to
step outside the prescriptive order of Scriptural literalism. Hence his
repeated insistence that Scripture comprehends all that is necessary
to Salvation – that is for the life of the *next* world – but not 'all

things simply'. This position, in denying the perpetual and immediate revelation of the Word, entails an acceptance of the radically different order of human temporality, in which understanding is not anchored through inspiration to the unproblematic significations of the Word. This cutting loose from certainty is a necessary polemical and theoretical manoeuvre, but it also means that the promise of order and stability – of a great settlement of Church and State – which the defence of Anglicanism announces is accompanied by the prospect of an uncontainable relativisation of meaning and knowledge. As Hooker writes of all attempts to change long-established laws: 'It amazeth [men], it causeth them to stand in doubt whether any thing be in itself by nature either good or evil, and not all things rather such as men at this or that time agree to account of them' (III, p. 422). The indefinite deferment of the Word produces the fear which haunts Hooker's discourse of a relativistic chaos of signs, values and desires which have been severed from any final determination, a vision of 'confusion and disorder in the affairs of this present world'.[6] That fear is articulated in Hooker's text in his discussion of three closely related topics – knowledge, signification, desire – where the threat of a relativistic *drifting* is felt with particular urgency.

To deny the efficacy of revelation, and with it the unmediated presence of the Word in history, Hooker insists, is to risk submitting knowledge to merely relative and differential criteria: 'For to make nothing evident of itself unto man's understanding were to take away all possibility of knowing any thing . . . ' (I, p. 177). The denial of revelation also produces a vision of the undoing of language through its alienation from the Signified, a question which emerges when Hooker discusses the problem of establishing criteria for the interpretation of Scripture:

> I hold it for a most infallible rule in expositions of sacred Scripture, that where a literal construction will stand, the farthest from the letter is commonly the worst. There is nothing more dangerous than this licentious and deluding art, which changeth the meaning of words, as alchymy doth or would do the substance of metals, making of any thing what it listeth, and bringeth in the end all truth to nothing . . . . (II, p. 241)

What Hooker asserts here as being a linguistic perversion is, on the basis of his own theoretical assumptions – as the hesitation in 'where a literal construction will stand' suggests – a local instance of the condition of human discourse as such, a condition which his own writing is obliged to confront in its pursuit of some non-metaphysical ground of linguistic authority and interpretative consensus.

The problem of desire, as it appears in the *Laws*, emerges from this loosening of the transcendental anchorage of knowledge and language. Hooker characterises desire as the rational appetite of the Will towards the Good, a definition which, in characteristically humanistic fashion, conflates the ethical and the epistemological. However, given Hooker's insistence upon the inaccessibility of the Word to human understanding, his account of desire stresses its perpetual deflection from the Good towards merely illusory objects of satisfaction. It is in his account of this deflection that Hooker provides his clearest and most extended description of the compromised human order within which the *Laws* situates its remedial project. A description of chains of illusory objects which are fully present neither to themselves nor to the desiring subject, existing merely in their relation to the other elements of the chain; of differential values without anchorage in any determining positive term; an image consequently of time as an eternity of unpunctuated succession, or, in other words, of repeated arrival at a false conclusion:

> Wherefore of good things desired some are such that for themselves we covet them not, but only because they serve as instruments unto that for which we are to seek; of this sort are riches. Another kind there is which although we desire for itself, as health, and virtue and knowledge, nevertheless they are not the last mark at which we aim, but have their further end whereunto they are referred, so as in them we are not satisfied as having attained the utmost we may, but our desires do still proceed. These things are linked, and as it were chained one to another; we labour to eat, and we eat to live, and we live to do good, and the good which we do is as seed sown with reference to a future harvest. But we must come at length to some pause. For, if everything were to be desired for some other without any stint, there could be no certain end proposed unto our actions, we should go on we know not whither; yea, whatsoever we do were in vain, or rather nothing at all were possible to be done . . . . (I, pp. 201–2)

This vision of chaos is compelled by Hooker's refusal of the Puritan model of unmediated access to the Word, but he takes pains to stress that it must not merely by submitted to as the inevitable condition of fallen humanity:

> So that unless the last good of all, which is desired altogether for itself, be also infinite, we do evil in making it our end; even as they placed their felicity in wealth or honour or pleasure or any thing here attained; because in desiring anything as our final perfection which is not so, we do amiss . . . . (I, p. 202)

The central problem of Hooker's writing is to preserve the punctuation and redemption of the human order by the Word – to abandon it would be to court anarchy – but to articulate a relation between the worldly and the transcendental dimensions which does not arrest human time and action in a repetition of the origin, whether that repetition is lodged in the pre-scriptions of an authoritarian Scripture, or in the inspired convictions of the Puritan saint. What is required is a rewriting of temporality which will avoid both the predetermined patterns of Puritan eschatology and the indeterminacy of a sceptical relativism. Hooker finds this in a temporal model of discovery and disclosure which is reminiscent of the narrative structure of the Quest:

> In the matter of knowledge, there is between the angels of God and the children of men this difference: angels already have full and complete knowledge in the highest degree that can be imparted unto them; men, if we view them in their spring, are at the first without understanding and knowledge at all. Nevertheless from this utter vacuity they grow by degrees, till they come at length to be even as the angels themselves are . . . . (I, p. 166)

In this progression from ignorance to knowledge, the human protagonist discovers gradually the initially hidden, but already inscribed coherence of the temporal sequence which it is traversing. In this sense, the restoration of the Word at the termination of the quest is the result of human determinations and initiatives, at the same time as it is the discovery of a metaphysical principle which precedes and structures the time of the quest itself. What the children of men will come to know by their own disciplined exertions is always already known by the angels of God.

The paradoxical relation of the subject–object relation in this temporal model – each appearing both to precede and to be produced by the other – also characterises Reason and Law, which are the linked primary subjects of Hooker's discourse in the *Laws*. In following the law of his own nature, Hooker argues, man discovers the eternal law which is its paradigm; in the same way, the operation of reason leads to knowledge of the Divine reason which it reflects:

> . . . by force of the light of Reason, wherewith God illuminateth every one which cometh into the world, men being enabled to know truth from falsehood, and good from evil, do thereby learn in many things what the will of God is; which will himself not revealing by any extraordinary means unto them, but they by natural discourse attaining the knowledge thereof, seem the makers of those Laws which indeed are his, and they but only the finders of them out . . . . (I, pp. 176–7)

Poised between the predestined and the aleatory, the transitive and the intransitive, Hooker's hermeneutic temporality, structured by Law and Reason, is the medium through which the metaphysical and the worldly maintain a necessary communication while preserving their difference. In this it reproduces the paradoxical nature of Christ's incarnation which involves a union between corruptible flesh and a being 'for ever one and the self-same':

> . . . two natures [which] have knit themselves the one to the other, and are in that nearness as uncapable of confusion as of distraction. Their coherence hath not taken away the difference between them. (II, p. 210)

If we turn now to a detailed consideration of the first of these pardoxical categories – the Law – we find that Hooker derives his conception of it from a fundamental axiom of negative theology:

> The particular drift of every act proceeding externally from God we are not able to discern, and therefore cannot always give the proper and certain reason of his works. Howbeit undoubtedly a proper and certain reason there is of every finite work of God, inasmuch as there is a law imposed upon it, which if there were not, it should be infinite, even as the worker himself is . . . . (I, p. 153)

For an entity to be finite, it must be subject to a restriction: the positing of finitude thus entails that of a prior intentionality or agency. As finite entities must by definition differ (the limit is also necessarily a boundary demarcating discrete categories) the setting of restrictions must also be an act of differentiation or discrimination according to particular cases:

> Measure is that which perfecteth all things, because every thing is for some end, neither can that thing be available to any end which is not proportionable thereunto, and to proportion as well excesses as defects are opposite. Again, forasmuch as nothing doth perish but only through excess or defect of that, the due proportioned measure whereof doth give perfection, it followeth that measure is likewise the preservation of all things . . . . (II, p. 214)

As this terminology of measure, proportion and preservation implies, the differentiation of the infinite into discrete and finite entities determines Hooker's characterisation of the causal agent as rational in its operations. It has only to be added that for an entity to have an end it must also have a beginning, and we have arrived at the three essential components of the Law, logically derived from the positing of the finite entity: it is the product of a pre-existing determining agent, it is rational, and it operates across time. The Law in short is the expression within the order of finite categories and entities – the world of created things – of a purposive temporal logic or rational teleology:

> So that no certain end could ever be attained, unless the actions whereby it is attained were regular; that is to say, made suitable, fit and correspondent unto their end, by some canon, rule or law. Which thing doth first take place in the works even of God himself . . . . (I, p. 150)

The Law, then, as that logic which informs the development of sensible things, is not itself available to sense. Its discovery is consequently the result of an excavation, a penetration beneath the deceptive surface of sensation and appearance:

> . . . that which hath greatest force in the very things we see is notwithstanding itself oftentimes not seen. The stateliness of houses, the goodliness of trees, when we behold them delighteth the eye; but that foundation which beareth up the one, that root which ministereth unto the other nourishment and life, is in the bosom of the earth concealed; and if there be at any time

occasion to search into it, such labour is then more necessary than pleasant, both to them which undertake it and for the lookers-on. In like manner, the use and benefit of good laws all that live under them may enjoy with delight and comfort, albeit the grounds and first original causes from whence they have sprung be unknown, as to the greatest part of men they are . . . . (I, pp. 148–9)

As a being distinguished from others by the supra-sensible operation of reason, it is precisely in this excavation beneath sense that man may follow the law of his own distinctive nature:

The soul of man therefore being capable of a more divine perfection, hath (besides the faculties of growing unto sensible knowledge which is common unto us with beasts) a further ability, whereof in them there is no show at all, the ability of reaching higher than unto sensible things . . . . (I, p. 167)

As the realisation of a Law – that of human nature – this work of reason implies the imposition of a logic upon human time: the logic of the quest, of the gradual disclosure of knowledge to the enquiring subject.

The logic of the quest is one means by which the concept of Law allows a defence of historical tradition, of the accumulated rational testimony of the human past. The concept of Law also answers the requirement for a criterion by which the rational status of that testimony may be assessed. Hooker's position is that because it is the underlying structural principle of a universal human nature, the law of reason demands that for a proposition to be judged rational, it should command the assent of all men:

The general and perpetual voice of men is as the sentence of God himself. For that which all men have at all times learned, Nature herself must needs have taught; and God being the author of Nature, her voice is but His instrument . . . . (I, p. 176)

With this question of universal assent we reach a crux in Hooker's argument which returns us to the polemical context of his writing. Clearly the reasonable propositions which Hooker himself advances through his work do not command universal assent – they face a vociferous Puritan opposition. It is here that Hooker's theoretical premises can be seen most clearly at work in support of specific political intentions. As the law of reason takes the form of a qualitative development of the human subject over time, it follows that not every man 'may be said to have attained so far forth the use of reason, as sufficeth to make him capable of those Laws, whereby he is then bound to guide his actions . . . '(I, p. 168). Those who have reached this stage and have attuned their reason to the divine reason constitute a collectivity which is in a distinctive and close relation to the Deity. The name of this collectivity is the Church; a body of the elect, where election is both the effect of an eternal predestination and the product of rational self-enlightenment:

> Our being in Christ by eternal foreknowledge saveth us not without our actual and real adoption into the fellowship of his saints in this present world. For in him we actually are by our actual incorporation into that society which hath him for their head, and doth make together with him one Body . . . . (II, p. 228)

Visible, and invisible, spiritual and corporeal, eternally ordained and historically determined, the Church partakes of the paradoxical mediating function of the Son[7] because it represents the point at which human and divine reason intersect. As the bearer of a divinely sanctioned rational consensus, it is the agency through which the Law of Reason unfolds itself in history; the arbiter of what has constituted the authentic human narrative in the past, and of what contributes to that development in the present. It is the Church which represents the Word in history, and so allows an authoritative punctuation of the proliferating chains of signification and differential value. Hooker exemplifies this stabilising activity of the Church through the following instances: its determination of the 'true signs and tokens of goodness' (I, p. 176), the fixing of Scriptural interpretations,[8] the choice of correct forms of government,[9] the identification of false doctrine,[10] the definitive interpretation of the signs of the sacraments,[11] and the silencing of debate by 'definitive sentence'. As this last example suggests, the arrest and authorisation of meaning by the Church is inseparable from the exercise of its 'political' authority: 'definitive sentence' is the epistemological ground from which the challenge of militant Puritanism may be repelled:

> For the public approbation given by the body of this whole Church unto those things which are established, doth make it but probable that they are good . . . . (I, p. 121)

It is in this role that the Church appears throughout the *Laws*, sifting the components of a rational collective history from the dross of actions and convictions distorted by the sub-rational elements of human nature. What troubles that historical consensus in its unfolding is, for Hooker, always the assertion of a minority or 'singular' perspective:

> So that of peace and quietness there is not any way possible, unless the probable voice of every entire society or body politic overrule all private of like nature in the same body . . . . (I, p. 121)

Given that the 'mature use of reason' is marked, according to Hooker, by its general adoption, such singularity is named as the product of a lower stage of human development; a fixation of the mind upon the seductive play of appearances, a privileging of surface over depth, of the sensible over the Law which informs it, of the immediate satisfactions of appetite over the deferred rewards of rational desire:

> There is not that good which concerneth us, but it hath evidence enough for itself, if Reason were diligent to search it out. Through neglect thereof, abused we are with the show of that which is not; sometimes the subtilty of Satan inveigling us as it did Eve, sometimes the hastiness of our Wills preventing the more considerate advice of sound Reason, as in the Apostles, when they no sooner saw what they liked not, but they forthwith were desirous of fire from heaven . . . . For which cause the Apostle, who knew right well that the weariness of the flesh is an heavy clog to the Will, striketh mightily upon this key, 'Awake thou that sleepest; Cast off all which presseth down; Watch; Labour; Strive to go forward, and to grow in knowledge . . . .; (I, p. 173–4)

As the double nature of man admits no divorce between the 'understanding part' and its corporeal instruments, so too it implies that there will always be another human history parallel to the rational history of the Law's unfolding. A history uninformed by the temporal and epistemological structure of the quest, unpunctuated by any transcendental term, motivated merely by the endless cycle of appetitive excitement and exhaustion, veering between a perpetual succession of illusory conclusions: a history, in short, of the body.

Hooker's name for this history is Custom; an accumulation of merely habitual, sub-rational determinations, propelled by a purely internal momentum, and, in his chief example, fixated upon the sensible entity rather than the eternal order which it rightly signifies:

> I deny not but lewd and wicked custom, beginning perhaps at the first among few, afterwards spreading into greater multitudes, and so continuing from time to time, may be of force even in plain things to smother the light of natural understanding; because men will not bend their wits to examine other things wherewith they have been accustomed, whether they be good or evil. For example's sake, that grosser kind of heathenish idolatry, whereby they worshipped the very works of their own hands, was an absurdity to reason so palpable, that the Prophet David comparing idols and idolaters together maketh almost no odds between them, but the one in a manner as much without wit and sense as the other; 'They that make them are like unto them, and so are all that trust in them . . . . (I, p. 184)

The bad signification of the idol involves a short-circuiting of the referential process by which, according to Hooker, the righteous penetrate the material husk of things in order to read the imprint of natural and divine law which declares their true origin. In opposition to this illicit order of signs, Hooker introduces sacramental signification; a semiotic mode in which the priority of the meta-physical signified over the material signifier is preserved. This mode is represented both by the sacraments themselves, and by all those sensible forms and observances through which the visible Church declares itself:

> Signs must resemble the things they signify . . . . Duties of religion performed by whole societies of men, ought to have in them according to our power a sensible excellency, correspondent to the majesty of Him who we worship. Yea then are the public duties of religion best ordered, when the militant Church doth resemble by sensible means, as it may be in such cases, that hidden dignity and glory wherewith the church triumphant in heaven is beautified . . . . (II, p. 37)

Hooker here is defending the luxuriance of Church ritual and appurtenances which was under attack by Puritans in campaigns like the one against vestments. Hooker's defence is based in a distinction between an ostentation of the signifier which curtails metaphysical referentiality – as typified by the idol – and a proportionality which links the 'excellency' of the worldly signifier to the majesty of the transcendental signified, and so legitimates it.[12]

The internal economy of the sacramental sign represents an interdependence of material and metaphysical components which finds a different articulation in the isomorphic relation between the Laws rational, natural and divine:

> And the truth is, that all our controversy in this cause concerning the orders of the Church is, what particulars the Church may appoint. That which doth find them out is the force of man's reason. That which doth guide and direct his reason is first the general law of nature; which law of nature and the moral law of Scripture are in the substance of law all one . . . . So that laws human must be made according to the general laws of nature, and without contradiction unto any positive law in Scripture . . . . (I, p. 38)

Hooker's difficult task in the *Laws* is to defend the self-constituting, innovating initiatives of the emergent Elizabethan Church in the name of universality, the eternal truth of the Word, and the authority of Apostolic tradition. The characterisation of reason which I have just quoted is an essential part of Hooker's strategy in tackling this paradoxical requirement. For reason, as Hooker describes it, is the medium through which the transcendental order of the Signified communicates with the consensual determinations of the historical Church, and as such, it sanctions the generation by men of new signs – verbal and ceremonial – which, paradoxically, do not supplement the eternal prescriptions of the Word. This is the key to Hooker's rebuttal of the attack mounted by Calvinists against the institution of new sacraments, as here by Beza:

> They sinned right greevously, as often as they brought any Sacramentalles (that is to say, any ceremonies to import signification to spiritual things) into the Church of God.[13]

For Beza, to supplement the Word is to imply its insufficiency; to multiply signs is to multiply the 'spiritual' things which they 'import'; as if men were to usurp the creative prerogative of God and imply a lack in his primal ordering of things. For Hooker, however, the sacramental sign and the Law represent a mode of signification in which the Word is at once conserved and capable of elaboration, where the eternal integrity of the Signified is reconciled with the historical mutability of the signifier. It is in this regime of the sign that Hooker discovers the possibility and the legitimation of a Church which may both rupture and regenerate tradition, both violate and reconfirm the grounds of its own authority.

* * *

Hooker's great work exemplifies the concerns of this study in a number of ways. In its attempt to develop a philosophical framework which reconciles the conservation of the Word with a responsiveness to historical contingencies, the *Laws* articulates the central ideological problem which resonates across the different discursive domains which are addressed here – how the dynamic processes of secular change are to be accommodated or managed within the static framework of transcendentalist orthodoxy. Another of this study's primary themes is introduced in Hooker's working out of this ideological dilemma around and through the bipartite structure of the sign. In a less conscious fashion, the *Laws* also reveals the mutual implication of these philosophical and semiotic manoeuvrings with the tactical adjustments and strategic reorientations of political, religious and social authority. For Hooker, the interpretative community of the righteous, with its commitment to the reading of the Law enciphered within the phenomenal forms of the world, is also the caste of the legitimately empowered, elevated above those arrested at a merely perceptual ('sensual') apprehension.[14] In its social and political applications, the hierarchical structure of the sign (the material 'body' of the signifier in its subordination to the 'soul' of the signified) underwrites a hierarchy of reading which corresponds to the distinction between those within and without the central 'reservation' of the socially and politically powerful.

Hooker maintains this clear underwriting of established social and political structures by natural law even as he attempts to legitimate a State and Church which have been wilfully detached from their 'natural' basis of legitimation in the universal authority of the Catholic succession. This amelioration of apparently contradictory demands – the need for a displacement of authority if it is to renew itself in the face of historical change – is typical of the strategies of mediation which we will encounter throughout this book. Such strategies are required by all those in the period who seek to legitimate metaphysically their pragmatic responses to the flux of historical transformation: by governments trying to channel new social and economic forces within the existing hierarchical structures, by government opponents seeking to justify policy innovation by appeal to immutable cosmic law, by individuals seeking magically to enter the inner circles of social power while remaining loyal to the principles of decorum and degree.

We will meet all these cases in the following pages. In each of them, a challenge is presented to the prevailing ideology's elevation of metaphysical being over secular becoming; in each case an attempt is made to neutralise that challenge by rethinking or rewriting the relationship between the metaphysical and the secular, thereby renegotiating the legitimation of secular authority while appearing to leave its metaphysical anchorage unshaken.

2

Narcissus and the Usurer

The Two Economies

Anima plus quam corpus et corpus plus quam vestimentum.

A Treatise concerning the staple[1]

In its recommendations for the management of the Royal Household, the Household Ordinance of 1478 proposes an Aristotelian avoidance of the extremes of parsimony and extravagance, and the adoption of a policy of the *mean* 'to be grounded and established upon the vertue called . . . liberalitie'.[2] Edward IV's reform divided the Household into two departments – the Domus Regie Magnificencie under the Lord Chamberlain, and the Domus Regie Providencie under the Lord Steward. The first, in the words of Gordon Kipling, was 'charged with impressing the outside world with ostentatious display'.[3] The second, on the contrary, operated discreetly and beyond public attention to make the extravagances of the other agency possible 'by means of economy and prudent management'.[4] Under Henry VII the Domus Regie Magnificencie was strengthened and elaborated, and the new office of Royal Librarian was added to it; an office which was to be the focus of Court culture – of literary production, education, the development of the revels – through this and the next reign.

Inseparable from its practical effects upon the organisation of the Household is the way in which this mechanism institutes a conceptual economy whose binary terms are externality/inwardness, surface/depth, ostentation/prudence, expenditure/husbandry, visual display/invisible labour. What it proposes is not so much an economy *within* the order of worldly forms, but a division of the worldly – the external, the surface, the visible, the expended – against that which founds/funds and regulates it, namely the invisible order of inwardness and depth, rational management and retention which is placed under the sign of Providence. It is this insensible Providential husbandry which secures the flotation of the monarchy's temporal power – the latter being a worldly presence operating upon the senses through the force of display and conspicuous consumption, and through the investment and manipulation of surfaces.

An insistence that there can be no development of the surface without its underwriting and authorisation in another scene; no luxury of exfoliation without anchorage in the networks of the root; this is the essential injunction enacted in Edward's Household reform. The economy which it represents is one of two terms hierarchically disposed: an immaterial term prior to and determining a sensible. As I hope to show in this chapter, this binary structure is capable of being brought to bear as a principle of organisation upon a number of fields, but at this point I want to stress the readiness of its application to the field of signification and the production of discourse.

The hierarchical structure I have just outlined is one central product of the interaction of Christian and Platonic ideologies over a number of centuries. The antithetical relation of its binary terms is traceable at once to the Christian opposition between the divine and the temporal and the Platonic antinomy between the orders of Being and Becoming. It is the parallel nature of these oppositions which forms the ground for the development of the Neoplatonism of the fifth century, and which finds its major synthetic statement in St Augustine's *City of God*.[5]

One major ideological activity of the medieval Church is the effort to discover modes of communication between these radically discontinuous spheres, in order to establish the nature of the relationship between Divine authority and human affairs; a process which is also, crucially, a means of confirming the power of the Church as the authorised mediator. The names of Aquinas, Duns Scotus and Ockham mark out one stage in the debates around this issue; the revival of Neoplatonism and negative theology in Renaissance Italy represents another; the return to Paul and St Augustine in the work of Luther ensures its continuing pertinence into the sixteenth century.[6]

One area of concern remains of central importance throughout this continuing labour of definition and dispute – that of the theory of signification. As it emerges in the philosophy of the Stoics and is developed in the work of the Neoplatonists and the Church Fathers, the theory of the sign is grounded in a binary structure which is strictly homologous to the structure of oppositions which govern cosmological speculation.[7] The supposed incorporation of an immaterial and a sensible component in the sign (signified/signifier) placed its analysis into an intimate relation with those cosmological questions which focused around the relationship between the material and the metaphysical orders.

This conceptual intimacy is in fact sufficient to make it difficult to maintain what I have described, for clarity's sake, as the priority of cosmological over semiological enquiry. The cosmological question is in fact persistently posed as a question of *representation*. How can the Divine presence be read in the signs which compose the Book of the World? How is the Idea represented by its material simulacra? In this sense the question of the sign *is* the question of fundamental cosmological relations, and this identity can be traced in a number of major discursive tendencies which are carried over from the medieval period into the sixteenth century: in the persistence of the trope of the World-as-Book, in the development of the medieval system of allegorical exegesis as a practice for mapping not only the levels of meaning recoverable from a text, but also the regions of an ontological/cosmological topography, or in the Renaissance fascination with the symbolic media of emblem, hieroglyph and numerological structure as means by which the enciphered forms of the Truth find a fleeting and evasive incarnation within the order of human discourse.[8] It is this same semiotic-cosmological relation which is revealed by the insistence of the literary analogy and the language of signification in the discourses on general economy which I will be considering in this chapter.

As we have seen, the Household economy instituted by Edward IV aligns the central institutions of the emerging English state with a dominant economy of cosmological relations and its attendant economy of the sign. In view of the latter, it is entirely appropriate that the reformed Wardrobe should be the source of the increasingly organised production of official representations in literature, painting, pageantry and festive/dramatic performance, as well as being the place for the licensing and authorisation of other literary work.[9]

I take the economy of the Wardrobe – in which worldly expenditure is sanctioned by its anchorage in the eternal stability of Providential wisdom – as exemplifying a conceptual strategy by which worldly practices in a variety of spheres – philosophical, political, industrial, commercial, semiotic, behavioural – are legitimated in sixteenth-century discourses, by an appeal to their conformity with the eternal structures of metaphysical Truth, as articulated by the Word. It is this nexus of associated ideal economies – and the principle of diseconomy which threatens them all – which is the subject of this book. In the present chapter, I want to trace one axis of relation between questions of national economics and the associated economies of the sign and of subjectivity; the axis, that is, which links the usurer and Narcissus.

The Sun and the Seal

You are not born to yourself,
Neither may you take
That thing for your own,
Whereof God did you make
But steward and bailiff.

Robert Crowley, *One and Thirty Epigrams* (1550)[10]

The importance of the usurer as a trope in the economic literature of the sixteenth century can be approached indirectly through a consideration of two texts written between 1519 and 1536: *A treatise concerning the staple and the commodities of this realm* (c.1519–35), and *How to reform the realm in setting them to work and to restore tillage* (c.1535–6).[11] The central economic problems addressed in *A treatise concerning the staple* are those which recur throughout the economic writing of the mid-century: inflation (or 'dearth'), rural depopulation, a poor balance of payments, and the instability of the cloth industry. The key to this treatise's analysis is the concept of an original Divine dispensation or 'gift' of resources, a distribution which sets the 'natural' limits and conditions of legitimate and prudent economic practices:

> . . . that is with the werke of housbondry to receyve the speciall gift of the fynes and goodness of the staple wolle, which Godd by his first day of everlasting light by vertu of his holy spirit gaff into the erth for the comon welth of Englande, befor sone, moone and sters were made, which are but the mynesteres of the gift of the same . . . . (p. 90)

The economic health of any historical moment consists in the confirmation and reproduction of this original gift. The divine distribution of different resources to particular geographical and national locations at the Creation acts as a structural constraint which persists beneath the variables of historical change, and only actions and policies which are shaped in reference to it can be considered either righteous or likely to prosper:

> As all inordinate companies made by mens wisdom, increasing into singular weale, hath but a beeng and endyng for a certain age, induryng such out of right contrary Gods ordinancie cannot endure, like as nothing under the sun is of itself ever after but as vanity. (p. 91)

The name of the economy in which the original just distribution of resources is represented is *common weal*. It is opposed, as in this passage, to actions which block that representation – actions, that is, which are dedicated to *singularity*. This opposition of terms is central to all the texts I will be considering in this chapter: here I want to stress that in the passage just quoted, 'singular weale' is termed inordinate not merely on ethical grounds. It is also that the agents of singularity consign themselves to an order of existence which, because it is unintegrated with the order which endures beyond history, is of a lesser and impoverished reality in comparison with the structures of Commonwealth. The order of singularity is also – and this term will also recur throughout this chapter – that of *vanity*, a term which in the contexts we will encounter connotes insubstantiality, brevity and abortiveness.

In the treatise's analysis, it is the direction of desire towards this singular order of ontologically deficient objects which is posited as the cause of economic malfunctions – one of the difficulties of restoring economic health is that the authentic object of desire is not a thing available to the senses but a structure of distributive relationships, the paradigm of commonwealth. I shall discuss later how this problem of redirecting desire from the sensible to the immaterial involves educational discourse in the question of economics, as well as assuring the theory of the sign a central place in that involvement.[12]

The contemporary Staple of the treatise's title is a mechanism of economic regulation whose function is to secure the relation between the contemporary economic system and the eternal structure of Commonwealth, ensuring that the local historical phenomenon fully represents the original paradigm. This congruence of phenomenon

and origin is also figured as the transparency of the phenomenon to
a distant source of light:

> . . . the fynes and goodness of the staple wolle, which God by his
> first day of everlasting light gaff into the erth for the common
> welth of Englande . . . . (p. 90)

The persistence or re-presentation of Commonwealth assures the
continued availability of this original illumination despite the inter-
posed forms of historical phenomena. If the historically specific
economic system, policy or action is structurally congruent with
the origin then light is not impeded by it; its incongruity is also
its opacity or imperviousness to divine illumination. If we shift into
the other terminology offered by the treatise – that of Spirit – the
opposition becomes one between matter which accepts the imprint
of Spirit and matter which persists as mere matter.

As I will show in my discussion of the Jonsonian masque, the
association of light and Spirit, and the question of the transparency or
opacity of phenomena, are central to Christian Platonist speculation
upon cosmic/semiotic economy. In a writer such as Maximus of Tyre,
for example, the relation of phenomenon to Creator is that of a
reflector or veil to a light source, or of signifier to signified.[13] It
is the perspicuity of the viewing subject which decides whether the
object will reveal – reflect – or obscure – veil – the divine radiance.
In terms of Maximus's alternative semiotic terminology, the problem
is one of *reading* and whether the reader of Nature's book is capable
of rendering the text transparent to the light of its meaning. The
difference introduced into this theme by the *Treatise concerning the
staple* is that of human agency – the object which admits or occludes
the light of the Signified is here not a given natural phenomenon but
a human construction whose transparency is determined by the will
of the constructor. The foundation of economic policy and practice in
the human faculties of will and invention means that the relationship
between ideal and worldly economies acquires an ethical dimension,
in which the initiatives of men may be judged according to their
conformity with the paradigm of the Divine Gift. As we shall see
in the next chapter, this is another area in which the question of
the economy of the sign links together sixteenth-century discourses
on both the system of national economics and the literary text: the
dangers of singularity – of a willed deviation from a metaphysical

paradigm – are held to be present for strictly analogous reasons in both cases.

The point at which the treatise's discourse on the national economy connects most clearly with questions of signification and the regulation of language is in its deployment of the associated tropes of the Sun and the Seal. It is through these rhetorical figures that a conceptual mediation is performed between the Gift, understood as the original moment of Divine illumination, and the orders of natural phenomena and human communication. The mediating agency of the first figure is intensified by an implicit pun on the terms Sun and Son – Christ being invoked as the exemplary instance of the translation of Spirit into matter, and of the Word into human discourse.[14]

The Sun appears in the treatise as one of the primary 'ministers' of the original dispensation, its role being to regulate patterns of labour and production in accordance with natural and Divine law, and to compensate for the disequilibrium and inequity introduced by 'singular' human policy:

> It is to see, how every reame hath serchid to robbe oon another. England hath geten owte of Spayne and other contreys the roth and fruyts of olives, figges, almonds, dates and orynges and such other thyngs, and hath sette and plantid theym in the erth in England, which hath brought forth to bodyly stokk and braunchis and levys by the risyng of the sonne in the spryng of the yere. But whan the sonne cometh to the mystery of his gift at the mydsomer, beholdyng England soo wylling to robbe Spayn to gette it Goddes gifts, the sonne turnyth from the northe towards the southe and not giff no vertu of good to non of the comodites of Spayn, soo removid into England . . . nor no propertie that shuld help and encrease England to the hurt and hynderaunce of Spayn. So evident to see, how the office of the sonne is not only to mynester alle the gifts of Godd yerly to every reame, region or contrey on the erth accordyng lyke as Godd in the first begynnyng gaff it, but also the sonne by his office holdith and kepith every reame and contrey in his own right, that noo oon robbe nor hurt another. What a lorde is Godd, that so rightwisly mynesterith right to all reames and contreis rown abowt all the holl erthe by his oonly oon grete brode seale of his law of sone of man, gevyng mete for bodyly levyng to all men in this world . . . . (pp. 99–100)

It is this regulation of resources in relation to their Divine distribution which makes the sun a conveyor of the original light. The sun's light, as the figure of an absolute and undeviating cosmic enstructuration – as, that is, the radiance of the Real – carries with it the assurance of illumination in the sense of secure knowledge or the unimpeded availability of the Signified. So by a visual pun the sun becomes the 'grete brode seale' of Divine righteousness, the definitive pictographic mark of authority which founds a system of value and exchange exempt from the possibility of deceit, ambiguity or the uncoupling of price from value. The stability and authority of the sign of the Seal is then opposed in the treatise to the obscurity, ambiguity and inconclusiveness of that legal writing by which the secular monarch articulates 'singular' policies:

> What a wisdome is of erthly kynges, that in oon litle reame, which is but as a howse in comparison to the kyngdom of sone of man, that in so litle quantite cannot giff to every man right and kepe every man in his right by oon ordinary hedd-seale, but for a sory cotage of a noble rent by yere must have many writings and many seales, and therby can nother see nor know how to have right clerly nor suerly. So false is mens wisdome and policy. (p. 100)

The absence of 'right order' in England is a question of the multiplication of 'singular' policies ('many writings and many seales') and the dissemination of their associated legal discourse, without regulation through reference to the authoritative imprint of the 'hedd-seal' which illuminates beyond dispute the fundamental categories of right and wrong policy. To live under this confusion, the treatise implies, is to descend to the sub-rational condition of the beasts, exposed to the hazards of sensory experience but powerless to organise that experience into the rational and linguistic order of *description*:

> A mervelous sight to see, England for lakke of the lyvely grace of Godd lyveth lyke as a beste, which beeng woundyd, of the sore greff and smert the members hath sensible felyng, but of the cause therof they have no descrivyng. (pp. 100–1)

The treatise's image of the Seal – as a trademark, and as an earthly delegate of the Signified – is the point at which two apparently disparate areas of concern intersect – the practical mechanisms for the regulation of economic markets, and the question of the metaphysical grounding of discourse. That the metaphoric force of the Seal does derive in part from a reference to existing regulatory machinery is underlined in the exposition of the function of a national staple in the second treatise, *How to reform the realm* . . . :[15]

> Wherupon it may please our gracious king of Englond to make a staple of all wollen clothes in London . . . and that every market towne of clothe making have a common seale and every wollen clothe made within the presinct and libertie and fredome of the towne, to recourde the true making of all wollen clothes to be sealed with the sealles of the townes wherin they be made; theruppon to be brought to the kinges staple of wollen clothe in London, ther to be sealed with the kinges seale of his staple, to recorde all the wollen clothes in Englond . . . shal be openly knowen to be trewe made clothes, whersoever they be bought and sold. So shall all Englishe clothers never be slaundered in no other realmes and contries for false making . . . . And their untrue saying slaunderith the sale of English clothes for lake that their true making of theym is not recordyd by a staple seale. (p. 119)

The practical function of the seal is to perform a fundamental semiotic stabilisation – it marks each cloth as being in fact what it claims or seems to be. This authentication of 'true making' is the basis upon which the Staple operates to regulate quality and price, which is in turn seen as the basis of a properly and equitably functioning market, and so too of reduced inflation and restored employment. The stability of the sign, as realised in a fully effective system of seals, is then at the heart of the reformed economy envisaged in the two treatises. The Staple and the Seal are both metonymic representations of two archetypal economies whose reproduction in contemporary practices is held to be crucial to the health of the social body – an economy of natural resources and an economy of the sign.

The authoritative pictogram of the 'great broad seal' functions within this economic discourse as a practical instance of that archetypal hieroglyphic or pictographic script which was the quarry of much sixteenth- and seventeenth-century speculation about language – a script in which signifier and signified are united and which is therefore exempted from the dubieties of interpretation and dissemination.[16] The theorists of the hieroglyph see it as a sign which resists the corrosive impact of temporality which destabilises ordinary language, because it does away with the syntagmatic dimension of discourse – the dimension in which meaning is temporally articulated – in favour of an extreme paradigmatic condensation. In the same way, the discourse of Seal and Staple proposes a negation of history by the immediate and perpetual recapture of the Origin, or Divine Gift.

In the terms of that discourse, the detour into history is also a diversion from nature into the artificial order of culture; from the 'right order' of naturally implanted resources to the chaotic contention of 'singular' policies. The reformed economic and social order envisaged by the treatises is accordingly conservative and organicist – in opposition to the disorder of policy and innovation they put in place the concept of 'husbandry',[17] an ensemble of customary measures and techniques immemorially attuned to the constraints of the original Gift and consequently assured in its production of staple goods for all citizens.

It is in the light of this organicist vision that the contemporary decline of the English economy is seen as deriving from an uncoupling of certain human agents from their naturally ordained places, and their consequent precipitation into a space or level of economic activity which is estranged from nature – a space conceived of as artificial, imaginary, insubstantial.

This detour from nature begins, according to the *Treatise on the Staple*, with the increase of wool production beyond what is socially necessary, in pursuit of private profit; a disruption of natural equilibrium and a shift into 'singularity' and the disorder of the artificial. The overproduction of staple wool determines an increase, again deemed artificial, in the number of staplers or wool merchants. Part of this surplus is supplied by 'por mens sons natural born to labour for their living' (p. 126), who instead of remaining in their natural vocation are placed as apprentices to London merchants:

The bredyng of so many marchaunts in London, risen owt of pore mens sonnes, hath bene a mervelous distruction to the holl reame . . . . So wer all yong merchaunts, comyng owt of ther prentishod and cowd have no wages of ther masters, compellid to borrow clothes of clothe makers for respite, and caried the same clothes to the marts beyonde see to sell, and ther must nedes sell theym, and the money to bestow it on wares to bryng home to sell, to make money to pay ther creditors at ther dayes . . . that in short time they distroyed the price of wollen

clothes, causyng all the old merchaunts to fall from byeng
and sellyng clothes. Than began old merchaunts to forsake
occupieng of clothes to occupie their money by exchaunge,
which is not only pleyn usury, but also it hath and yit doth
helpe to distroye the welth of the kyng, of his lords and comons,
for that occupieng hynderith the reame both ways outward and
inward. (pp. 106–7)

The 'bad' economic cycle described here – the novice's borrowed
stock, the cheap sale abroad, the import of luxury goods, the sale
to creditors – with its destruction of 'natural' cloth prices and its
forcing of established merchants into exchange transactions for
their profits, exemplifies for the writer an artificial system, a
chain of economic relations which is self-generative, ungrounded
(not 'stapled') in any relation to the naturally instituted structure
relating resources, labour, distribution and the circulation of money.
The fact that this artificial process is seen as ending in a manipulation
of money on the exchanges characterised as 'plegn usury' points to
the conceptual connection within Commonwealth discourse between
credit and the processes of industrial and economic innovation – a
connection which produces the demonisation of the usurer, which I
will consider later in this chapter.

The diversion from nature into artifice is focused in the treatise
in two images of the artificial subduing the organic, of surface
obliterating substance, and of technique exceeding nature. The first
relates to the cause of the original overproduction of wool which
initiates the cycle of economic decline:

So as all people should work the earth to receive both meat for
bodily living and clothing together, not for clothing to destroy
bodily living, for the less to destroy the more. (p. 104)

The inversion of the natural relation between essence and accident,
substance and surface, turns clothing from a sustainer of life into
its destroyer; I shall discuss this conceptual structure – and the
associated critique of superfluous apparel – at greater length later
in this chapter. The same concern emerges when the treatise deals
with the exchange of English exports for luxury imports:

All nacions sittyng in the contreys deviseth fantasies to make
English men foles to get the riches owt of the reame, in
experience as well French men and others, that in London

> shewith ware howsis full of trifell sold and bought for a hundred
> pownde; if the werkmanship of makyng therof takyn away, the
> very substance beside the werk is not werth a hundred shilling,
> but boones, hornes, sakkes, ledder peces, heres, papers, erthyn
> potts, bottels, glassis and such other trifells; yhe, and daily
> carieth owt of England old shoes, hornes and bones, and
> bryngith it into the reame ageyn made in to fantasies, wherby
> they get the riches owt of the reame . . . . (p. 110)

Here the reality of substance is displaced by a double artificiality
of workmanship and price; monetary inflation is inseparable from
an inflation or excess of form in relation to the object's organic
content. The opening up of a difference between the natural order
of commonwealth, with its stable (or stapled) relation of substance
to value, and the artificial system of mercantile economy, involves,
then, what is seen as an artificial differentiation of substance and
value, content and form, and the possibility of a transformation
of material without any reference to 'natural' function or use. We
will see these terms, and particularly the language of fantasy and
dissimulation, return in our discussion of the economy of literary
representation.

The logic of the intermediate

> . . . men that live as thoughe there were no god at all, men
> that would have all in their owne handes, men that would leave
> nothing for others, men that would be alone on the earth, men
> that bee never satisfied . . .
>
> Robert Crowley, *The Way to Wealth*[18]

The vision of an artificial order of socio-economic activity generating
itself within the customary structure of Commonwealth is extended
in the treatise *How to restore the realm* . . . . The dominant terms
of the treatise on the Staple – the head, the gift of grace, right order,
the bodily members – are redeployed here so as to produce an image of
the ideal integration of the monarch and common people in the feudal
economic and political system. The malfunctioning of that system is
portrayed as the result of the singular desires and policies of the
intermediate ranks between King and common people, the ranks
represented in the House of Commons:

Therfor cane they make no acte nor good order for the welth
of the common people, but remytteth all causes to pass by the
wisdome, content, will and agrement of theym which are in the
common howse, thinking that such as are in the common howse
shuld especially entende the welthe of all coommon people, the
kynges bodyly members. Who woll serch may prove, whether
suche sortes are not in the common howse, which hath distroyed
the welth of the king and his lordes and common people, getting
every yere above 200000 poundes out of the common weale into
their singler weale . . . . And whether the enclosiers of pastures
for shepe, and graciers and regraters of corne and catalles, ar
not in the common howse, and merchauntes, byers and sellers,
which gettyth their richis out of the common weale . . . . And yf
the king and his lordes in the hedd howse wold mynester the rich
giftes of grace to the common people . . . they in the common
howse, which hath and doth distroy the common weale, cannot
suffer no acte passe for the common weale, but they must nedes
distroy their owne singuler weale. (pp. 121–2)

The repetition of key terms here signals the structural homology
which, it is implied, exists between the original divine dispensation
of resources discussed in the first treatise, and the mechanisms –
political, juridical, distributive – of an idealised feudal order. The
'head house' of monarch and lords ('head' carrying with it the
connotations of authoritative declaration and rational illumination
involved in the first treatise's imagery of 'head-seal' and the Sun)
must communicate directly with the king's 'bodily members' or
common people. This union of head and members in an integrated
body is another version of the organicist vision we discussed earlier, a
vision of natural social dependencies and distributive harmony.[19] The
unification of the feudal social body qualifies it – by homology with
the structure of the divine Gift – as a 'minister', a true conveyor or
representative of the divine light. What obstructs this continuity is the
development of an intermediate sphere (between head and members)
of specifically political activity focused in the House of Commons.
The Commons is the seat of singularity and its familiar agents;
merchants, buyers and sellers, lawyers, engrossers and enclosers of
land. It acts as an obstruction to the natural circulation of wealth
between King and common people, which is to be restored by the
unmediated collaboration of national and local government:

> Therfor the king and his lords of the erth hath nede to
> ordeyn that the common weale of the hole realme may by
> his mynesters be mynysterd in all market townes, wherin all
> wollen clothes are wrought and made, for therin the common
> welth restith. (p. 122)

The Commons focuses and articulates the anti-social energies of
the middleman; indeed it represents the pernicious nature of the
intermediate as such – of any category, that is, which intervenes
to disrupt or sophisticate the unambiguous relations and communications which sustain natural order. It is appropriate, then, that the
Commons should also be represented as the source of the juridical
writing – the Statutes – by which 'singularity' articulates its manifold
and incoherent policies.[20] Writing, in the kind of economy (national
and cosmic) which I have been considering, is a principal type of
bad intermediacy, diverting direct oral communication into an area
of deceit, contention and disputed meaning.[21] This suspicion finds
in Statutes and legal discourse a malign agency at the heart of
the nation's political and economic systems. It is another of the
Staple's remedial functions to replace these writings with the direct
intercourse of ministers and local officials:

> And by that reason the king and his lordes shall never more
> be trobeled with no workes nor actes of parliament for the
> common weale, but to the governors and rewlers of his riche
> townes, which shall have gold and silver brought out of all
> other contries for our wolles and wollen clothes, etc., value
> for value. (p. 122)

In this treatise, politics is the name for the systematic articulation
of 'singular' policies; an order of artificiality and intermediacy which
is to be excised from the England regenerated by economic reform.
Government in the new order is an unmediated expression of the
natural bond between King and commoners, the state being funded
directly out of the fecundity of the organic society. The political nation
represented in the House of Commons is in this way made redundant
as a source of levy and taxation, and so as an influence upon policy:

> . . . and so shall the king and his lordes be riche as in old tyme,
> to have no nede to study how to gader money out of that little
> quantitie of money which is in the handes of the commons, in
> the realme to make scarsite. (p. 122)

The exclusion of the middle and the middleman represents an imagined curtailment of those forces whose tendency in the economic history of this period was towards the liberation of the market from social restraints. In the 'bad' market of the middleman, as the treatises represent it, exchange is a moment of dislocation and slippage, in which the relationship between substance and value, quantity and price, the thing and its monetary representation, appears to have escaped any natural or absolute determination. The Staple, on the contrary, is an image of the regulation of exchange according to the natural paradigm of the Gift – a regulation, that is, which effaces itself, and becomes only another moment in the natural circulation of self-equilibrating quantities and values which is the organic society.

For the defenders of Commonwealth, the artificial economy of the middleman is dominated by two processes: inflation and the dislocation of social agents from their customary or natural places. The relationship between the stability of prices and of social categorisation in medieval economic theory (and, I would add, in the medievalist economic and social criticism of the sixteenth century) is described by the economists Hunt and Sherman:

> A just price was one that would compensate the seller for his efforts in transporting the good and finding the buyer at a rate that was just sufficient to maintain the seller at his customary or traditional station in life.[22]

The link which this implies between inflation and social dislocation is strengthened by the fact that sixteenth-century commentators believe both to involve an effect of semiotic disruption. Both introduce a principle of slippage and insecurity into the process of reading the Book of the World. Inflation does this by uncoupling value from substance; social dislocation by severing social actions and appearances from customary vocational position or 'degree'. So, for Thomas Lever, the agent of inflation insinuates himself between natural categories, contriving a place for himself where nature offers none:

> I say these merchants of mischief, coming betwixt the bark and the tree, do make all things dere to the buyer . . . these have every mans living, and no mans duty.[23]

The middleman here breaks the natural linkage between living and duty; between, that is, personal gain and vocational integration into the structure of Commonwealth. Lever's specific target is the credit transaction and its brokers. The growing necessity of this kind of finance in all the principal spheres of national economic activity is a central development in sixteenth-century England.[24] One of its principal consequences is the development of a new level of economic activity and relationship which has no relation to the customary categories around which the discourse of Commonwealth is articulated. The result is a crisis in the denomination of social agents and relations:

> . . . men that have no name because they are doares in al thinges that ani gaine hangeth upon . . . O good maisters, what shuld I call you? You that have no name, you that have so many occupacions and trads that ther is no name for you![25]

The namelessness which Robert Crowley complains of here has three main types – the namelessness of the intermediate or mobile, of the multiple, and of the interloper. We have already considered some of the agents of the intermediate as the first Treatise represented them congregating in the House of Commons. The associated anxiety attached to mobility is best expressed in the proposed regulatory machinery of the Statute of Artificers, whose measures frequently conflate the restriction of physical and of social mobility:

> #2. Labourers and Servants. – That the Statutes 12 Richard II, chap iii, 'That no servant or labourer at the end of his term depart out of the hundred or place where he dwells, etc.' . . . be confirmed, with the addition that 'no man hereafter receive into service any servant without a testimonial from the master he last dwelt with, sealed with a parish seal kept by the constable or church warden, witnessing he left with the free licence of his master, penalty 10l.' So, by the head of the masters, servants may be reduced to obedience, which shall reduce obedience to the Prince and to God also.[26]

Here the judicial geography of hundred and place reproduces 'horizontally' the 'vertical' topography of degree and obedience. The vagrancy of the masterless man erases the judicial frontiers of local geography and in doing so disrupts the categorical demarcations which map out the topography of 'degree'. It is this second form of disruption which concerns Crowley in his complaint against a blurring of nomination through a multiplication of the economic roles of individual agents. At one level the target is again the middleman, shifting his function according to the nature of the individual transaction, but Crowley is aiming particularly at 'the gentlemen, the knight, the lordes'.[27] The diversification of economic and social roles among the aristocracy is one response, along with rack-renting, the raising of entry fines, and the engrossing and enclosing of land, to the erosion of its traditional income from land. Francis Bacon points to the consequent broadening of the definition of aristocratic 'husbandry':

> I knew a nobleman in England that had the greatest audits of any man in my time, a great grazier, a great sheep-master, a great timber-man, a great collier, a great corn-master, a great lead man, and so of iron, and a number of the like points of husbandry; so as the earth seemed as a sea to him in respect of the perpetual importation.[28]

The qualitative or conceptual shift involved in this diversification of economic roles is implied in Bacon's concluding image: the customary relation between the husband and the land has modulated into that of the merchant to his overseas markets. The relationship in which the economic, social and political harmonies of Commonwealth are literally grounded – that between the nobility and gentry, and the land – has taken on not only the profitability, but also some of the hazardousness and contingency – the outlandishness – of that between merchant capital and the world market.

Bacon's metaphor harbours a connection between an alienation from customary socio-economic roles and a growing commerce with the alien itself: the erosion of Commonwealth is intimately connected, according to many sixteenth-century commentators, to England's increasing implication in foreign trade and the associated cultural exposures and infections which are believed to follow from it. One focus for this concern about the effects of foreignness on domestic stability is the alien merchant or worker based in England.[29] All the fears of placelessness and namelessness which haunt the discourse on Commonwealth are concentrated here: the alien has no origin or customary location within the categories of domestic Commonwealth, and his social 'invisibility' is inevitably compounded by the inscrutability of his language, manners and native customary structures. Moreover, the consolidation of national and ethnic groups in particular urban quarters and ghettos intensifies the

commentators' fears of social disintegration: the alien communities
are seen to represent not merely an evasion of the systems of domestic
commonwealth, but the entrenchment of counter-systems: '. . . they
are a commonwealth within themselves'.[30]

One particularly visible alien commonwealth, which potently
combines the dangers of self-integration with those of collective
vagrancy, is that of the gypsies. Philip and Mary's *Act for the
Punishment of certain Persons calling themselves Egiptians* draws
attention in its title to an illegitimate self-nomination – the assertion
of an identity outside the ordained nominations of degree. The Act
proceeds to allow for the waiving of its sanctions if the gypsies
renounce their autonomy and integrate themselves into the customary
structure of service and calling:

> For thavoyding and banishing out of this Realme of certaine
> outlandishe People calling themselves Egiptians, using no crafte
> nor feate of marchaundises for to lyve by, but going from place
> to place in greate Companies, using greate suttle and craftye
> meanes to deceyve the Kinges Subjectes . . . using their olde
> accustomed develishe and noughty practises and devises, withe
> suche abhominable lyving as is not in any Christian Realme to
> be permitted named or knowen . . . . That this present Acte nor
> anything therein contained, shall not extend nor be hurtfull to
> any of the said persons . . . which within the saide time . . . shall
> leave that noughty idle and ungodly lyef and company, and be
> placed in the service of some honest and able Inhabitante or
> Inhabitantes within this Realme, or that shall honestly exercise
> himself in some lawfull worck or occupacion.[31]

The economy of 'lawfull worck or occupacion' confronts that of 'craft
and subtiltie'; the divinely sanctioned system of commonwealth stands
against 'olde accustomed develish . . . practises and devises'. The
contemporary gypsy is affiliated with the Egyptian of Old Testament
narrative whose polytheism and alien observances fall within the
categories of idolatry, necromancy and devil-worship. The Devil, as
the Father of Lies, presides over the economics of deception and fraud;
God, as Clerk of the Market, over the just order of Commonwealth.

The idleness of the gypsy is in part a function of his or her
placelessness; another instance of the vagrant's evasion of the
organised visible field of 'official' geographical and social space.
The idleness of the gypsy's 'noughty practises and devises', however,

is to be understood as a *temporal* delinquency. The statute of Philip and Mary specifically charges that the 'Egiptians' 'bear . . . in hande that they by Palmestrye could tell Mens and Womens Fortune'.[32] The telling (and hearing) of fortunes represents an attempted evasion or usurpation of the Providential structuring of time, and in this it is typical of the delinquent arts and recreations of *idleness* identified by moralists in the period. Idleness is the state suffered (or perhaps enjoyed) by all those who are detached, whether by choice or force of circumstance, from the productive duties of vocation or degree. In the moral discourses of the period it is always a question of choice: redundancy is the result of a perverse act of will, a manifestation of the inertial tendency which attends all human subjects since the Fall. As such, idleness is properly an object for regimes of self-discipline and personal reformation. It is at this point also that idleness, and the regulation of subjective temporality according to the demands of vocation and duty, become central preoccupations of another discourse, that of the humanist educational theorists.

Making haste slowly: the economy of temperance

Veritas filia temporis.
Classical topos

The worde flyeth from us irrevocably. The tyme flyeth from us irredeemably.

George Gascoigne, *The Shame of Sinne*[33]

Thomas Elyot's *Book of the Governour* exemplifies this Humanist preoccupation, as it returns compulsively to the question of the economical regulation of time, the epicentre of the topic being located in his discussion of games and recreation. In Elyot's hierarchy of games according to their educational value the lowest rung is occupied by dice, which he associates intimately with idleness. Dice for Elyot is an entertainment and re-creation of randomness – in its celebration of the haphazard and the contingent it represents the antithesis of the dance, whose elaborately structured temporal measures, happily analogous to the patterning of Providential time, place dancing at the top of Elyot's recreational hierarchy. Card-playing is placed above dice because 'therin wytte is more used, and lasse truste is in fortune'. It is also preferred because its elements are more readily rendered significant – 'as devising a bataile, or contention between vertue and vice'.[34] These recommendations of card-playing are important because they associate criteria of rationality ('wytte') and significance with that of temporal coherence. The hierarchical ascent from randomness to Providential order is accompanied by two parallel gradations, as follows:

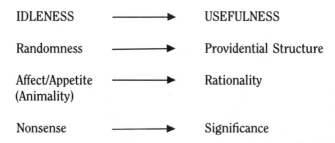

IDLENESS	⟶	USEFULNESS
Randomness	⟶	Providential Structure
Affect/Appetite (Animality)	⟶	Rationality
Nonsense	⟶	Significance

It is unusual to find a discussion of idleness and usefulness in this period – a discussion, that is, of the criteria for the social legitimation of the subject – which does not issue from this ideological structure. Elyot, for example, rescues the dance from charges of redundancy or triviality by establishing a triple claim for its usefulness: as an imitation of cosmic harmony and Providential temporality, as an exercise of rational self-discipline, and as a signifying practice which articulates a body of orthodox knowledge:

> Now it behoveth the daunsers and also the beholders of them to know all the qualities incident to a man, and also all qualities to a woman lyke wyse appertayninge . . . I have devised howe in the forme of daunsinge . . . the hole description of this vertue prudence may be founden out and well perceyved, as well by the daunsers as by them whiche standinge by, wyll be diligent beholders and markers, havyng first myne instruction suerly graven in the table of their remembrance. (I, pp. 236, 240)

Other pastimes fulfil one or other of the criteria of profit without matching the comprehensive educational value of the dance. Chess is commended principally for its signifying potential – 'it is the more commendable and also commodiouse if the players have radde the moralisation of the chesse, and whenne they playe, do thinke ypon it' (I, p. 283). Archery and tennis in their turn are judged according to their scope for rational self-regulation; archery being approved because the archer regulates his own exercise around a standard of 'mediocritie' or moderation, unlike tennis, where the dependence of the player upon his opponent means that 'neither of them is at his owne libertie to measure the exercise'. At the other extreme from archery is football, 'wherin is nothinge but beastly furie and extreme violence' (I, p. 292); a judgement which stresses the link between sub-rationality (the 'beastly') and chaotic violence, the latter standing in antithesis to rational and Providential order. From this series of assessments it is possible to extrapolate some further dimensions of the Idleness/Usefulness structure:

IDLENESS		USEFULNESS
IDLENESS	⟶	USEFULNESS
Randomness	⟶	Providence
Appetite	⟶	Rationality
Nonsense	⟶	Significance
Chaos/Violence	⟶	Order/Self-regulation
The Many (Football)	⟶	The One (Archery)
Democracy	⟶	Monarchy

I want to stress the structural link between the conservation and ordering of time, psychic economy and signification with a final quotation from Elyot, in which he is emphasising the necessity of rendering all elements of the student governor's domestic environment significant:

> In likewise his plates and vessels would be engraved with histories, fables, or quick and wise sentences . . . so wisdom may be ingested with food, or fruitful disputation or reasoning, wherby some part of time shall be saved, which else by superfluous eating and drinking would be idly consumed.
> (II, p. 103)

The strategic pre-emption of idleness, its conversion into *re-creation*, is exemplified in this regime of feeding: the vacant moment and the sensual appetite are reclaimed from their tendency to eventuate sin and become instead agents of profit or usefulness. The diseconomy of 'lost' time and 'superfluous' consumption is transformed into an economy of retention, of the active reproduction of the contents of knowledge ('sentences') and the forms of discourse and rationality ('disputation and reasoning').

We should note that this whole operation, by which the subject's sensual experience and consciousness of time are submitted to social discipline, is founded upon the submission of the vacancy of material objects – their semantic inertia – to the economy and discipline of *interpretation*. The force of the social discipline outlined by Elyot resides in this energising of the material environment: the consolidation of the subject within established and authorised systems of knowledge operates not as an imprisonment but as an incitement to explore, to read the environment productively so that the familiar is discovered in the ciphered forms of the novel or alien. The discipline which opposes the 'wanderings' of the delinquent, the vagrant and the idle in the name of education is a strategy of harmonisation by which the conflicting energies of the appetites and the reason, the undisciplined prodigality of materiality and the stabilising authority of spirit, are brought into equilibrium. The educational strategies of the Humanists attempt to establish an *economy of the mean* at the level of the subject which is analogous to the economies of time and signification in Hooker's work, or the Household economy instituted by the Ordinance of 1478. In this case the strategy secures orthodox forms of knowledge, moral and social discipline, while inciting the student to exercise initiative and curiosity, to engage cunningly and productively, in other words, with the snares of worldly circumstance.

In the case of Elyot, this union of conservation at the level of the system and experiment at that of the individual is produced in response to important changes in the social character of education and government.[35] With the centralisation and professionalisation of national and regional administration under the Tudors, and the initial hostility or indifference of the aristocratic response to the new developments, the necessity of enlisting and training personnel from hitherto under-exploited social strata was inescapable. Elyot's *Governour* is one direct response to the potential difficulties and risks of this process; its strategies of dynamic conservation attempt to manage a regulated incorporation of 'new men', new ideas and new areas of experience into a secure domain of orthodoxy.

This educational effect is reproduced within the texture of individual experience, providing a regime by which the subject too manages the incorporation and familiarisation of new experience. This double purchase – both macro- and microcosmic – is also the case in education's economising of time, through which it makes a central contribution to the broader policing of idleness. For if education seeks to reconcile conservation and innovation at a macrocosmic level, then that modulation of divergent temporal rhythms has its equivalent in the temporal experience of the subject: that is in Elyot's newly-introduced and Englished category of *maturity*,[36] meaning the virtue of economy, of prudent expenditure, in the management of subjective temporality. Elyot's mature governor exercises his personal capacities in that 'due time and measure' which finds its socially symbolic articulation in the dance.

The sumptuary and the supplementary: diseconomies of attire

> Persons having less than £20. a Year &c. shall
> not wear Silk;
> Penalty £10. and Three Months' Imprisonment.[37]

Tudor educational theory is supported by an institutional framework which allows for the rigorous supervision and control of the process by which the system admits innovation. In other contemporary ideological and disciplinary domains, mechanisms for the reproduction of orthodoxy are less developed. As we have already seen in relation to the policing of social mobility and economic innovation, the measures of social discipline here tend to be gestures of disavowal; attempts to sustain the coherence of a disintegrating ideological system through the drama of exclusion and reintegration which is performed around such figures as the gypsy and the vagabond. From this perspective, the incorporative tendency of the education system can appear as dangerous, as here, in Burghley's 1559 *Considerations*:

> #8. Education of the nobility. – That an ordinance be made
> to bind the nobility to bring up their children in learning at
> some university in England or beyond the sea from the age of
> 12 to 18 at least; and that one third of all the scholarships at

the universities be filled by the poorer sort of gentlemen's sons. The wanton bringing up and ignorance of the nobility forces the Prince to advance new men that can serve, which for the most part neither affecting true honour, because the glory thereof descended not to them, nor yet the commonwealth (through coveting to be hastily in wealth and honour), forget their duty and old estate and subvert the noble houses to have their rooms themselves, etc.

#9. That none study the laws, temporal or civil, except he be immediately descended from a nobleman or gentleman, for they are the entries to rule and government, and generation is the chiefest foundation of inclination.[38]

The dissociation of 'generation' from 'inclination' – in other words of the 'natural' bond between noble birth and administrative aptitude – which these measures confront is one manifestation of that larger dislocation of 'natural' order from the actual circumstances of economic development which we have been considering. The attempt to reassert the priority of 'generation' is typical of Burleigh's *Considerations*, of the Statute of Artificers into which they feed, and of the ideological tone of Tudor social and economic legislation generally. We can suggest this continuity by considering an earlier statute, that of Henry VIII concerning apparel.

The primary intention of *1 Henry VIII c.14* is to prohibit the wearing of apparel which exaggerates the wearer's social standing. In this it attempts to reassert a comprehensive structural alignment between strictly graded hierarchies of rank, cost and sumptuousness of apparel, and income. One section of the statute will characterise its overall procedure:

> Nor no persone other then be above named were Velvet in their Dublett nor Satten nor Damaske in their gownes nor Cotes, excepte he be a Lordes Sone or a Gentilman havyng in his possession or other to his use Landes or Tenements or annuytes at the leste for Terme of Lyffe to the yerely valewe of an hundreth pounde above all repryses . . . .[39]

What this procedure aims at is the assertion of a continuity between essence and accident, between the core of degree and the superficies of personal ornament. By attempting to resecure this continuity, the Act seeks to regulate the semiotic function of apparel; to ensure, that is, that the nuances of fashion are tied in strict representational relation to those of rank:

> And that no manne under the degree of a Baron use in his Apparell of his body or of his Horses eny clothe of golde or clothe of Sylver or tynsyn Satten ne no other Sylke or Clothe myxte or broderd wyth Golde or Sylver . . . . (p. 8)

We have met this regime already in the bipartite structure of the Royal Wardrobe: the implied determination is that there will be no ungrounded or unrooted exfoliation of ornament, no expenditure of the signifier which is not founded in the signified (the signified being that 'truth' of things which is fixed by their location within the hierarchy of degree). In the unhinging of apparel from the categories of 'truth' there appears a dangerous convergence of two kinds of idleness: idleness as a delinquency of the *sign*, a vacancy or redundancy of the signifier which has wandered from its anchorage in the signified, and idleness as social decomposition, an atrophy of the linkages which bind the subject to a determined category or degree. Idleness as 'vanity' and idleness as vagrancy are bound together in the groundless significations of 'bad' apparel.

Because of this placement at the intersection of the two main axes which organise the question of idleness – the social and the semiotic – the issue of apparel is frequently the point at which there occurs a powerful condensation of the various tropes of dislocation/innovation which we have been considering. One example, of central ideological importance, is to be found in the 'Sermon against Excess of Apparel' in the 1547 *Book of Homilies*.

The sermon begins with a powerful conjoining of the question of apparel with those of social mobility and economic decay:

> All may not look to wear like apparel, but everyone according to his degree, as God hath placed him. Which, if it were observed, many a one doubtless would be compelled to wear a russet-coat, which now ruffleth in silks and velvets, spending more by the year in sumptuous apparel, than their fathers received for the whole revenue of their lands. But, alas! nowadays, how many may we behold occupied wholly in pampering the flesh, taking no care at all, but only how to deck themselves, setting their affection altogether on worldly bravery, abusing God's goodness when he sendeth plenty, to satisfy their wanton lusts, having no regard to the degree wherein God hath placed them.[40]

The superseded economy of the fathers which is appealed to here represents a strict proportionality or ratio between economic base ('lands'), revenue, consumption, and 'degree'. It is such a proportionality, regulating expenditure in relation to divinely established resources, which we have seen as the organising principle of the Royal Wardrobe and of the economics of Staple and Seal. The Homily sees such proportionality being disrupted in the mobility of the subject who dresses above his degree, and in the escalation of expenditure over revenue typical of the landed classes. It is unclear whether the sermon's second sentence consciously conflates or simply confuses these two categories of disruption, but in either case, there is a term which the Homily does not use which links the two categories together – *credit*.

It is credit which bridges the increasing gap between aristocratic revenues and expenditure in the period, and in doing so also funds the rapid social mobility of the broker or money lender, making him a principal villain of the discourse against pretentious apparel.[41] A link is established, then, between the disruption of monetary semiotics in the credit transaction and that of the semiotic relation between degree and apparel. I will pursue this further in my discussion of the usurer.

The diseconomy of apparel and revenue which the Homily addresses is traced to a breakdown of subjective economy – an assertion of the body and the sub-rational faculties at the expense of reason. The rational order of degree is displaced by the claims of 'flesh', 'affections' and 'lusts'. Concomitantly, that 'regard to . . . degree' by which the subject should look to its structural location is overcome by a self-regard which is fixated upon the surface of flesh and 'bravery'. This opposition of looks, between the through-seeing, categorical regard of reason and the self-/surface-fixated gaze of 'affection', is developed fully in the language of mirroring, bedazzlement and blindness which circulates about the figure of Narcissus, which I will consider later in this chapter. The *Homily on Apparel* develops not towards Narcissus (although the image of self-regard in the mirror remains latent) but into a diatribe against women and the use of cosmetics, which is another of the primary themes of the discourse on apparel.

The full array of disruptions and delinquencies which the discourse on apparel addresses accumulates about the figure of the painted woman:

What do these women, but go about to reform that which God

hath made? not knowing that all things natural are the works of God, and things disguised and unnatural be the works of the devil: and as though a wise and Christian husband should delight to see his wife in such painted and flourished visages, which common harlots most do use, to train therewith their lovers to naughtiness . . . . Nay, nay, these be but vain excuses of such as go about to please rather others than their husbands. And such attires be but to provoke her to show herself abroad, to entice others . . . . She doth but waste superfluously her husband's stock by such sumptuousness, and sometimes she is the cause of much bribery, extortion and deceit in her husband's dealings, that she may be the more gorgeously set out to the sight of the vain world, to please the Devil's eyes, and not God's . . . . (p. 61)

From the wife's painting to the husband's extortion, what is outlined here is a chain of causally linked violations of natural order and propriety. From the adornment of the face to the malpractices of the market, the disruptive principle is identified as a deviation into artifice, an egregious supplementation or complication of the organic. If the wife who paints commits a primary dislocation of appearance from reality, then this violation of ontological propriety determines a disruption in the natural economy of sexual generation, appetite and matrimony.

The married state exists, the Homily implies, to direct sexual appetite to its natural end in procreation: the use of cosmetics incites appetite in excess of procreative function, a surplus which directly reflects the supplementarity or artifice of the cosmetic. This contamination of the natural arena of sexuality by artifice is also a contamination of nature by the market, represented by the monetarised sexuality of the harlot. The harlot 'train[s] . . . to *naught*-iness': the vacuousness or redundancy of the aroused appetite is another name for its sophistication, its outstripping of natural function. As arenas for the incitement and exploitation of such appetites, prostitution and the 'free' market are equivalents in the ethical and economic discourses which we are considering.

The opening up of 'natural' matrimony to the artificial incitements of the market is accompanied by a reorientation of the wife from her 'natural' place within marriage to a delinquent sociability (a shift which the Homily also represents as being from 'Christianity' to 'Jewishness' and 'ethnicity', or in other words from the divinely sanctioned to the secular). The vanity of the wife in her painting is also her admission to that broader culture of vanity which I have already considered:

> No sooner are they varnished, but they forsake their home . . .
> Jezebel, (I am sure) proves Jezebel, when all is done, fit for
> nothing but to look out at a window towards the place and
> instruments of her destruction, unfit to stir or travel in her
> vocation.[42]

As we have seen, the culture of vanity is the negation of all divinely instituted economies; as this quotation from the preacher John Hoskins implies, by her defection to it the housewife strikes economy at the root,[43] turning herself from the centre of a prudent household economics to the provoker of 'waste and wantonness' (p. 61). It is this household diseconomy which in turn disrupts the husband's business and provokes, in his recourse to 'bribery, extortion and deceit', a practice of disguise at the economic level which completes the series of homologies which the sermon derives from the practice of disguising the face.

Cosmetics, then, are seen as a potent threat to the regulation of sexual, social and economic energies which is the function of the patriarchal household. The breakdown of patriarchal authority in a chaos of unregulated and 'artificial' appetites is prefigured later in the Homily as a catastrophe of *effemination*: a collapse of rational men into the sub-rational condition of women:

> Yea many men are become so effeminate, that they care not
> what they spend in disguising themselves, ever desiring new
> toys, and inventing new fashions. (p. 60)

Here the feminine is not merely another of the categories which is marked negatively, as participating in the counter-Commonwealth of vanity and singularity – it is the mark of that negativity itself, the condition into which men fall when they have dislodged themselves from the fully human order of Commonwealth. The same vision of the feminine informs the discourse against luxury imports, which I will discuss in detail shortly:

> Oftentimes by good policy merchants are forbidden to bring in
> certain kinds of wares which appertain to the effeminating of
> the people in wanton riotous life and the attire of the body.[44]

Woman as housewife, or woman as pure diseconomy, the revolt of the body's wantonness against the rational disciplines of the godly citizen. The feminine can only be countenanced when contained and disciplined by patriarchal structures – the sacramental bond of marriage, the dutiful sphere of the housewife – because it is conceptualised as inherently destructive of all structures, all economy, all discipline. Woman – each individual, the essentialist category – is therefore always two-faced, because even when presenting the appearance of virtue, duty and obedience, there lurks beneath that surface the barely restrained energies of the essential feminine – 'wantonness', 'riot', 'desire' and 'invention' – forces which the Homily against Adultery sums up under the title of Whoredom, a principle of negativity which perpetually shadows and threatens that of patriarchal economy:

> What patrimony (or livelihood), what substance, what goods, what riches doth whoredom shortly consume and bring to naught.[45]

Certain vagrant or outcast women – the whore, the gypsy, the vagrant, the frequenter of stage-plays, the cross-dresser – function as signs of pure negativity, of the realised potential of the feminine when it escapes, wanders from, the disciplinary enclosure of the patriarchal household.[46] Within that enclosure, as I have said, an unstable binary economy is posited – woman appears (under discipline) as Housewife, but is always potentially to be revealed as Whore, the reality of the feminine.[47] That economy is another which can be assimilated to the binary structure of the sign, and through that to other forms of social disturbance and diseconomy which are conceived semiotically. So, for example, Thomas Wilson condemns usurers in terms which interconnect the doubleness of the usurer and of the feminine through a figure of semiotic division:

> These be marmaids, not merchaunts, singing sweetly to confusion.[48]

Wilson's metaphor relies on the traditional post-classical confusion between mermaids and the Sirens who lured mariners to their destruction in the *Odyssey*.[49] The confusion allows the moral lesson of sensual allurement leading to spiritual destruction which is drawn conventionally from the Siren episode to be condensed into a single emblematic visual image – the 'woman' divided between the alluring human half above the waist, and the rebarbative animal half below. From the Pythagoreans through the Christian Platonists and Church Fathers to the moralists of the sixteenth century, the discourses of patriarchal discipline, of *contemptus mundi* and self-transcendence, focus their attacks upon the unlegitimated secular order through such binary figures of femininity, so that the unveiled or disclosed horror of the female genitalia (the mermaid's 'animal' part) is the priveleged index of the horror of unredeemed materiality and sensual engagement.

The binary semiotic of the mermaid

$$\frac{s}{S} = \frac{woman}{beast}$$

is one particularly hard-worked and authoritative version of the semiotic of female duplicity through which the discourses against the culture of vanity and singularity are articulated. That more general binary structure

$$\frac{\textit{Feminine Appearance}}{\text{Carnal Degradation}} = \frac{\textit{Worldly Allurements}}{\text{Temporal Decay}}$$

stands in an antithetical, almost parodic, relation to the semiotic of transendence which guides the godly citizen 'upwards' from the material entity to the Divine truth which it veils:

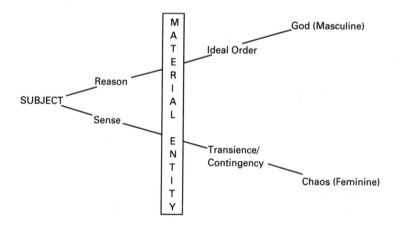

The (unconfined) feminine is the vain, the transient, the singular, the vagrant, the superfluous; all those negatively marked terms which we have met and will meet in this study when a discourse of patriarchal fixity and transcendence believes itself to confront the mobility and contingent materiality of 'unlegitimated' secular process. We have seen how the trope of the mermaid can connect femininity to the usurer's supposed immersion in this-worldliness; here Fulke Greville organises an attack on Rhetoric around the same figure:

> *Rhetorike* to this [logic] a sister and a
> twinne,
> Is growne a Siren in the forms of pleading,
> Captiving reason, with the painted skinne
> Of many words; with empty sounds misleading
> Us to false ends[50]

This participates in a conventional discourse against rhetoric; the divorce of rhetoric from logic is a deviation from the truth of essences and universals (of which logic is the science) into the falsehood of surfaces and the contingent particular. The negativity of the verbal surface, the vacancy of the Siren's 'empty sounds' – the dangers of rhetoric, like those of usury, are assimilated to the semiotic economy of the feminine, which modulates here from the aural duplicity of the Sirens' song into the visual duplicity of the woman who uses cosmetics. I discuss this quotation, and the links between the attack on rhetoric and that on cosmetics, in more detail below;[51] I want to use this example here to emphasise the ubiquitousness of tropes of feminine diseconomy in all the fields of discourse which this book considers. In the case of the discourse against rhetoric, the negatively marked feminine is installed at the centre of this book's concerns – rhetoric which is believed to have escaped its anchorage in logic is a writing which has abrogated its duty to reproduce the fixed and 'universal' truths of patriarchal orthodoxy in order to articulate the mobile, unforeseen, protean 'surface' events of contemporary secular process. That writing, negatively marked as feminine, is the vagrant writing which my title invokes, and whose potentiality I discuss at a number of points in the book. For the present we will return to the state of 'effeminacy' as a condition of economic dysfunction.

The effeminate man is projected into that domain of illusory objects and proliferating desire which we identified earlier (when discussing the Staple) as that of singularity.[52] The temporal dimension of singularity is characterised here by a compulsive novelty ('ever desiring new toys, and inventing new fashions'): the restlessness of desire in its pursuit of persistently unsatisfactory objects promotes a systematic disruption of continuity or extended temporal rhythm. This in itself is a threat to the temporal structure – placid, conservative, uniform – of patriarchy. The Homily focuses this concern in its repeated opposition of the hectic rhythms of fashion to the traditions of the fathers:

> . . . spending more by the year in apparel, than their fathers received for the whole revenue of their lands . . . . yea, and those clothes which [the Israelites'] fathers had worn, their children were contented to use afterward . . . . We are loth to wear such as our fathers have left us . . . . We must have one gown for the day, another for the night . . . one for winter, another for summer . . . while one spendeth his patrimony upon pounces and cuts . . . (p. 60)

The conversion of patrimony into pounces is, as it were, the diagnostic centre of the sermon, its condensed image for the various transformations which it castigates: of organic resources into frivolous expenditure, of the traditional into the fashionable, of patriarchal authority into effeminacy, of husbandry into harlotry. For the *pounce*, as Andrew Welsby's annotation of this passage tells us,[53] is a hole 'pinked or cut out for ornamenting a garment' and *cuts* are 'edges of a garment slashed for decoration': in these images, the Homily stresses the conversion of systemic energy into the vacancy and negativity of the culture of vanity.

This theme of negative, entropic transformation reaches its most intense homiletic development in the works of the London preacher Thomas Adams at the end of the century:

> Our monstrous pride, that turns hospitality into a dumb-show: that which fed the belly of hunger now feeds the eye of lust; acres of land are metamorphosed into trunks of apparel; and the soul of charity is transmigrated into the body of bravery: this is waste.[54]

The 'monstrous' announces a violation of natural structures and proportionalities; the 'real' (because systemically dedicated) practice of hospitality is replaced by a representation (the theatrical simulacrum of real hospitality, but probably also an allusion to the aristocratic employment of actors[55]); at the heart of this process of transformation is the metamorphosis of patrimonial substance into the nugatory appearances of 'apparel', an exchange which represents a triumph of body over soul, of expense misdirected to the material surface of the 'singular' body over expenditure spiritualised by its dedication to the uses of the Commonwealth ('charity'). As the imaginative range and condensation of this passage suggest, the trope of delinquent expenditure allows conceptual links to be made across the full array of socio-economic disruptions and malfunctions which obsess the commentators, from the individual body to the social body, including the economic force which is believed to underlie and animate them all, namely, inflation.[56]

Inflation (or 'dearth') is consistently identified by sixteenth-century commentators as a condition of impoverishment in times of plenty. This is precisely the kind of disjunction – between natural resources and their distribution – which can be subsumed under the figure of delinquent expenditure. Consequently the *Homily on Apparel* treats inflation as a fundamental expression of a universal malaise: the interruption of the circuits which transmit God-given resources through the customary structures of Commonwealth to maintain and nourish each subject in his or her degree:

> And every man, nothing considering his estate and condition, seeketh to excel others in costly attire. Whereby it cometh to pass, that, in abundance and plenty of all things, we yet complain of want and penury, while one man spendeth that which might serve a multitude, and no man distributeth of the abundance which he hath received, and all men excessively waste that which should serve to supply the necessities of others. (p. 60)

The ideological strength of this kind of analysis is in its tautological structure: if there is a disturbance of the system, it is the fault of anti-systemic behaviour. The system itself is unassailed, is indeed reinforced by a diagnosis which traces breakdowns to those who obstruct its normal functioning by diverting the flow of resources from the consolidating practices of husbandry and hospitality into the blind alleys of singularity.

If dearth is identified by commentators as the most dramatic disruption of the English economy's internal equilibrium, then it has its counterpart in the economy's external dimension, its interaction with foreign markets and producers. The analysis of England's poor balance of trade tends to be carried out in the same conceptual terms which organise the analysis of dearth and domestic dislocation.

The *Discourse of the Common Weal*,[57] which is strikingly un-representative of socio-economic commentary of the period in many respects, is entirely conventional when it notes as a principal cause of economic decline the exporting of 'substantial wares' in exchange for imported 'trifles'.[58] The language of the *Discourse* absorbs this question of exchange into the ontological–ethical discourse which we have been considering. The conversion of the substantial into the trifling is seen here as an abdication from authenticity, a deviation from the realm of necessity into that of vanity.

At the level of the consuming subject, the *Discourse* takes this to be a deviation from the experience of common need into that of personal or singular appetite. In discussing the influx of 'trifles' it states:

> Of the which sort I mean glasses as well looking as drinking . . .
> cards, bells, puppets, penhorns, inkhorns, toothpicks, gloves . . .
> brooches . . . buttons of silk and silver . . . ' (p. 63)

We should note that these are all items of personal ornament, entertainment or self-scrutiny; that they are chosen clearly for their material fragility or functional redundancy; that the entertainments (remembering Elyot) involve randomness, immoderation and the duplication of God's work; that the intoxications of drinking are joined – through the word 'glasses' – to those of a narcissistic self-regard; and that this catalogue of vanities includes the instruments of writing – penhorn and inkhorn. The return of the categories of vanity and singularity – ornamentation, sophistication, insubstantiality, redundancy, doubleness, the reflective, the intoxicating – is dis-tinguished here by their organisation around the central term of the glass or mirror:

> . . . their shops glitter and shine of glasses, as well looking as
> drinking, yea, all manner vessels of the same stuff – painted
> cruses, gay daggers, knives, swords and girdles – that is able [to]
> make any temperate man to gaze on them and buy somewhat
> though it serve no purpose necessary. (p. 64)

This, I think, is itself an intoxicating moment in the history of social and economic analysis. In this image of an array of (literally) alien-ated artefacts, an array which is also one of mirrors returning the consumer's own 'dressed' or elaborated image, there is prefigured the full paradoxical development of commodification.[59] The 'glass' is a rhetorical figure which allows the analysis of economic disturbance and that of social and psychic estrangement to coalesce powerfully – the commodity appears as an alienation of use-value through the intervention of foreign manufacture, and also as the medium of the consumer's self-alienation, a mirror which returns to him a groundless and intoxicating image. Through what Baudrillard would at one time have called its *symbolic exchange value*,[60] the personal accessory-as-commodity links the violation of an economics of the necessary with a collapse of the psychic economy of temperateness.

If the nature and value of goods available in England are increasingly subject to the influence of invisible European and ultimately world market forces, then the *Discourse* relates this fact to the invisibility of use-values behind the seductive display of commodities, and this in turn is seen as generating the disappearance of the 'real' self through its displacement by the consumer's intoxicated self-image. This complex articulation of disrupted economies – from the industrial to the subjective – centres upon the visual glamour of elaborated surfaces, a seductive look of things which blocks any attention to their utility. The 'gay daggers, knives, swords and girdles' have been converted from their martial function to one of spectacular and semiotic effect. The *Discourse* explains this shift as the result of the development of a 'time of Show' (p. 81), a time, that is, of aggravated status competition, in which the decline of the feudal aristocracy as a martial caste competing physically within the realm has led instead to the symbolic contest of status-presentation or display.[61]

In the figure of the glass the concerns of this chapter find a powerfully condensed articulation; a focusing of discourses on monetary, social and subjective economy – and diseconomy – upon the central issue of the economy of the sign. It is this convergence of issues that I now want to pursue through the figure of the usurer.

The Devil's word: usury and the economy of the sign

Mr. Molley: We are not, quoth he, so straitned to the Word of God, that every transgression should be surely punished here. Every vain word is here forbidden by God, yet the temporal law doth not so utterly condemn it.

Debate on the Usury Bill, 1571[62]

What we have been pursuing through the pages of economic treatises, homilies, statutes and educational tracts are the local emergences, the partial articulations of a broadly authoritative and generally distributed discourse on the opposed economies of Commonwealth and of singularity. This discourse comprehends an economics, a sociology and cultural pathology, and a psychology, but its force does not rest in the scientific elaboration of these fields of scrutiny. It is rather in a certain thematic condensation, a multiple investment in a few potent images, that the opposition is staged – in images, as we have seen, of the middleman, the alien worker, the gypsy, of superfluous attire, painted faces, and intoxicating reflections. Among these agents and agencies of singularity, there is one whose image involves a particularly dense thematic concentration, a strikingly comprehensive articulation of discursive levels: the usurer.

We have seen that the idea of singularity is produced in opposition to that of Commonwealth, and that this opposition is also understood as one between nature and artifice. It is in these terms that the case against usury, as it is summarised and elaborated in Sir Thomas Wilson's *A Discourse Upon Usury*, is pursued.

* * *

Wilson locates usury as the motivating force behind those interrelated developments – dearth, social mobility and displacement, excessive expenditure and the decline of husbandry – which threaten the integrated socio-economic system of Commonwealth:

> For if mony might not so soone bee had of those covetous usurers, moste men woulde lyve within their boundes and leave their wanton apparell, their unnecessarye feastynge, theire fonde gamynge, and theire lewde hazarding of great wealth and revenues without all wytte upon a mayne chance at dyce . . . . For so these unthriftes may have mony to serve theire lustes . . . they care not what they paye . . . .
>
> If men will conform themselves to the lawe of nature, and lyve as they ought to do uprightlie in their vocation, and remember there is a God . . . then plentie will followe, and goode cheape will bee of all thyngs, when every man lyveth uprightlie in his callinge and profession as God hath appoynted, and forsake these unlawfull shiftes . . . . (pp. 369–70)[63]

If the usurer's effect is to disrupt the vocational categories of Commonwealth by feeding the voraciousness of private appetites, then this reflects his own status as the prototype of antisocial desire:

> The Romaynes never began to decaye tyll usurie lorded amongst them, for then private gain thrust oute common profite, luste was holden for lawe, ydleness more used than labour, ryott in steede of diett, vice better regarded than vertue, no charity at all, no love betwixt man and man, but everie man for hymself, and the whorlepole of ryote overflowed in all thynges and in all places. (p. 180)

In accordance with this corrosive auto-affection, the usurer is a man without ties to the social body. He is not merely displaced from the locations of 'vocation' or degree: rather his activity undoes the very constitution of such relations:

> Wheras God willeth everye man to lyve in his vocation, and hee that will not laboure eyther with body or minde according to his callyng rightly should not eate at al, forbidding men to make lending a kinde of living. But these men [i.e. usurers] do not live in any vocation. (p. 178)

In the same vein, Wilson describes many 'leaving their former honest industry and resolving to live idly upon usury' (p. 104); and the Act against Usury of Elizabeth's reign describes the usurer, oxymoronically, as 'an unnecessary member of the commonwealth'.[64] The usurer's disintegration of the 'natural' link between 'living' and 'calling' is emphasised in Crowley's 'Epigram on Usurers' (1550), where 'calling' represents the generation of wealth as it is integrated into the natural order of 'corn' and 'cattle', and so too into the order of commonwealth through which wealth rightly should flow:

> 'Why, sir' (quod this Usurer) 'it is my
> living'.
> 'Yea, sir' (quod this Prophet) 'but it is not
> your calling;
> You are called to live after twenty pound by
> year,
> And after that rate ye should measure your
> cheer,
> Tyll God did increase you by his merciful ways,

By increasing your corn and your cattle in the
leyes;
Which increase with your lands you are bound to
employ,
To the profit of all them that do dwell you
by.[65]

This begins to suggest an explanation for the usurer's decisive
disqualification from the natural order of Commonwealth; his short-
circuiting of the channels of socially dedicated revenue so that
they issue in his own pocket, an exemplary action of singularity
at the expense of Commonwealth. There is also something more
fundamental even than this: his supplementation or sophistication
of a fundamental 'natural' relation; an action which places him first
among those practitioners of the artificial that we have considered:

Yea, he offendeth, sayeth this doctour, against the nature of
things, because it is impossible by the order and course of
nature that once one should bee twise one, whiche the usurers
goe about to make . . . for nature cannot afoord it, that once
one of dead things should become twise one . . . . (p. 327)

Usury disrupts monetary value at its very root, in the fundamental
matrix of mathematical values and proportions. Through this radical
dislocation, Nature itself becomes the first of those unable to afford
the supplementary expense of usury.

As with superfluousness of attire and the use of cosmetics, the
idleness or redundancy of usury is double: the social idleness of
the agent, and the ontological redundancy of the thing produced,
its doubling of the natural object. The artificial is then the doubled
or reproduced, a perverse self-generation of the inanimate. Perverse
also because artificial reproduction occurs precisely at points where
the circulation of reproductive energy through the system is blocked:
the socially consolidating expenditures of hospitality are diverted
into the excesses of apparel and gluttony, the sexual energies of
the housewife are redirected from the reproduction of patriarchal law
within matrimony to the provocation of licentiousness. In the same
way usury is held to convert money from a pure instrumentality – as
the transparent medium through which objectively grounded values
are exchanged – to a corrupt agency of the usurer's singular desire,
diverting systemic energy into its own perverse self-breeding:

So that by these twoe idle occupacions, great usurye and manye flockes of sheepe ... this noble Countrye is ... brought to greate ruyn and decay .... And, I pray you, what is more against nature than that money should beget or bring forth money, which was ordained to be a pledge or right betwixt man and man, in contracts or bargayning, and not to increase itself, as a woman dothe, that bringethe foorthe a childe, cleane contrarye to the firste institution of money? (p. 286)

The monstrous fertility of usurious money is also, conversely, a withering or dessication of the Commonwealth.[66] As a burgeoning of the artificial, this fertility is conceived paradoxically as parched and barren – the usurious manipulation of the money markets is termed *dry exchange* (in opposition to *natural exchange*) because, as Fenton would later state, 'having no more juice or sap than a painted tree either in charity or in equity, but being a griping usury under the title of exchange, it drieth up the fountain of both'.[67] In natural exchange, then, the sap flows – the energy which sustains the organism of Commonwealth circulates through its appointed channels without impediment. In dry exchange that energy is diverted into the creation of a fictional representation ('a painted tree') which mimics the transactions of equitable exchange:

... for the usurer beareth the countenance of an honest man ... and dealeth as though it were by law, being none other than a lawful theefe .... And thys ys very true, he undoeth as many as hee dealeth with all, under the colour of amitie and lawe. (p. 285)

In terms of the cosmology of Commonwealth, usury is anathema because it is the generative principle of artificiality; it embodies a constitutive fictionality which usurps the place and function of God the Maker. Wilson's case against usury rests on God's establishment of things in their particular natures and in their hierarchically ordained places – this, then, is also the establishment of definitive values for things in relation to each other, values which are grounded in the relation of each thing to God:

It is written Sap. 11: thou, O God, hast ordeyned all thinges in measure, nomber and weight. Now then, he that will not deal iustly, according to measure, nomber and weight, the same man is not worthy to lyve upon earthe .... Therefore

> let every man give value for value, pound for pound, ounce
> for ounce, as thynges are woorth, and the iust proporcion is
> kepte, as it shoulde bee, and everye mans necessitie served a
> ryghte without unlawfull gayning . . . . (p. 267–71)

On this basis money is the mere mark or registration of 'just
proportion': the crime of usury is to endow this pure representation of
objective value with the properties of object-hood, including value:

> For the occupiers [of usurious exchange] doe geeve and sell
> moneye for moneye, whiche was not invented and ordeyned
> for that ende that eyther it should price it selfe by it selfe, or
> bee valued and esteemed by waye of merchaundise, but that al
> other things shoulde receive their prices and value of it; and
> the valuation of money . . . to be perpetual and unchangeable,
> according to a knowne standard. (p. 307)

It is this self-referentiality, this pricing of itself by itself, which gives
to the usurer's money its malign substantiality, its status as a thing
actively creating itself as value and re-creating the values of the things
which it acts between.

In this systematic re-establishment of things in their value and
their mutual relations, usurious money is the originating energy of
a counter-Creation – 'an arte . . . altogether against nature' – whose
organising principle is singularity or private appetite:

> . . . these money men, and these merchants doe sett what price
> they list of moneye, and make it eyther of highe value or meane
> value as they please, for their owne singuler commoditie and
> private gaine. (p. 310)

The challenge offered by the usurer to God is absolute: a re-creation/
re-description of the cosmos in terms of singularity and artifice.
The usurer is not, then, merely another of the wanderers whose
transgression, like that of the gypsy, serves to confirm by conceptual
antithesis the categories of natural order and propriety: he is
impropriety itself, the negation of the proper and of established
proprieties, an absolute contrariety:

> So that I may well avowe, that lyght and darkenes, whyte
> and blacke, trueth and falshood, heaven and hell, are not so
> contrarye and so distant, as god and the usurer. (p. 288)

In harnessing an energy of de-creation, the usurer presides over a domain which has dispensed with God:

> Yea, so horrible is this sinne, that amongst al other sinnes it maketh menne to forget god, or rather to thinke there is no god. (p. 361)

Usury is, then, the achieved form of the power ascribed to money by Luther: 'Money is the word of the Devil, through which he creates all things, the way God created through the true Word'.[68]

It is this status of usurious money as the counter-Word – naming things contrary to the denominations declared by God in the hierarchical categories of degree – which leads to the persistent characterisation of the usurer as a liar, a manipulator of language, his double-talk matching the dubiety of his money's signification:

> Even so the usurer is a worme at the first handeling, softe and gentle in woordes, always pretending the charitable ayde of hys borrower, but in the ende he devoureth every mans patrimonye and enheritance that dealeth with hym. (p. 327)

Wilson stresses the relationship between this lying and the usurer's undoing of the Word by associating him with those whose social deviation consists of a denial of official religious doctrine:[69]

> There bee two sortes of men that are always to bee loked upon very narrowly, the one is the dissembling gospeller, and the other is the wilfull and indurate papistes . . . . And touching thys sinne of usurie, none doe more openly offende in thys behalfe than do these counterfaite professours of thys pure religion . . . . So that betwixt the secret dissembler and the open blasphemer, the world is made a praye . . . . (p. 178)

This charge of estrangement from and of the Word also underlies the persistent association of the usurer with the Jew, the heretic, the infidel and pagan, and of his 'art' with idolatry.[70] The idol – and here we might recall Hooker's discussion of idolatry[71] – represents an arrest of signification in the material, an excision of the immaterial referent of the sign, which is directly analogous to the curtailed and self-directed referentiality of the usurer's money.

The centrality of issues of signification and representation to the question of usury also accounts for the concern expressed by mid-sixteenth-century commentators at the increasing importance of the scrivener as an intermediary in credit transactions. The scrivener is frequently charged with claiming to represent a third-party lender when in reality he is the lender himself, an accusation which focuses a number of fears about intermediacy.[72] As we have seen, the ideology of commonwealth constitutes as dangerous all those who, as middlemen, evade the categories of degree and vocation. The scrivener confirms this suspicion by using the fact that he is neither one thing nor the other as a way of becoming two things at once – both lender and lender's agent. With this multiplication and disguising of himself the scrivener turns the moment of drafting the credit agreement – a moment, properly, of transparent communication – into the occasion of a malign fiction-making.

The scrivener's perversion of representation is a peculiarly over-determined instance of the threat which writing is believed to present to metaphysical systems such as that of Commonwealth. In such systems, as Derrida has shown, writing has the status of a technical supplement to the 'natural' process of oral communication, and it is the analogous supplementarity of money in relation to the 'natural' ordering of values which accounts for the anxieties which cluster about the figure of the scrivener – a middleman in the processes by which both monetary value and meaning are 'artificially' transmitted and exchanged.

We should particularly note that writing becomes dangerous in the hands of the scrivener at the point where it is believed to transform itself from an agent of transcription to one of representation and fictional creativity.[73] In this transformation, and in the capacity to generate a counter-reality which mimics and undoes 'natural' structures, writing declares its intimacy with the de-creating Word of the usurer. In the words of Philip Stubbes: 'The scrivener is the instrument whereby the devil worketh the frame of this wicked world of usury . . . .'[74]

The question of usury, then, is cast as an acute struggle between Word and Anti-Word. Despite the ideological authority of the Commonwealth orthodoxy, however, the debates on usury – and particularly those in Parliament – manifest an anxiety about recon-ciling a strict adherence to the prescriptions of the Word and an inescapable engagement with credit as an essential component of the developing economic environment:[75]

> That all should be well is to be wished: that all should be
> done well is beyond hope. For we are no saints: we are not

of perfection to follow the letter of the Gospel . . . . We are
not so straitened to the word of God that every transgression
should surely be punished here . . . . It is biting and over sharp
dealing which is disliked, and nothing else. (p. 160)

The speaker here combats the tyranny of the Word with word-play:
the reference to 'biting' is a common strategy by which etymological
precision is exploited to narrow down the current definition of the
word 'usury' and so excuse all but 'over sharp' practices.[76] What is
at stake here (and the issue is implied in much of the debate about
usury) is a contest between opposing conceptions of language, and,
by implication, of history.

On the one hand, as in my last quotation, the Word declares its
pan-temporal sufficiency, a fixedness and unequivocality of meaning
which announces itself authoritatively to each generation.[77] On the
other, etymology submits the word to history and deduces an ethical
relativism from the cultural and temporal specificity of the production
of meaning.

This contest is at its most explicit in the arguments of Wilson's
Civilian and Preacher. The Civilian speaks within a tradition of
humanistic philological and historical enquiry, and seeks to delimit
the meaning of 'usury'; the Preacher speaks for the immediacy
and authority of prophetic illumination and its continuity with
the unyielding Word:

> Ockerfoe: But what a worlde is thys, that men wyll make synne
> to bee but a flea bytyng, when they see gods word dyrectlye
> agaynste them! And thus you runne to the propertie of the word,
> and so trye it in divers languages, whiche indeede signifieth
> a bytynge. And nowe you tryumphe and say your pleasure,
> that a manne may bee a lytle naughte, so that hee bee not
> altogether starke naught. Well, god gave this name in divers
> languages after this sort, that suche vyce might bee the more
> abhorred . . . .
> Lawyer: . . . you shall not doe well to use suche argumentes,
> and to stande upon universalities.
> Ockerfoe: Indeede the woorde of god is my foundacion, whiche
> doth expounde itselfe playnelye ynough to my understandinge
> and to the satisfaction of my conscience. (pp. 259, 352)

The Civilian's humanistic response to this is a refusal to exempt the
Word in its Scriptural transcription from the historical process of the

production of meaning. The immediacy of the Preacher's relation to the Word is both temporal and cognitive: the humanist's opening of this relation to history is also a redefinition of it as a *hermeneutic* relation:

> I thinke you divines doe not well observe circumstances, when you will that the very bare letter shalbe plainelye taken as it lieth, and in one sort or manner to be applied to all men, without regarde of circumstance, degree, estate or condicion of any one. (p. 243)

The relationship of the Word to truth which is implied by this position replaces the immediacy of the 'bare letter' with the difficulty of a reading in which text, social context and historical conjuncture interact in perpetually unprecedented configurations. In the Preacher's model the circumstances and practices of the world are inimical to the Word and must bend themselves to its requirements: in the Civilian's, temporal circumstance is precisely the element within which the Word realises itself for human comprehension.

Usury provokes this contest of opposed linguistic paradigms because it is a central and emblematically potent factor in a fundamental shift in economic and social relations. Usury's estrangement of the monetary semiotic epitomises the rearticulation of ontological and social relations, the disruption of established categories of individual and collective being, which results from the emergence of a new economic (dis)order of inflationary cycles, credit transactions and commodity production within a world market. It is that historical process which poses a fundamental challenge to the ideology of Commonwealth, by recreating the world in a form which is uncontainable within its conceptual topography.

For Wilson, usury redefines the founding relation between thing and value, the object and its categorisation, and as the motor of inflation it disseminates this effect throughout the social order, animating and sustaining the culture of 'show' anatomised in the *Discourse of the Common Weal*:

> ... [these] men with theire maskynge maners and greate braveries shoulde seme for a time to be ioly felowes, wheras at length they discover themselves, and are become worse than naughte .... For if mony might not so sone bee had of those covetous usurers, moste men would lyve within theire boundes,

and leave their . . . lewde hazarding of great wealth and revenues
without all wytte upon a main chaunce at dyce . . . (p. 369)

The 'maskynge maners and great braveries' of the borrower identify
him as a social actor, and so a target of the discourses against
dissimulation which we have already seen being deployed against
the professional actor and the vagrant, as here in Wilson's attack
on the borrower:

> . . . rather would he seeme to bee that which he is not, than to
> bee in deede and in outward shewe that whiche hee is. (p. 369)

From the perspective of Commonwealth, then, the social domain
which centres upon usury is a chaos of ungrounded appearances
where any organising rational principle ('wytte') is usurped by the
randomness of the dicer's chance ('lewde hazarding . . . upon a main
chance at dyce', and compare Wilson (p. 369) on the borrower setting
'upon blynde fortune . . . all that they have').[78] The question of the
historial incarnation of the Word, of the possibility of accommodating
its prescriptions to this unprecedented social context, is not even
approached in critiques such as the *Discourse*, for what the Word is
held to confront is not some new mutation of the real, but disreality
itself, the collapse of a world underwritten by the Word into a chaos
of illegibility.

The culture of singularity which the usurer's money animates is,
then, a domain of images uncoupled from any anchorage in what
the discourse of Commonwealth defines as real social relations.
The uncoupling is held to occur when energy is diverted from
its circulation through the channels of Commonwealth and fuels
instead the self-generation of some *singular* component of the
system: a properly relational force becomes one of self-implication.
The removal of the component from its systemic position entails a
degradation of its ontological status: matter breeding upon itself is
figured paradoxically as insubstantial, a generation of shadows. The
trope which can include both the self-reflexiveness of singularity and
its supplementary insubstantiality, and which in consequence can
represent the matrix of forces which generates the culture of vanity,
is the *mirror*:

> . . . will [the usurer] have, when hee hath departed with his
> owne for tyme, for nothynge somethinge? for a shadowe a

perfite bodye? for moone shyne in the water a mans whole
treasure? (p. 287)

For Wilson, the substance which the usurer deals epitomises sublunar
insubstantiality; a reflection of the moon's reflected light, shadow of
a shadow, that third degree of the image which is for Plato the
illusory condition of Becoming. The type of the evacuated *object*
is a reflection in water; the typical *subject* of the domain of vanity
would, then, be one who looks into the water and takes the reflection
for the reality:

> Whoever wishes to understand this story, let him understand by
> Narcissus those who delight madly, senselessly, the haughty, the
> presumptuous, who affect temporal goods, who see themselves
> and take delight in the false mirrors of this world, which
> plunges them into madness and folly, intoxicates them with a
> drink full of bitterness and gall . . . . It is the perilous mirror,
> in which the proud look upon themselves, who covet earthly
> delights . . . . And the more they fix their thought on that
> mirror the more their thirst increases, which all the more
> destroys those who drink of the fountain full of false sweetness:
> it is the deceiving fountain, which makes the faint and mutable
> image seem real and permanent. And he thinks himself rich
> and powerful all the more as he gazes upon himself and is
> able to see in this deceiving mirror the false image in which
> he delights . . . .[79]

There is clearly a close relationship between a moralisation of the
Narcissus story such as this and the analytical image of the 'glass'
which appears in the *Discourse of the Common Weal*. In particular
we should remember the double sense of 'glass' in that passage, as
both mirror and drinking vessel; a sense which is repeated here in
the water as both reflecting surface and fountain of intoxication. It
is this double connotation which allows the discursive employment
of the Narcissus figure to mediate between macro- and microcosmic
disruption, between cosmic/social semiosis and the economy of the
passions.

Narcissus: the economy of reflection

Corruption in the skin, says Job; in the outward beauty, these be
the records of vellum, these be the parchments and indictments,

and the evidences that shall condemn many of us, at the last
day, our own skins; we have the Book of God, the Law, written
in our hearts; we have the image of God imprinted in our own
souls; we have the character, and the seal of God stamped in
us, in our baptism; and, all this is bound up in this vellum, in
this parchment in this skin of ours, and we neglect Book, and
image, and character, and seal, and all for the covering.

John Donne, *Sermon XIV*[80]

The tradition in which Ovid's tale of Narcissus is explicated and
rendered significant is also that of Neoplatonic speculation on the sign
in its relation to cosmic economy.[81] In the third century, Clement of
Alexandria initiates this development by linking Narcissus' encounter
with his reflection to the vanity of the woman who paints her face
before a mirror. Clement's citation of 2 Corinthians 4:18 on the
transience of visible things and the permanence of the invisible
establishes the ethical dimension of the Narcissus story as an
exemplification of *vanitas*: the insubstantiality of the visual image
serving as the term which links together vanity as self-regard and
vanity as impermanence.[82]

The philosophical implications of this convergence of themes are
elaborated by Plotinus. The disjunction of visible image and invisible
reality is extended by him into the philosophical opposition of
materiality and the ideal, while the emphasis on issues of image
and representation is maintained. The result is an exemplification
of Neoplatonic sign theory: the relation of matter to Ideal reality is
that of signifier to signified, and the error of Narcissus is to privilege
the signifier and so deny the real:

When he perceives those shapes of grace that show in body,
let him not pursue; he must know them for copies, vestiges,
shadows and hasten away towards That they tell of.[83]

The continuity of this Neoplatonic elaboration of the Narcissus
story into the sixteenth and seventeenth centuries is particularly
conspicuous in works dealing with the Pythagorean dicta. Neoplatonist debate about these arcana is pursued in Gyraldus's *De
Deis Gentium* (1548),[84] which considers in particular the eighth
dictum, translated here as 'One should pray to Echo when the
winds are blowing'. Gyraldus quotes the interpretation of the early
fourth-century commentator Iamblichus, who 'said that [Pythagoras]

suggested that one should love the image of the nature and power of the divine'. The connection between Echo and Narcissus and the symbolic mysteries is taken up again in Alexander Farra's *Settenario* (1571). In Farra's final section, 'Filosofia simbolica overo delle Imprese', he treats of contemplation and the attainment of ecstasy, and considers the Pythagorean dicta. The interpretation offered of the eighth is that Echo represents the 'reflex' of the image produced in the mind by the breath of God, which conduces to intellectual unity and the direction of the soul's parts towards God. Narcissus, on the contrary, is the soul which denies this process and attends instead to the reflection supplied by the senses and 'corporeal shadows':

> Iamblichus certifies that this symbol [Echo] is a theorem on divine wisdom, teaching us to love the images of divine ideas and divine virtues, and giving rise to deeds which contribute towards their message being honoured with the greatest zeal.[85]

We should note here the opposition between, on the one hand, the phonic signifier and the immediacy of self-present thought, and on the other the material iteration of the visual signifier and its association with self-alienation; an opposition which Derrida identifies as one important version of that between speech and writing in Western metaphysics. The Narcissus–Echo story becomes in this interpretation an allegorical account of the destruction of speech by writing. In terms of the present argument, the reference directs us back to the case against the scrivener, and forward to the narcissists of Jonson's *Cynthia's Revels* in my final chapter.[86]

The universality of the principle of divine reflection represented by Echo is underlined in the discussion of Iamblichus' statements on the eighth dictum in Athanasius Kircher's *Oedipus Aegyptiachus* of 1653, where Kircher writes:

> Iamblichus says that this dictum is a theorem on the divine wisdom in every single created thing which shines forth as in a kind of mirror, so that there are as many echoes of the divine voice as there are created things. They are, so to speak, reflections of that which urges us incessantly to sing about the goodness of the divine essence.[87]

There are then, according to this tradition of Neoplatonic specu-lation, two regimes of signification in universal opposition. One, represented by Echo, insists upon the status of material entities as signifiers of the divine essence, and posits reality as that which is read or seen through the superficies of matter; the other, represented by Narcissus, is in fact a denial of signification, a refusal of depth and seeing-through in favour of a fixation upon the surfaces of material being.

What Farra's elaboration of Iamblichus makes clear are the implications this opposition has for the internal economy of the subject. The mental 'reflex' which unites material thing and divine afflatus in the mind is accompanied by an integration of faculties and their unanimous direction towards God. This process then issues in action, in those 'deeds which contribute towards their message being honoured with the greatest zeal'.[88] Conversely, the result of Narcissus' fixation upon the sensible image is a dissipation and disintegration of internal forces, which is usually represented as the rebellion of appetite and passion against reason. It is this psychic decomposition which is identified as incapacitating Narcissus for any participation in the sphere of social action and duty: he is a man prostrated by love. In John of Salisbury's *Policraticus* (1159) this redundancy is figured as the fruitlessness of the Narcissus flower; henceforth a crucial trope whose resonance is increased by its association with images from the Psalms and the Book of Job. By the twelfth century the association in those biblical texts between flowers and shadows has become a homiletic commonplace. As Vinge notes: 'So *umbra* and *flos* have conventional symbolic values which are easily united with the . . . drawing of Narcissus's character in Ovid's fable.'[89] What the association produces for the explication of Narcissus is a link between the redundancy of the reflected image (the 'shadow') and the fruitlessness of those who are fixated upon the imaginary objects of worldly attainment: 'For they despise others in comparison to themselves and seek to attain the impossible, rejoicing in advance at the deceptiveness of things.'[90] The direction of desire towards an illusory object determines Narcissus' fruitlessness, his uncoupling from the circuits of socially integrative energy. It also determines another of his characteristics in the exegetical tradition – insatiability:

> And the more they fix their thought on that mirror the more their thirst increases, which all the more destroys those who drink of the fountain full of false sweetness.[91]

The desire which refuses direction towards depth and essence is condemned to an interminable tracking of the material surface. Each object it selects reveals itself as illusory, prompting a perpetually renewed pursuit of the sufficient object:

> The gainers themselves, never fortunate with the frute or benefite of the goods they possesse, but rather being most miserable and hungry, by a certain strange gredy desire to hepe them together, are swallowed up with the unsaciablenesse therof . . . .[92]

This is Wilson on usurers: as the epitome of those who, in desiring the material object, commit an erasure of metaphysical realities, the usurer also exemplifies the sins of Narcissus.[93] Wilson stresses the impermanence of the usurer's wealth, its insufficiency as an object of desire. What he opposes to it is not a material object, but a mode of relationship – 'charitable dealing':

> Therefore I say still, charitable dealing is the most assured and best wealth that a man can purchase uppon earth, for where all other worldly substaunce fayleth and consumeth awaye, this continueth for ever, and ys a token of perfit christianitye, when men shewe their faith and beliefe by their good lyving and well doyng. (p. 207)

What constitutes the usurer's Narcissism is the withdrawal of affect from the social order and into a perverse generation of self-referential signs. 'Charitable dealing' opposes this by a socialisation of affect ('Love thy neighbour as thyself') which restores the transparency of actions, making the life represent – become 'a token of' – faith, belief, perfect Christianity.

The frequent association of the usurer with the whore and the pimp originates in what is seen as their common appropriation of affect – of an energy which is properly directed to the generation and regeneration of the social organism – for their private ends:

> Neither oughte men to make the moste of theire owne that they can . . . for soe, the evill woman may saye, that because her body is her own, shee may doe with it what shee list, and company with whome she pleaseth for her best profit and avayle; wheras god hath commaunded that every body should keepe hys owne vessel pure unto holyness, because we are all the images of god, created to his likenes. (p. 268)

The citizen is responsible in so far as he exercises stewardship, acting merely as an agent for the transmission of resources through the social network; the body is legitimated in so far as it signifies God. In both cases there is a structure of representation – citizen and body stand in for God. In both cases desire is legitimated only as it circulates within this structure, directing the worldly towards its origin in the ideal. Images of the usurer and Narcissus are key points at which these discourses on social responsibility, semiotic hygiene and affective economy reveal their mutual implication: in the images of usurious and Narcissistic fruitlessness the discourse of Commonwealth dramatises a force of de-creation which challenges its own generative power at the root

> So that, yf there be not as quicke wedyng hookes, and as sharpe yron forkes, readye at hande to clense the soyle from tyme to tyme, as the weedes are and wilbee readye to spring up and growe, in the ende all wilbee wedes, and antichrist hymselfe will be lorde of the harveste.[94]

3

George Gascoigne:
Writing Vagrantly

If it were not for Writers, there should be no feare of God, no
law nor order: every one would live after his own maner.
John Florio, *First Fruits*

Go little Booke, God graunt thou none offende.
George Gascoigne, 'Dulce Bellum Inexpertis'.[1]

What profit might there be for a bankrupt poet in lecturing his
sovereign on the subject of allegory? Why might an approach
through that subject bear fruit where other modes of courtly address
have proved barren? And what relation holds between allegory and
the other subject in question, George Gascoigne, when in 1576 he
presents himself and his text of *Hemetes the Heremyte* before the
eyes of royal judgement?

The sword and the pen equably rendered to the service of an
accommodating and vigorous sovereign power; images such as
Gascoigne proffers here have had their broader resonances, their
function in anchoring a certain representation of the history of our
national culture: a representation invoked, for example, in the title
of C. T. Prouty's 1942 biography, *George Gascoigne: Elizabethan
Courtier, Soldier and Poet*.[2] Here, as Prouty's commentary affirms,
is that integration of potentially divergent roles and spheres of
activity which has been celebrated in the idea of Renaissance Man:
an organisation of active and contemplative faculties, of aesthetic and
political imperatives, into a balanced economy. It is an economy of
both the individual subject and the culture as a whole, for what is also
celebrated here is that happy moment before the fall into dissociated
sensibility; the moment of organic society, psychic integration and

linguistic fecundity, oblivious to the coming barbarisms of revolution and Miltonic style.[3]

If Gascoigne's life and work are exemplary, however, it is not as they represent the organic integration and fertility of a mythical Renaissance England, but in their intimate registration of the contradictions and disequilibrium produced by the drive towards the establishment of a centrally regulated national culture.

Gascoigne's literary career spans the decades in which central authority, working through its agencies in Court, universities, Inns of Court and grammar schools, encouraged a massive and extraordinarily rapid accumulation of cultural capital. The translation and educational dissemination of classical and contemporary European texts, the domestication of forms such as the novella, sonnet, romance, masque and pageant and the importation of foreign and classical terms into the English lexicon[4] are among the principal modes of this process. Its aim, declared most explicitly in the declarations of the translators,[5] was the urgent formation and consolidation of resources for a newly conceived and organised national culture which might rival the fecundity and prestige of the French or Italian, and lay claim to a similar authoritative continuity with the classical archetypes.

The remarkable impulse towards innovation which marks Gascoigne's work – he is responsible for the first treatise on poetry in English, the first adaptation of Greek tragedy, the first entirely English prose novella, the first translation of Italian prose comedy – represents one resourceful contribution to this process by which the fruits of the new and the alien were dedicated to the uses of the Commonwealth.

It is precisely this relationship between innovation and public utility, however, which is a crucial site of contradiction, both for the emergent national culture and for its individual literary outworkers. On the one hand the writer is enjoined to plunder rival cultures without reservation to ensure that no significant or fashionable body of knowledge or expertise, no established literary genre or technique, remains unavailable to the repertoire of English. At the same time, it is equally imperative that this prodigal maximisation of resources should not disturb the essentially conservative ideological framework of Commonwealth which it is intended to reinforce.[6]

As we have already seen, the idea of Commonwealth is powerful precisely in its exclusion of historical change or development. The idea of order which it encodes is of such force and clarity exactly because it represents the original and eternal disposition of the cosmic structure by God. Its mutually supporting hierarchies of subjective, social and natural orders map out the incorruptible order of the Real, in relation to which the innovations of history are a play of illusion, the merest epiphenomena. For the Elizabethan State, this was still the most developed and comprehensive system of places in which things and subjects could be kept. Yet, as I have suggested, the Elizabethan State in its self-formation presides over and incites the very process which is proscribed by its conservative ideology – the process of historical innovation, of comprehensive cultural restructuration.

The contradictions of this position are clearly exposed in the vacillations and inconsistencies of Elizabethan economic policy.[7] Here government is obliged for its own financial survival to accommodate those proto-capitalist forces whose advance is increasingly inimical to the socially regulated market enshrined in the idea of Commonwealth. State revenues come increasingly to depend on the encouragement of monopolisitic practices and intensive capitalisation in the textile industry, mining and manufacturing, on monopolies in import, export and wholesale trade, and on the manipulation of exchange markets.[8] All these are tendencies which are criticised by Commonwealth commentators and which are thought by modern historians to have contributed to the economic dislocation and accompanying immiseration and unrest which recurred throughout the Elizabethan decades. Yet these threats of social breakdown were met by statutes aimed at social and economic regulation which rearticulated the ideal of Commonwealth and its supporting cosmology, in an increasingly futile attempt to keep that system in its place and its subjects in their places.[9] This precarious attempt to reconcile the demands of systems-maintenance and economic innovation, to manage a regulated intercourse between stability and mobility, is the normal state of Elizabethan government.

If we consider the cultural sphere in this context, it is the Court, either directly or through a few mediating agencies, which is the primary instigator of literary innovation, and the place in which the criteria of public utility are announced and enforced.[10] The literary judgements passed at Court are also judgements of the subject who writes, an assessment of public character and potential utility in the spheres of administration, diplomacy, Court entertainment and propaganda, or, in a case such as Donne's, the Church.

For the ambitious writer who attempts to break into this central domain of patronage and social endorsement, the text is a secondary artefact, the mere representative of personal credentials in the service of extra-literary ambitions. However, to present the self for ratification through a text admits an exclusion from unmediated personal contact with the prospective patron and subjects the presentation of the self to the hazards of reading and interpretation.

The hazardousness of this process is ensured by two factors determining the encounter between the uninitiated writer and the Court. The Court acts as an interpretative community whose judgements are definitive. The aspiring writer from outside that community has only more or less informed inferences and secondary information on which to base his fashioning of the text to fit current standards. This uncertainty about the criteria of acceptable writing is compounded by the indecisiveness of the Court itself. This derives not only from the contradictory imperatives of literary innovation and ideological conservation which I have already outlined, but also from the volatile and contentious nature of internal Court politics. The Court is neither stable nor undivided, and the text which enters its circuit is open to valorisations and imputations of meaning incited by some current internal crisis or factional dispute of which the writer is ignorant or inadequately informed.

This double hazard is illustrated by the case of Gascoigne's first collection of verse, *A Hundreth Sundrie Floweres*, published in 1572 when the author was fighting in the Dutch wars against the Spanish. The collection presents verses of amatory sophistication calculated to conform to current fashions of leisured, luxurious courtly discourse. It plays ingeniously with authorial persona, reportage and auto-biographical modes to produce the implication that Gascoigne is an adept not merely of writing, but also of the amorous intrigues and contests which the writing describes. On his return to London in 1574, however, Gascoigne found the Court's reponse to have been directed by the requirements of moral and social regulation. The text had been seized by the Court of High Commission on the grounds of licentiousness and the imputation of aristocratic morals; certain episodes in the prose narrative 'The Adventures of Master F.J.' having been taken to allude to recent minor scandals at Court.[11]

Gascoigne (and we might add – different crises, different texts – Raleigh, Chapman, Fulke Greville and the compulsively inept Harvey) falls foul of an opposition between two economies, both of them centring upon the Court. The first, which I shall term 'mundane', is that of patronage, competition for office and status, and cultural ostentation. It represents one circuit which connects the Court to the forces of economic expansion and modernisation, of social mobility and dislocation, and of national centralisation. The other, 'ideal' economy is that of Commonwealth and its associated cosmology. Here the Court appears as the custodian of stasis, the conserver of degree and hierarchy, maintaining the social regulation of economic activity, and securing the authority and clarity of official Christian doctrine.

From this second perspective the mundane economy is an arena of worldliness, pride and private commodity. It is in the mundane that Gascoigne (and this is true of all ambitious 'unplaced' Elizabethan writers) is fully implicated by his orientation towards Court patronage, his economic insecurity and social displacement, and his commitment to cultural innovation. At the same time his aspiration to official status requires that he appears as an agent of the ideal; a conserver of doctrinal integrity, his texts confirming and restating the eternal order, his skills selflessly dedicated to the Commonwealth. To find some way of operating within this contradiction, and to anticipate the Court's concomitant oscillations and ambiguities – this is the precarious and laborious task of the Elizabethan writer.[12]

* * *

The fracas of 1572–4 seemed to mark Gascoigne's conspicuous failure in this task, serving merely to dramatise and confirm the dubious reputation he had been acquiring over the previous decade.[13] In 1559 Gascoigne had abandoned his legal studies at Gray's Inn to spend four years in a fruitless and financially ruinous attempt to make an impact at Court. Heavily in debt, he retired to Bedfordshire, becoming embroiled in a series of cantankerous lawsuits. The cost of relaunching himself at Gray's Inn from 1564, compounded by the expenses on the loss of all his lawsuits, led to his confinement for debt in Bedford jail in 1570. In 1572 anonymous detractors condemned him in a letter to the Privy Council as a notorious debtor, 'a defamed person . . . a common Rymer and deviser of slanderous Pasquelles . . . a notorious Ruffian and especially noted to be both a spie, an atheist and a godlesse person'.[14] Pursued by creditors and desperate for any employment, it was at this point that Gascoigne fled to the Low Countries, leaving his *A Hundreth Sundrie Floweres* in the hands of the printer. On his return in 1574 he had participated in several disastrous English campaigns, and had received no pay from the army.

Gascoigne's response to his continuing public embarrassments was this time not forced retirement but the circulation of a new public persona through a new sequence of texts. 1574 sees the emergence of a series of prose tracts and religious poems which present Gascoigne the penitent sinner and prophetic scourge. What these works develop is a systematic and theologically grounded opposition between the mundane and ideal economies.

The satirical poem 'The Steel Glas' makes it clear that this, in other terms, is the opposition which we discussed earlier between Commonwealth and singularity. The poem situates itself within a tradition of Commonwealth writings which includes the *Discourse of the Common Weal* and the *Utopia*. As in the works which we have already considered, the analysis of social and economic dislocations in the poem is closely bound to questions of vision, epistemology and representation, a condensation which is fixed in the opposition between the Steel and the Crystal Glass, a variation on the trope of the mirror which we encountered in the *Discourse of the Common Weal*:

> Lucylius, this worthy man was namde,
> Who at his death, bequeathed the christal
> glasse,
> To such as love, to seme but not to be,
> And unto those, that love to see themselves,
> How foul or fayre, soever that they are,
> He gan bequeath, a glasse of trustie Steele,
> Wherin they may be bolde alwayes to looke,
> Bycause it shewes, all things in their degree.
> . . . And therwithal, to comfort me againe,
> I see a world, of worthy government,
> A common welth, with policy so rulde,
> As neither lawes are sold, nor justice bought,
> Nor riches sought, unlesse it be by right.
>
> (II, 149–75)[15]

The unambiguous and divinely grounded nature of identity and relationship within the ideology of Commonwealth is celebrated here as the clarity with which things appear in the steel glass or mirror, an absolute fit between object and image which Gascoigne laments as lost in contemporary England:

> I see and sigh (bycause it makes me sadde)
> That pevishe pryde doth al the world possesse.
> And every wight, will have a looking glasse
> To see himselfe, yet so he seeth him not . . .
> That age is deade, and vanisht long ago,
> Which thought that steele, both trusty was and
> true,
> And needed not a foyle of contraries,
> But shewde al things, even as they were in
> deede. (II, 147)

The poet makes this clarification of identity beyond difference (the 'foyle of contraries') available again through his satire, a 'glass of trustie steele' which affords also an authentic presentation of personal identity. Beside the marginal title of 'The aucthor himselfe', Gascoigne describes the image which the glass offers of his own dubious career: 'An age suspect, bycause of youthes misdeedes./A poets brayne, possest with layes of love' (II, 140). The retrospective narrative of inconsistencies and self-difference concludes as follows:

> And to be playne, I see myself so playne,
> And yet so much unlike that most I seemde . . .
> I should in rage, this face of mine deface,
> And cast this corps, downe headlong in
> dispaire,
> Bycause it is, so farre unlike it selfe.
> (II, 149)

Later ideologies of the subject would take the contradictions and slippages in Gascoigne's narrative self-image as the marks of authenticity; here they are the occasions of the self's dissolution. The integrity of the subject – its full presence – is located not in existential immediacy but in the impersonal categories of degree and vocation to which Gascoigne's inconstant experience fails to conform. So the truth of Gascoigne's life is not for him in the autobiographical account derived from the mirror, but in the satirical persona through which he frames and evaluates it. It is that persona which, in its pointing of morals, its impartial criticism, its proposals for reform, is dedicated to the uses of the Commonwealth, and so announces the writer's assumption of the duties proper to his vocation. By this social redefinition, the self is grounded in system and hierarchy and so assumes its authenticity.[16]

As Helgerson suggests, this self-loathing 'authentic' subjectivity is also one immobilised in its conformity to the disciplinary discourse of the Father:

> . . . remembrance as the key to self-knowledge. Remember your father and his precepts, and remember who you are . . . . To be . . . means to emulate your father and to obey his counsel. Not to be means to stand in your own conceit, and to follow the bent of your own disposition.[17]

The repetition of the Same is enforced, while any deviation into difference is anathematised as a grotesque or sub-human shifting of the self:

> The threat of a Circean transformation, of a metamorphosis from the self decreed by duty, haunted the mid-century Humanists.[18]

Helgerson supports this point with references to the Elizabethan taste for allegorised transformation tales such as the *Metamorphoses*, Apuleius' *The Golden Ass* and the Circe episode of the *Odyssey*. Such transformation stories are indeed made to carry the superscription of patriarchal moralism, but what Helgerson does not explore is the way in which the need for the moralising 'apparatus' betrays a fear that the texts themselves embody or generate the metamorphic energy which, paradoxically, the 'moral' invariably claims they are intended to denounce. In other words, it is not only the subject of metamorphic representation – the actions of intemperate or delinquent characters within the fiction – which the patriarchal discourse of the moralisation is called upon to police, but the medium of representation itself, which is deemed to have the power to transform the godly reader into his or her delinquent or 'bestial' antitype. Witness Golding's characterisation of the *Metamorphoses* even as he introduces his own translation of it:

> Behold, by sent of reason and by perfect syght
> I find

A panther heere, whose painted cote with yellow
spots like gold
And pleasant smell allure mine eyes and senses
to behold.
But well I know his face is grim and feerce,
which he doth hyde
To this intent, that whyle I thus stand gazing
on his hyde,
He may devour mee unbewares . . . [19]

Ovid's text here is supposed to exert the short-lived and catastrophic allure of sensual pleasures which, according to the text's moral commentary, causes the downfall of the characters of whom it tells. Ovid's narratives are deemed to teach the necessity of transcending sensuality and living 'under awe/ Of reasons rule continually . . . in vertues law' (p. 21), and this is precisely the discipline which Golding enjoins upon his readers as they are faced with the perilously sensual Ovidian text:

The readers therefore earnestly admonisht are
to bee
To seeke a further meaning then the letter
gives to see.
The travail tane in that behalf although it
have some payne
Yt makes it double recompense with pleasure and
with gayne.

(p. 23)

In its transcendence of sense-experience and the materiality of the 'letter', the allegorical hermeneutic offers the reader a route to transcendence which is denied the similarly assailed, but hapless, actors of Ovid's fiction. In a similar fashion, William Adlington introduces his translation of another pagan tale of metamorphosis, Apuleius' *The Golden Ass*,[20] by asserting that 'the jesting and sportfull matter of the booke, [is] unfit to be offered to any man of gravity and wisedome' (p. 4). However, he continues, 'considering that although the matter therein seeme very light and merry, yet the effect thereof tendeth to a good and vertuous moral, as in the following Epistle to the Reader may be declared' (p. 4). The Epistle duly informs us that

in this feined jest of Lucius Apuleius is comprehended a figure of man's life, ministring most sweet and delectable matter, to such as shall be desirous to read the same. (p. 6)

The Epistle supplies the allegorical key which allows the reader to metamorphose the 'light and merry' matter of the text into the 'sweet and delectable matter' of the text's initially hidden significance, a significance which the text 'ministers', a verb with reassuringly righteous and dutiful connotations. This righteous or 'upward' re-formation of the text (in opposition to the 'downward' metamorphosis of man into beast of which the text tells) is the means by which a corresponding upward transformation may be undertaken by the unrighteous or unreformed reader. Adlington states that he will 'open the meaning' of Apuleius' narrative so that the ignorant

> may not take the same as a thing only to jest and laugh at . . . but by the pleasantnesse thereof bee rather induced to the knowledge of their present state, and therby transforme themselves into the right and perfect shape of man. (p. 6)

The implication here is that the 'ignorant' who are initially fixated upon the mere material or sensual letter of the text have themselves already undergone a 'downward' transformation from the 'right and perfect shape of man'; a transformation which Golding describes in his epistle to the *Metamorphoses*, when he discusses those who do not live 'under awe/Of reason rule continually':

> And that the rest do differ naught from beasts,
> but rather bee
> Much worse than beasts, bicause they doo abace
> theyr owne degree.
>
> (p. 21)

In both these cases, then, the unmoralised pagan text is itself a Circe which has the power to lure men by sensual attraction, and, having ensnared them, transform them to a bestial condition. The magical agent – or *moly* – which protects the reader from bewitchment by the metamorphic text is the allegorical method, whose counter-metamorphic agency reclaims both text and reader from the domain of sensuality into the order of reason and virtue, a state of 'erection' towards God.[21] These parallel relationships between the situations of the narrative and the situation of reading – between protagonist and reader – may be summarised in the following table:

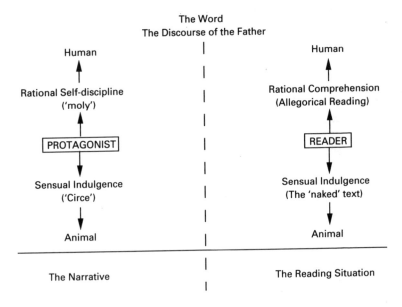

The mode of reading which corresponds to the self-discipline of a Ulysses or Guyon[22] in the face of sensual temptation is an allegorical one which abolishes the 'dangerous' text even as its makes it available to an increased readership in the vernacular. The text which is believed to diverge from the monological discipline of patriarchal orthodoxy is re-formed into a restatement of that orthodoxy. This hermeneutic drama – in which the fixity and singularity of the Word is reasserted in the face of a feared plurality and vagrancy of words within fictions – reproduces the moral and epistemological drama of human existence 'outside' the reading transaction which the allegorised text allegedly is 'about'. Like the text, the world too is seen as being composed of sensually apprehended elements, and the emotional and imaginative states to which they give rise, which are perpetually threatening to escape or exceed the disciplinary enclosure of patriarchal orthodoxy. The struggles to reclaim the text and the world of secular contingency are one and the same: an attempt to reduce difference, heterogeneity and process to the prescriptive certitudes and singular 'truths' of a discursive regime centred upon the Logos. As we shall see shortly, the metamorphic text represents an extreme case in a more general struggle around literature as a whole; for the moment we will return to the parallel contention between the Word and the contingencies of secular circumstance, between ideal and mundane economies.

The violence of self-mutilation which Gascoigne imagines in 'The Steel Glas' is provoked by the radical divorce between the truth of the self and its mundane existence. The figure of the glass allows Gascoigne to connect this diseconomy of the subject to dislocations of social and cosmic order, the mediating term being that of visual imagery or representation. The divorce between the ideal and the mundane at both micro- and macrocosmic levels is also a dissociation of the worldly signifier from its grounding in the Signified.

I have already discussed the centrality of theories of the sign to a long tradition of speculation upon cosmic economy.[23] The Neoplatonic doctrine which informs much of this tradition is essentially optimistic and progressive in orientation: if the earthly signifier veils the radiance of the Signified, it also dimly reflects it, and these faint glimmerings of the Divine Light can be pursued and magnified by a dedication of the initiate to esoteric disciplines, and the progression towards a state of ecstasy or *furor* in which a revelation of the Divine Incandescence may be granted.[24] The relationship of sixteenth-century, and in particular Northern European, writers to this tradition, however, is crucially modified by the emergence of Lutheran fideism and the predestinarian doctrines of Calvin.

Militant Protestantism fiercely contradicts any possibility of mediation between the divine and earthly orders. Luther and Calvin both insist upon a rigorous separation of spheres in which the rigours of faith mark precisely the non-presence of the Divine and the deferment of the accession to truth to a moment beyond this life and the abolition of the world. Calvinist predestinarianism confirms this harsh dispensation in the perpetual and inscrutable separation of the elect from the damned.

The tendency of militant Protestantism is, then, towards a vision of the world as a disorder of ungrounded signification which is incapable of arrest or regulation through referral to the eternal order of the Signified. This tendency is forcefully present in the relentless fideism and predestinarian gloom of Gascoigne's penitential works. It is confirmed by Gascoigne's confusion in the face of the economic, social and cultural processes which I have outlined: the rapid and seemingly uncontrollable increase in material and cultural productivity, the flooding of England with new things, words, ideologies and cultural artefacts among which new relationships obtain. The inability of the established ideology of Commonwealth to contain or render comprehensible this implosion of innovatory forces was readily conceived as the engulfment of the settled categories and syntax of 'natural' order by a deluge of non-meaning, an erasure of the Signified which grounds the intelligibility of things; a triumph, in short, of the illegible.

Gascoigne's response in his penitential tracts is a fulsome contempt of the world, a total retreat from any embroilment with the duplicities of the mundane. The regime of abstention which the tracts recommend to the righteous Christian involves a discipline which is at once epistemological, semiotic and discursive.

The title of Gascoigne's *The Needle's Eye* immediately suggests, through its allusion to the parable, a connection between a rectification of mundane values and magnitudes and a discipline or rigorous refocusing of vision. Indeed the radical Neoplatonism of the tract establishes the scene of truth, of achieved grace, as one in which the signifier is abolished and the apparent multiplicity of things evaporates in the face of an original unitary meaning which, in truth, they merely represent:

> We know that when he apeareth we shalbe lyke unto him, for we shal see him as he is . . . clearly and perfectly in his forme and proper kynde. For the intellectual sight, is and consisteth by view of the intellygible forme or shape, whereby we see what is the lykenesse of the thing ones understoode. Neyther can that lykenesse playnely represent the thinge, unlesse it be made equall unto the thinge it selfe. But every shape, lykenesse or forme created, dooth infinitely fayle and come short of the full representacion of the divine essence or being, and therefore God is seene onely in the heavenly kingedome, bicause then the very divyne essence it selfe is unyted unto the myndes of the blessed in the steede of the intellygyble forme or shapes. (II, p. 414)

The proliferation of differences which generates a mundane order of purely relational values is to be combated by a systematic referral of things to the true, spiritual object which they signify, an object whose value is self-instituted and self-declarative, and depends upon no relational or diacritical definition:

> Now it is certeyne that temporall thinges are directed, and ordered, unto, and by the spirituall thinges, as unto theyr

ende and onely skope. But thend and terminable skope is loved
and desyred one waye and the meanes and degrees whereby
we atteyne to the ende . . . another way. For the ende is of
it selfe and by it selfe to be desyred and loved . . . . But the
meanes and degrees . . . are to be desyred and loved, in that
they are profitable or availeable to the attayning of the ende or
skope . . . . (II, pp. 419–20)

This discipline of vision, semiosis and desire arrests the production
of differences and restores similitude; an economic stabilisation of
the sign upon an original and unitary principle of intelligibility. The
lateral, metonymic generation of the signifier is curtailed by a forced
displacement on to the axis of metaphor, and as a result the perpetual
onward rush of the new and the different is replaced by the endless
return of the Same:

> For simylitude and lykenesse are cause of love, as dissymilitude
> and unlykenesse are cause of rancor and hatred. Yea the
> perfection of any creature . . . is to be proportionately made
> lyke unto his creator. (II, p. 417)

This restoration of monological integrity is achieved in practice by
a rigorous Scriptural literalism, reinforced by mnemonic disciplines.
The process is described in the poem 'Gascoigne's Good Night':

> Ere sleepe close up thyne eye to fast, do not
> thy God forget,
> But searche within thy secret thoughts, what
> deeds did thee befal:
> And if thou find amisse in ought, to God for
> mercy call.
> Yea though thou find nothing amisse, which thou
> canst cal to mind,
> Yet ever more remember this, there is the more
> behind:
> . . . The stretching armes, ye yauning breath,
> which I to bedward use,
> Are patternes of the pangs of death, when life
> will me refuse:
> And of my bed each sundrye part in shaddowes
> doth resemble,

The sundry shapes of deth, whose dart shall
make my flesh to tremble.
. . . The hungry fleas which friske so freshe, to
wormes I can compare,
Which greedily shall gnaw my fleshe, and leave
the bones ful bare:
. . . And as I ryse up lustily, when sluggish
sleepe is past,
So hope I to rise joyfully, to Judgement at the
last.

(I, ll. 58–9)

Through this 'affectionate recollection or repetition of mind towards god' each component of experience is converted into a metaphor. As a result the sequentiality of existential time is arrested in a static repetitive rehearsal of the moment of Judgement, and the narrative of daily particularities is revealed as an encoding of Scriptural commonplace.[25] Whether as speaker or listener, writer or reader, the subject's encounters with discourse become purely mnemonic and reiterative: in Gascoigne's words, 'the conversation must be made conformable unto the prayer' (II, p. 426). This entails a wary restraint of the signifier, a curbing of any discursive elaboration which threatens the unimpeded transmission of the 'sense':

> For it is requisite in tyme of prayer to behave our selves purely . . . . Yea and that wee may desire to please God onely, and bee more delighted in the sence, then in the galantnesse of the wordes, and more in devotion, then in warblyng with the voyce, lest we commit any wanton gesture or action.
>
> For Augustine sayeth: whensoever it happeneth that I am more delyghted with the musicke, then with the effect of the wordes that are sung, I confess . . . that I doe offend greevously . . . . For what prevayleth the noise of the lippes when the harte is dombe? (II, pp. 427–8)[26]

The disciplined integration of the subject and the regulation of the sign come together in this authority of the Word, which underwrites the natural orders of cosmos, society and self. The educational discipline which Gascoigne describes registers the Word in the most intimate recesses of self-consciousness, and so realises the claim which he makes elsewhere:

For the worde of god is most plentyfull, conteyning in it all
delights. And therin (as in a myrrour) when we doo looke and
gaze with the eyes of our inward mynde, we doo also see and
behold the secret shape of our soules. (II, p. 336)

Those who resist the registration of the Word in the lineaments
of the self are condemned to that earthly wandering which is one
of Gascoigne's persistent themes.[27] This restless pursuit of illusory
partial objects is accompanied by an internal divagation of faculties, a
dispersal of affective energies through a wanton dissemination among
worldly objects:

> ... sinne maketh a manne unstable. For a sinner is over-
> throwne, tossed, and caryed about with every wynde of
> passiones, temptations and vices. As it is written, the wicked
> shall walke aboute; for they are as the dust which the wynde
> driveth from the face of the earth: because their herts are
> not made faste unto the highest, unchangeable, onely true
> and most perfect goodnesse. Therefore they wander in thinges
> created, and are divided in mynde, and are most inordinately
> affected. (p. 318)

The sinner is unanchored, a wanderer or vagrant, driven by desires
and appetites which are doomed only to find inadequate objects.
As a remedy to this state of dissipation, the ethical discipline of
monological concentration and conservation assumes a powerful
libidinal dimension, and is transposed into a discourse of collected
and undiverted phallic potency. In this erotic register, the paradox of
male power focused and secured by submission to a higher authority
engenders an imagery of interpenetration, in which the soul is both
the 'erected', 'active' male member and the 'passive' female 'vessell'
to be 'filled and satisfied':

> For virtue is both greater and of more force when it is united,
> then when it is dispersed and divyded into the inordinate
> love of worldly creatures .... If the outward wandering
> be shut up, the inward accesse to God is opened, for the
> lesse that the soul be dispersed in it self, the straighter it
> is erected to things above .... Hee will associate thee unto
> him for ever. So that thou mayest enjoy him thy fill most
> sweetly and abundantly .... For he which is capable of GOD

cannot be filled and satisfied with anything that is less than
God. (II, pp. 386–7)

The discourse which validates God as the only satisfactory 'anchor' for
human activity, the one adequate object of men's desires, produces
at the same time a powerful endorsement of the priority and
authority of sexual relations between 'normally' gendered subjects.
This association between the legitimation and hierarchical subordination of the subject and the hierarchically organised domain of
heterosexual intercourse (as legitimated, of course, by the sacramental
framework of marriage) contributes powerfully to the ambivalence
of dominant representations of female sexuality in the period –
as we have already seen,[28] an agent of order and conservation
when sacramentally contained and directed, but a provocation to
'wandering' and self-dispersal when unconstrained – and to the
demonisation of divergent or 'supplementary' sexual practices. In all
these areas the disciplinary discourses which play upon the subject
operate a primary distinction between the anchored and the 'unloosed'
or vagrant.

A good place to look for delineations of those who, in departing
from the disciplines of the Word, suffer the wandering disposition of
worldliness is in the self-castigations of the professional Elizabethan
writer:

> . . . being a man wholy addicted to all gracelesse indeuors, giuen
> from my youth to wantonnes, brought up in riot, who as I grew
> in yeares, so I waxed more ripe in ungodlines, that I was the
> mirrour of mischiefe, and the very patterne of all preiudiciall
> actions . . . so that herein I seemed a mere reprobate, the child
> of Sathan, one wipt out of the booke of life: and as an outcast
> from the face and fauour of God.[29]

This is Robert Greene, a specialist in repentance and self-excoriation.
A later confession – *Greene's Vision* – makes clear that if the writer
is wiped out of the book of life, it is his own books which have done
most to disqualify him:

> . . . then the discommodities that grew from my vaine pam-
> phlets began to muster in my sight: then I called to mind,
> how many idle fancies I had made to passe the presse, how
> I had pestered gentlemens eyes and minds, with the infection
> of many fond passions . . . a sudain fear tainted every limb,

and I felt a horror in my conscience, for the follys of my pen . . . . (p. 203)

It is this vanity of the pen that figures most prominently in Gascoigne's own confessions:

> I must needs confess both unto your honour and to the whole world, that . . . I find myself guilty of much time mispent, and of greater curiosity than was convenient, in penning and endighting sundry toyes and trifles. So that looking back (with inward grief) . . . I find that both the time, and my duty do challenge in me the fruits of repentance. (II, p. 376)

It is in this intimately associated delinquency of the writer's life and work that the disciplines of the Word find their object. The denial of the Word delivers the self up to the chaos of unregulated affect and passion whose seat is the body, and, as Greene testifies, through its reproduction in the writer's words the same disorder is visited upon the reader:

> . . . so the outward phrase is not to be measured by pleasing the eare, but the inward matter by profiting the minde: the puffing glorie of the loftie stile shadowing wanton conceipts is like to the skin of a serpent that contriues impoysoned flesh . . . so bookes that contriue scurilitie, may for a while breed a pleasing conceit and a merrie passion: but for euery dram of mirth, they leaue behind them in the readers minde, a Tunfull of infecting mischiefs, like to the Scorpion, that flatters with his head and stings with his taile. (p. 203)

The other figure who flatters with *her* head and (metaphorically) stings with her tail is the mermaid/Siren, whose function as one of the tropes which lodges the *feminine* at the centre of discourses against singularity and vanity I discussed earlier.[30] There we saw Fulke Greville in his *Treatie of Humane Learning* mounting a conventional case against rhetoric (a case derived ultimately from Plato's *Gorgias*[31]) which modulates from rhetoric as a Siren into rhetoric as 'the painted skinne of many words'.[32] It is through this trope of cosmesis that rhetoric is linked to the other delinquent or vagrant practices which patriarchal discourses associate with the archetypal delinquency and vanity of the feminine. The 'painted skinne of . . . words' is an aesthetic supplementation which supposedly shifts language away from the unadorned transmission of the *sense* (*res*, matter, *doxa*, the Signified) – the discipline by which discourse affiliates itself to the Logos – and into an unlegitimated field of discourse where the elaboration of the signifier is deemed to have cast off its proper subordination, the natural, proportional, 'decorous' bonding to the Signified in which it finds its only legitimation. The painted face of a woman is similarly constituted within these discourses as the field of a dangerous supplementarity, or vagrancy, of the signifier. Philip Stubbes's *Anatomy of Abuses* cites the Church Father Ambrose thus:

> For what a dotage is it to change thy natural face which God hath made thee for a painted face, which thou hast made thyself.[33]

Vanity as a self-absorption before a mirror; vanity as vagrant practice, unanchored in the natural order of God's making, producing an object which is therefore deficient in its artificiality, ontologically 'thin', an egregious and dangerous supplement. Cosmesis serves as a rhetorical junction point at which disciplinary discourses can establish connections between different delinquent practices and objects, one of the intersections out of which the all-encompassing textile web of the discourse on *vanitas*, singularity, vagrancy, is composed.

So, if for Fulke Greville rhetoric is cosmetic (a 'painted skinne of ... words'), for Richard Rainolds, that association connects it to the delinquent femininity of the whore: '... singed with harlot's curling irons, smeared with dripping perfumes, daubed with pigments'.[34] George Downame, a sixteenth-century commentator on the rhetorician Ramus, brings us back to the struggle of the classical hero against a monstrous femininity (recalling Fulke Greville's Siren rhetoric). Madeleine Doran writes of the 'comparison made by George Downame ... of invention, disposition, and memory to Hercules, of elocution (style), and delivery to "merely the Hydra and the skin of eloquence ..."'.[35] Here the analysis of the component parts of rhetoric is submitted to a binary logic which is continuous with that of the sign (and of the human subject): inward rational parts (invention, disposition, memory) against external, bodily ones (elocution, delivery).

Behind the urbanity of Downame's formulation the classical allusion reveals a model of discourse (and therefore of the speaking subject) as divided and at war with itself. Just as the economic subject is enjoined to discipline a vagrant propensity of the self towards the artificial, supplementary, vain commodities of personal (bodily) adornment (an internal contention between the conservative force of *patrimony* and the dissipative energies of *effemination*), so too the subject of discourse must resist the allurements of the verbal surface, the supplementary 'body' of speech; a struggle between the reiterative discourses of patriarchal orthodoxy and an excessive or divagatory potential of language which is associated with an unconfined, unplaced or undisciplined, vagrant femininity:

> Yet since, she [Rhetoric] playes the wanton
> with this need,
> And staines the Matrone with the Harlot's
> weed.[36]

This is Fulke Greville's second stanza on Logic's 'sister', Rhetoric: she starts as the chaste and dutiful sister, becomes a Siren, ends a whore. The binary pair of sister/harlot (varied here as Matron/harlot) is supported by that of 'natural' face/painted skin, and in this final line by another opposition which sets the Matron's implicitly sober apparel against 'the Harlot's weed'. So the discourse against excessive apparel also finds a place in this matrix of associated tropes which interlock around the central figure of the painted woman.

Another link is to be found in the late second-/early third-century *Paedagogus* of Clement of Alexandria, who warns women against vanity, and particularly against applying cosmetics before a mirror: '. . . for not even the beautiful Narcissus . . . gained any happiness from becoming an observer of his own image.'[37] As Louise Vinge comments: 'When, as far as one can see, Narcissus appears for the first time in a Christian context, his reflection is thus made to illustrate *Vanitas*, the emptiness of outward, perishable beauty.'[38] And *vanitas* itself is imagined as female cosmesis and self-regard. The semiotic and economic binarisms which arise out of the Christian allegorisation of Narcissus, establishing him, as we have seen, as the archetype of the man fixated upon the illusory epiphenomenal surfaces of the secular world, is grounded here, in its first emergence, in the image of the supplementarity of a cosmetic feminine appearance, of that appearance's detachment from the sphere of divine making.

I have already shown how the trope of Narcissus is able to assimilate the figure of the usurer, and with the usurer, the matrix of interconnected tropes out of which the discourses of patriarchal authority, patrimonial economy, Commonwealth hierarchy and logocentric orthodoxy are generated is almost complete. Any of these figures – vagrant, usurer, narcissist, middleman, scrivener, excessive dresser, face-painter, actor, harlot, writer – may be linked with, displaced by, or illuminated through, any of the others, because all are generated within the binary economy of the discourse upon *vanitas* or singularity. Each, therefore, may also be exchanged with the figure which founds and fuels that discourse – the figure of an untamed, extroverted, corporeally unregulated femininity. As one last loop to secure the multi-filamented knot I am attempting to tie, let me thread Bishop Drant's statement in the preface to his 1566 translation of Horace's *Sermones*:

> I have done as the people of god were commanded to do with their captive women that were handsome and beautifull: I have shaved of his heare, and payred of his nayles (that is) I have wyped awaye all his vanitie and superfluitie of matter.[39]

A startling passage: the dangerousness *and attractiveness* of the pagan text is that of the alien woman and her practices of self-adornment. The imperialistic capture of the text, its domestication within the signifying regime of the Word – the forcible conversion, that is, of the 'vanitie and superfluitie of matter' into, one infers, the imperishability and essentiality of *spirit* – is, then, also a reconversion of the gendered text ('his heare', 'his nayles') from an assumed state of 'wild' effeminacy to its 'proper' masculine condition. The preacher of the Word confronts and tames the rhetoric of the unbeliever; it is a peculiarly explicit instance of the struggle which is played out in the period around a dominant conception of rhetoric; explicit too in the way it reveals the ideological violence implicit in the practice of translation in the period, be it translation between languages, or the intra-lingual conversion of unlegitimated practices of the signifier to conformity with the Word. Above all, the passage captures the gendered nature of this ideological struggle in a single remarkable image: the unlegitimated text as 'uncaptive' woman, attractive ('handsome and beautifull') and dangerous precisely in so far as it/she escapes, wanders free of, the shavings, pairings and wipings of patriarchal 'hygiene'. Drant allows an unusually direct glimpse of the normally unacknowledged politics of vanity, superfluity, matter, and the unlegitimated word.

The contamination which begins in the dissipations of the writer and proceeds through the diseconomy of the sign ends in the creation of a society of the vagrant, as invoked by Gascoigne:

> And therefore the Psalmist sayeth: of the reprobate and un-thankful sort: I have let them loose even according to the desires of their hartes, and they shall wander in their own inventions. (II, p. 422)

In the terms of sixteenth-century rhetorical theory, *inventio* or invention is the first and fundamental 'part' in the fivefold division of rhetoric. As D. J. Gordon defines it, 'Invention is literally the finding of the subject of the poem . . . [it] is also equated with the fable or fiction of the poem.'[40] To identify a subject or fable in a written work is already to locate a depth in which the work is grounded. Renaissance rhetorical theory elaborates this as a distinction between the subject and the subordinate act of expression, or the stylistic development of the verbal surface. *Inventio* demands that the subject be selected from the already formulated orthodox wisdom abundantly gathered in the system of *places*,[41] while the principle of decorum insists that the stylistic treatment of the subject should ensure its unimpeded and forceful transmission.[42] So when Richard Rainolde writes a treatise of rhetoric, it is also a compendium of orthodox doctrine concerning social and political duty:

> I have compiled this work . . . wherin are set forth such orations, as are right profitable to be read, for knowledge also necessary. The duty of a subject, the worthy state of nobility, the preeminent dignity and majesty of a prince . . . are here set forth.[43]

When the emphasis is shifted from the work to the writer, the ability to subordinate verbal performance to the transmission of the subject is a question of the writer's rational control of his physical faculties of expression. As Puttenham puts it:

> . . . therefore there be that have called stile, the image of man . . . for man is but his mind, and as his mind is tempered and qualified, so are his speeches and language at large, and his inward conceits be the mettal of his mind, and his manner and utterance the very warp and woofe of his conceits.[44]

Integrated writing represents the integration of the writer's self. When integration means securing the priority of reason, and reason is the transmission of commonplace or orthodox knowledge, the implications of a bad style are extended. As Roger Ascham has it:

> . . . all such writers as be fullest of good matter and right judgement in doctrine be always most proper in words, most apt in sentence, most pure and plain in uttering the same . . . . [Therefore] Stoics, Anabaptists, and Friars, with Epicures, Libertines and monks . . . [are] rude and barbarous in their writings.[45]

Ascham supports this argument with John Cheke's explanation of the stylistic incoherence of Sallust's work:

> . . . [he] spent the most part of his youth very misorderly in riot and lechery, in the company of such, who, never giving their mind to honest doing, could never inure their toung to wise speaking. (p. 40)

The integration of the text, then, reproduces and is linked to that of the self. Both are reinforced by the writer's orientation towards his vocation; that is his place in the hierarchies of duty and function which make up the established order of Commonwealth. There are two ways in which this proper orientation of writing is stressed; one relating to the production of the work, and one to its consumption.

The first concerns the idea of writing as the spontaneous effusion of the aristocrat. This image of the gentleman amateur preserves the idea of writing as an impersonal emanation of natural order by disentangling it at source from human labour and the compromising implications of artifice.[46] So, by implication, to work at writing for money is to invent spuriously at the dictation of the forces of appetite working through the artificial mechanisms of the literary market.[47] As George Pettie observes:

> Those which mislike that a gentleman should publish the fruits of his learning . . . think it most commendable in a gentleman, to cloak his art and skill in everything, and to seem to do all things of his own mother wit as it were.[48]

Issuing from the natural order through the conduit of aristocratic 'wit', writing returns to it by being dedicated to the Commonwealth. Few books, however scurrilous or depraved, fail to advertise their usefulness to the Commonwealth in this period. By doing so, writers assert the congruity of their words with those of the Book of Nature, and so with the Word of God. In this spirit Henry Peacham writes of the proper self-effacement of poetry:

> . . . the fathers of the Church teach us the true use and end [of poetry], which is to compose the Songs of Sion, and addresse the fruite of our invention to his glorie, who is the author of so goodly a gift, which we abuse to our loves, light fancies, and basest affections.[49]

This expulsion of affect in the dutiful act of writing also has implications for the question of the writer's audience, for as I have already suggested, the commercial literary market is represented as a mechanism of chaotic affect, sensuality and fancy, through which appetite challenges the Word as the primary determination upon writing:

> Idle toyes tending to sensualitie, or other lyke lycensious follie, are set forth upon their [i.e. booksellers] Stalles, in bright and glistering covers, when those bookes that are eyther drawing to vertue or godlinesse, are throwne into dustie corners.[50]

As Dekker apologises to his gentleman readers:

> If I put into your hands a homely piece of work, I must entreat you to blame the vanity of our times, which are so phantastical, that they covet stuffs, rather slight, to feed the eye with show, than substantial for enduring . . . . I have therefore not . . . swum against the stream, but followed the humorous tides of this Age.[51]

Through the sway of the humours, the market represents the assertion of the body at the expense of the mind; a sub-rational condition which is shared by the commercial audience. As Richard Rich makes clear, body to mind is as the multitude to the elite:

> To make myself sociable with the multitude, I have mingled matters of importance, with matters of small regard: I know this is the humorous age . . . and a man that can but tattle this and that (though to little purpose) shall have audience.[52]

Rich describes his text as being heterogeneous ('mingled matters'), purposeless, and determined not by himself, but by the 'humours' of the mass audience. All these points represent violations of the logocentric ideology of 'legitimate' writing, which is required to be self-consistent, profitable to the Commonwealth, and the product of the poet's own sovereign reason and invention. As literature is progressively implicated in the process of commodity production for the market, so its character diverges more dramatically from the logocentric paradigm. As Miller notes,[53] in the extreme (but increasingly common) case of the Elizabethan hack-writer, writing is characterised by speed (in response to 'news' events and to rapidly shifting market trends); brevity and an episodic, discontinuous form (to meet the need for short and therefore cheap material; Miller ascribes to this the hack-writer's incapacity in consecutive narrative); a multiplication of the individual writer's professional personae, attending a diversification of his practice; and a mechanical reprocessing of other writing (a kind of perverse parody or demystifying replication of the 'legitimate' practice of classical and Scriptural allusion). Here Miller cites the cony-catching literature, which from Greene's plagiarising of Awdeby, Harman and the original 'A Manifest Detection . . . of Dice Play', through the 'borrowing' of chunks of his own work by writers well into the 1630s, represents an unbroken seventy-five year span of plagiaristic reinvestment of literary capital. Associated with the last point, the hacks' compositional method tends towards a scissors-and-paste bricolage of ready-made and market-tested textual bits, rather than the 'legitimate' ideals of classical unity or organic cohesion.

These shifts in the organisation of literary production, within the context of a printing industry increasingly organised on a capitalistic basis, represent a growing exposure of the writer to the forces of economic and vocational reorganisation which are reordering the Elizabethan-Jacobean social order as a whole. The newly felt precariousness of the writer's identity, which I will discuss shortly, is one particularly visible (because eloquently lamented) instance of a more general reinscription of subjectivity which takes place as the forces of social change and mobility place the ideological system of identity as conferred by degree or estate under strain.

We can clarify this issue of the literary market and its relationship to the writer's self-inscription further if we return to the figure of the gentleman amateur. By his spontaneous transmission of the truth (or the commonplace material of orthodoxy) the aristocratic writer announces his own self-integration, the congruity between his natural wit and the imperatives of natural order. His elite audience, it is assumed, is unambiguously committed to the same order of 'natural' truths and social orthodoxies, and so their reception of his meaning is relatively assured, and with it the social confirmation of his subjective coherence, his integration as a person. The mutually confirming nature of this circuit depends upon its restricted scale; the consolidation of meaning and subjectivity is secured by elite solidarity around shared orthodoxies, codes and styles.

The writer such as Gascoigne, who is as yet outside this courtly circuit, is exposed to a double risk deriving from his two possible sources of income and employment. Firstly, if Gascoigne has displayed an instability and indecorousness of character, these dubious qualities have been elicited by the scramble for employment at Court, which has established itself as the dominant source of patronage and status, and has incited competition for preferment. Paradoxically, it is also the Court which, in the name of ideological orthodoxy, condemns Gascoigne for his conspicuous embroilment with worldly circumstance. Similarly, Gascoigne's contentious poems have been shaped in accordance with courtly fashion and to display those virtuosities of rhetoric, sophistical ingenuity and polished manner which the Court requires in its agents. Again it is the Court which may condemn those very qualities as compromising to the systems of ethical and discursive sobriety which it maintains. Both Court and writer-candidate are fully implicated in a worldly economy of patronage, status-seeking and cultural ostentation; both are also principal agents in the reproduction of an ideology which anathematises such systems as arenas of chaotic and misdirected desire.

In turning to publication as a means of financial survival and of bringing his work to notice, the writer exposes himself to the associated insecurity which attends the dissemination of work through the public presses.[54] By losing all knowledge of his audience, the writer abandons himself to hazards of misreading and malicious interpretation far worse than those inherent in his commerce with the Court. It is in this alienation of meaning from its customary self-confirming channels that the writer experiences a historically unprecedented alienation of self:

What though the sacred issue of my soule
I hear expose to Idiots control?
What though I bare to lewd opinion,
Lay ope to vulgar prophanation

My very genius . . . .
Spight of despite, and rancor's villany,
I am my self, so is my poesie.[55]

Marston here asserts a threatened self-identity against the usurping *alter ego* generated in the (mis-)reading of his texts. This is the condition of any writer without assured aristocratic status and income at the end of the sixteenth century: caught between an ideology of writing which asserts the continuity of text and self, the full representation of the person by his writing, and a situation in which the production of writing, and with it the public persona of the writer, is increasingly determined by market forces. The disintegration of any stable image of the self and its representative productions, the impulse to a perpetual diversification of the work and by implication of the persona, is lamented by Nashe in, appropriately, his role of Pierce Penilesse:

> New herrings, new, we must cry, every time we make ourselves public, or else we shall be christened with a hundred new titles of Idiotism . . . [when] the bottom of my purse is turned downward, and my conduit of ink will no longer flow for want of reparations . . . I am fain to . . . follow some of these newfangled Galiardos . . . and Fantasticos, to whose amorous Villanellas and Quipassos I prostitute my pen in hope of gain; but otherwise there is no newfangledness in me but poverty, which alone makes me inconstant to my determined studies.[56]

Nashe articulates the writer's dilemma in an exemplary form: the newfangledness which makes him marketable is from the perspective of the patronage circle a disabling inconstancy, the mark of an unstable candidate in the contest for employment.

It is in this context that the text comes to be apprehended by its author as incriminating evidence against him. So the printer of Pettie's *A Petite Pallace of Pettie his Pleasure* announces that the author 'was not willing to have it common, as thinking certain points in it to be too wanton to be wrought by that wit which by this work appeared to be in him'.[57] The contradictory relation of writer to text could not be more clearly stated: the work advertises the author's wit, but through a wantonness which is self-disabling. So too in his repentance Greene can condemn his early works as

so many parricides . . . for now they kill their father, and every lewd line in them written, is a deep piercing wound to my heart . . . . Black is the remembrance of my black works, blacker than night, blacker than death, blacker than hell.[58]

We are back with Greene, then, still repenting. For Greene, who developed a profitable line in deathbed retraction, the repentance is a form which allows the contradictory investment of the self in the text to be negotiated. It allows the dubious material of the life to be retold and retailed, while recasting it in the exemplary form of the morality tale. It represents the incoherence and flux of the body and the passions, while staging forcefully the final triumph of the mind, the restitution of meaning, and the definitive closure imposed by a final Judgement. It dramatises the writer in terms of existential immediacy, and at the same time establishes him as an exemplary moral figure. It is in short one mode through which self and text can be strategically placed in suspension between the contradictory imperatives of the market and the Commonwealth.

The repentance is Greene's distinctive method for rendering the compromised position of the Elizabethan writer profitable. As such it takes its place among an array of strategies for the disavowal or reclamation of delinquent writings which is to be found in the material prefacing Elizabethan literature. These include the simple disowning of youthful folly and trifling, and the claim that dubious matter is included precisely as a warning to the reader. Or there is the common argument that as life is mixed, so is art, which is illustrated usually by the imagery of gardens, where weeds, flowers, fruits and medicinal herbs are all available, depending upon the discernment of the gatherer. Gascoigne, desperately, uses all these in his 1574 letter to the Commissioners, adding to them the common argument that 'out of everie floure the industrious bee may gather honie, yet by proofe the Spider thereout also sucks mischeevous poyson' and the Horatian doctrine of the conjunction of pleasure and utility in the text.[59]

The problem with these strategies is that they are concessionary; they acknowledge the dubious components of the text while arguing that they should be simply discounted or balanced out against its more wholesome elements. The exception is the spider and bee argument, which turns on the audience and ascribes any depravity of meaning to the latter's corrupt interpretative inclinations. This is a serviceable device when it is directed against the rabble who cruise the market-place for scandal and sensation; it is less readily deployed against Her Majesty's High Commissioners when they detect wanton or contentious material in one's work. These limitations are sadly revealed in Gascoigne's revision and second publication of *An Hundreth Sundrie Floweres*, soberly retitled *The Poesies*. The contentious matter is left substantially intact, but is divided into sections headed Flowers, Weeds, and Herbs, and the implied injunction to horticultural discretion is reinforced by the three apologetic prefatory letters from which I have quoted. Despite these precautionary measures, the revised volume was seized in 1576 by the Court of High Commission.

* * *

Sir Hugh Platt, in 1594, lamented the Court's neglect of 'a secret number of choice wits, being full fraught of more necessarie, yea more invaluable commodities, then either the East or West Indies are able to afford'.[60] Yet this is precisely the problem; the incorporation of alien and potentially estranging materials into the unworldly economy of courtly ideology, dedicated as it is to spiritual rather than material profit. What is required, it seems, is some mechanism which can resolve the self-contradictory orientations of Court, writer, and courtly text. Such a mechanism would perform a number of strategic mediations; between the Court as innovator and as conserver of cultural order, between the writer as the divided subject of mundane fortune and as the loyal subject and underwriter of the ideal, between the text as delinquent surface and as virtuous depth.

For a writer such as Gascoigne who faces at Court the full rigours both of this set of contradictions and of an implacable justice, such a mechanism will also be a means of ameliorating judgement, of reconciling its arrest of the subject in a definitive category with the possibility of development, self-reformation and reversal:

> For as I can be content to confesse the lightnesse wherewith I have bene (in times past) worthie to be burdened, so woulde I be gladde, if nowe when I am otherwise bent, my better endevors might be accepted . . . . And . . . when the vertuous shall perceive indeede how I am occupied, then . . . Gravitie

the judge shal not be abashed to cancel the sentence unjustly pronounced in my condemnation. (II, pp. 136–7)

The definitive pre-emptive sentences – linguistic and judicial – of Lutheran and Calvinist discourse are here replaced by the provisionally articulated sentence of a moderate Humanism: a sentence whose interpretation is fixed only at the arrival of its final term. The state of rational maturity punctuates and retroactively orders the preceding terms into coherence and meaning, converting mere sequentiality into syntactic definition. This is the logos of Erasmus or Hooker, a gradual declaration of the Word in and through human time and circumstantiality.[61] The introduction of a certain deferral into the process of sentencing implies also a modification of the regime of the sign which was exemplified in Gascoigne's penitiential works. There the earthly signifier was negated by an immediate referral to the Signified. Rather than any temporal generation of meaning there was an abrupt monological encoding, which reproduced similitude at the expense of the proliferation of differences.

The Humanist model, however, introduces a provisionality into the relationship of signifier and signified, a regulated deferral of meaning whose modality is not the code but, as I have suggested, the sentence. For Erasmus or Hooker the production of meaning occurs precisely through a development of human reason towards the possibility of consensual definition: the Word manifests itself as the product of an accumulation of interpretative hypotheses in which error and revision contribute to the formation of authoritative meanings. This is the principle of *collatio* (comparison) which Erasmus opposes to Luther's *assertio* (the definitive declarations of the inspired) in their dispute over free will; precisely in order to keep open the possibility of self-reformation and the postponement of definitive judgement to which Gascoigne appeals.

In preparing yet another approach to the Court at the end of 1575, Gascoigne takes a step beyond the concessionary devices that he used in the previous year, by isolating a discursive strategy which corresponds to this melioristic regime of sentence and sign. What is required is a literary figure which rather than negating the signifier will place it in suspension, and so will replace the peremptoriness of Judgement with the deferred sentencing of interpretation. A figure which will represent the recuperation of the signifier through the unfolding of a narrative, so that the apparent excesses and diseconomies of the surface – of a text or a life – are resolved by the eventual emergence of a structural economy at depth. It is this figure which Gascoigne discovers in his preface to *Hemetes the Heremyte*; what George Puttenham describes as 'the chiefe ring-leader and captaine of all other figures', asserting that 'no man can pleasantly utter and perswade without it, but in effect is sure never or very seldome to thrive and prosper in the world that cannot skilfully put in use . . . the Courtly figure Allegoria'.[62]

* * *

The original *Tale of Hemetes the Heremyte* had been delivered before the Queen during the collaborative entertainment given at Woodstock, the terminus of the royal progress of 1575. Gascoigne had been one of the writers involved, although the *Tale* seems not to have been his work. Towards the end of the year Gascoigne took the *Tale* and worked it up into an ostentatious manuscript, supplementing it with his own translations into Latin, Italian and French, his own emblematic illustrations, and the prefatory disquisition on allegory which I will be discussing here. This package of Humanist virtuosity was then presented to the Queen as a New Year's gift for 1576.

Gascoigne's prefatory address first presents to the Queen the following paradoxical adage which represents, he writes, 'a rare and strange adventure':

> . . . thonder 'often tymes bruseth the bones, without blemishing of ye flesh, or . . . yt hath byn sene to breke the sword, without hurt don to the scaberd'. (II, p. 474)

The obscurity of this observation, Gascoigne continues, associates it with the apparent arbitrariness and senselessness of earthly contingencies:

> The chaunces which happen unto man are infynyte, and full of wonderfull varyetie, yet are theare none of them (in my judgement) so sleight or ridiculous, but that they carry with them some presage or forewarnying. (II, p. 474)

Gascoigne now proposes to demonstrate how the obscured meaning of the adage can be extracted from its seemingly recalcitrant surface so that it 'may become profitable to the willing minde' (p. 474). He will, that is, proceed 'to allegoryse this Adage' (p. 474).

The subject of the adage – thunder – appears to be the natural event most inimical to profit and fruitfulness: it 'do beat down corne grasse and fruite, [and] consume the foyson of ye earth' (p. 475). Thunder strikes and renders things infertile, but Gascoigne's *reading* of the thunderbolt redeems this infertility by harvesting its spiritual import: '. . . wheareby we may playnlye perceyve, that it is a type, or perfecte token, of gods wrath and indignacon conceyved against us' (p. 475). Gascoigne now returns to the adage, asking, 'Shall we then take this Text grossley or litterally as yt standeth . . . . God forbyd.' God forbids because His existence implies that of the spiritual dimension which He inhabits, a dimension which is hollowed out beneath or as a hidden depth within all seemingly opaque surfaces, including the linguistic surface of the adage.

So the adage, which speaks of thunder leaving surfaces intact as it penetrates to disturb interiors, is met by a reading which preserves the verbal surface while opening up an interiority of meaning. So the adage comes in truth – at depth – to speak of God's hurtless penetration of the flesh to reveal the hidden interior truth of his subjects:[63]

> . . . the wrath of god breaketh the blade of his rash deter-mynacyons, though ytt leave the skaberd of dissimulacon whole . . . . [it] doth . . . punyshe the sowle of man, when his body seemeth to florishe in greatest prosperytie. (p. 475)

God, like the allegorical reader, opens up the region of truth beneath the dissimulating surface. Gascoigne proceeds:

> And this allegorycall exposition of Thoonder, have I pretely pycked owt of myne owne youthfull pranks . . . [for] he hath brused my bones with the scourge of repentance, though my body beare the shew of a wanton and waveryng worlding. (p. 475)

What is also opened up, then, is the possibility of a rereading of Gascoigne's compromising life; a reading at depth, where the narrative is revealed as one of continual repentance and spiritual sobriety. The penitence and sobriety of a sinner, nevertheless: God opens Gascoigne up in order to judge him strictly, and Gascoigne is still in search of a softening of justice, despite the fact that 'the judgements of thallmighty are not moveable' (p. 475). Gascoigne requires God to be inconsistent, but how can this be granted when it is precisely God as unity, consistency and constancy who opposes and exposes the doubleness, dissimulation and variability of matter?

Gascoigne resolves this difficulty through a reading of another paradoxical adage: '. . . that one self same soonshyne doth both harden the clay, and dissolve the waxe'. Here the integrity of the sun itself is not compromised by the doubleness of its effect. What appears as double at the material level is resolved into the mysterious unity of the spiritual; for does not God resolve the Many into the One and through his Son reconcile body and spirit, history and eternity, judgement and grace?

Having in this way facilitated a rereading of his wanton life and the possibility of revising justice without compromising the judge, Gascoigne proceeds to install Elizabeth in the position of God as judge and penetrating reader. The compromising facts of Gascoigne's biography are drawn 'in sequens, before the skylfull eyes of your lerned majestie . . . being of God, godly, and (on earth) owr god (by god) appoynted' (p. 476). Recalling the thunder of the adage, Gascoigne admits his fruitlessness: 'I tylled the soil of fancy, and reaped the fruits of folly' (p. 476). His hope is that, as in the case of thunder, this fruitlessness will be redeemed through a skilful reading by Elizabeth, and that as a result 'your highnes will sett me on worke' (p. 476). If this requires a revision of earlier judgements, no matter. In assuming the position and perspective of God, Elizabeth also assumes his 'mysterious' integrity, his capacity to resolve contradictions into spiritual unity and to reconcile justice and grace.

Moreover, in fashioning this situation through his demonstration of allegory, Gascoigne has shown himself to be a master of linguistic interiority; a mastery which testifies to an intimacy with the depths both textual and personal, in whose name he makes his plea. Gascoigne's youthful waste of time can now be discounted: his unchanging interior truth meets Elizabeth's eternal, divine judgement in a dimension beyond the vacillations of historical and biographical time.

The effects of Gascoigne's allegorising are reinforced when he turns to speak of his translations of the original tale. Here he works a variation upon his basic paradox – that although a worthless sinner he is still worthy of employment – and his success again depends upon Elizabeth being located as divine judge and linguistic arbiter.

Gascoigne's case is based in an analogy between the shortcomings of the sinner and the translator. Gascoigne declares that he is good enough to enter service; but if he is sufficient only to serve, does not this acknowledge a deficiency? The position of the good servant is also that of the elect puritan whose works, however sufficient, only indicate the disposition towards election, depending finally upon the freely given grace of God. As translator too, Gascoigne's works may be good, but the continuity of meaning which they attempt to fix is accomplished in fact only by Elizabeth's reading: having heard the original at Woodstock, she is in the position to reconcile the differences between it and the translations, to restore divergent meanings to unity. As in the question of works and grace, the subject supplies the materials through which the Spirit manifests itself in the world, but it is the Spirit which redeems the deficiencies of the material and renders it complete. As with the allegorical instance, an incoherence at the level of the signifier and the substantial is resolved by the ideal reading performed by the Sovereign.

Elizabeth has now been placed in the same position of through-seeing, synthesising, absolving reader in relation to the adage, Gascoigne's biography and his translations. So Gascoigne is able finally to elide any difference between the composite text which he is offering and his own contradictory life, because it is the 'self-same' spiritual power which judges, resolves and pardons their strictly analogous deficiencies:

> But yet suche Itallyan as I have lerned . . . such lattyn . . . frenche . . . and English . . . have I . . . poured forth before you, most humbly beseching your majesty, that you will vouchsafe gracyowsly to looke into your loyall subject, and behold me . . . nott as I have byn, butt as I am, or rather not as I am, but as I would be, for I spare not here to protest, that I have no will to be, but as I should be. (p. 476)

* * *

The Elizabethan decades see a considerable investment in metaphysical representations of both the Court and the courtly writer: the Court as source of the eternal Law and guardian of arcane knowledge, the writer as moral legislator and underwriter of the ideal. The central authority of the Court and the effectiveness of its ideological agents are powerfully supported by these images of a metaphysical dimension in which Court and writer conserve and rearticulate the eternal order of 'things in their degree'. It is in these decades too, however, that Court and writer become embroiled in historical forces profoundly disruptive of ideas of stasis and immutable Law.

In *The Veil of Allegory* Michael Murrin writes that for the Renaissance writer

> allegory automatically reveals cosmic relationships, particularly in its combination of the two *logoi*, the invisible and visible words which imitate the combination of appearance and invisible power which make up the cosmos and the human being.[64]

It is this characteristic of allegory, along with its deferment of interpretative closure, which makes it an essential strategy of courtiership. The compromising worldly involvement of Court and writer is sublimed and exalted by the operation of allegory: the writer is able to move from material bankruptcy to spiritual solvency, the text from the redundancy of the letter to the fruitfulness of the sense, and the Court may admit both to its ethereal circuits without fear of contamination. In this way allegory contrives transcendence – to the material profit of all concerned.[65]

4

'The Instrumentality of Ornament': George Puttenham's *Arte of English Poesie*

> For the talke of the tongue, is the image of the hart . . . . Such as the man is, such is his communicacion.
>
> George Gascoigne, *The Needles Eye*

> It is learning and knowledge which are the onely ornaments of a man, which furnisheth the tongue with wisedome, and the hart with understanding, which maketh the children of the needy poore to become noble Peers, and men of obscure parentage to be equall with Princes in possessions.
>
> Thomas Nashe, *The Anatomie of Absurditie*[1]

Puttenham's *Arte of English Poesie*, in its solicitation of the 'courtly maker', teaches the art of successful communication within the Court, and yet the most forceful examples with which it supports its teaching are to be found in the sphere of communication *between* Courts:

> . . . a Herald at armes sent by Charles the fifth Emperor to Fraunces the first French king, bring him a message of defiance, and thinking to qualifie the bitternesse of his message with words pompous and magnificent for the kings honor, used much this terme (sacred Maiestie) which was not usually geuen to the French king, but to say for the most part (Sire). The French king neither liking of his errant, nor yet of his pompous speech, said somewhat sharply, I praye thee good fellow clawe me not where I itch not with thy sacred maiestie, but goe to thy businesse, and tell thine errand in such termes as are decent betwixt enemies, for thy master is not my frend, and turned him to a prince of the bloud who stood by, saying, me thinks this fellow speakes like Bishop Nicholas, for on Saint Nicholas night commonly the Scholars of the Countrey make them a Bishop,

who like a foolish boy, goeth about blessing and preaching with so childish termes, as maketh the people laugh at his foolish counterfaite speeches.[2]

This is one of several consecutive examples which Puttenham assembles to illustrate the breakdown of diplomatic communication. In relation to the central argument of Puttenham's *Arte* the function of these failures is to demonstrate, by default, the necessity for all communication to be governed by the principle of *decorum*, which Puttenham defines as 'this good grace of every thing in his kinde . . . . This lovely conformitie, or proportion, or conveniencie between the sense and the sensible'. As this makes clear, Puttenham, in common with other rhetoricians of the period, means by decorum a relation of fitness or appropriateness between the thought to be expressed and the vehicle or mode of expression. The purpose of Puttenham's treatise is to teach the techniques of successful communication, and the inculcation of this governing principle is, accordingly, its primary task.

It is important here to stress the particular function of the Ambassadorial cases in this educational project – they are negative instances, examples of the failure or absence of method, which serve to confirm antithetically the sphere of adequate, rule-governed communication to which the treatise will supply the methodological key:

> . . . I see no way so fit to enable a man truly to estimate of [decencie] as example, by whose veritie we may deeme the differences of things and their proportion, and by particular discussions come at length to sentence of it generally, and also in our behaviours the more easily to put it in execution. (p. 263)

If we consider more precisely what confounds the speech of Charles the Fifth's Herald at Arms, we can define the problem as one of contextual complication. The example's initial clause can stand as an instance of the simple communication model which underpins Puttenham's treatise:

Sender	—	*Message/Vehicle*	—	*Addressee*
Emperor		Defiance/Herald		Francis I

As Puttenham's anecdote proceeds, this model is immediately disrupted by the play, around and upon the message, of contradictory and diversionary contexts. The principal opposition is between the context of international hostility and that of courtly deferential address, which produces an initial disjunction between the message and its expression. Operating within this is another opposition between the socio-political ranks of the sender and messenger – the intrusion of deference upon defiance would have been less, we can assume, if the Emperor had faced the King himself. Complicating his difficulties, the herald next falls foul of the conventions governing courtly address in an alien political/cultural context: he lacks the insider's knowledge of the usual forms and protocols. As well as a familiarity with local conventions, this would also include knowledge of the disposition of the particular prince – Puttenham has examples of other princes whose addiction to deference in their inferiors is unswerving, and (to add to the difficulty) of those whose disposition changes at will.

The French King's aside to the prince of the blood underlines the theme of the herald's social misplacement, his exclusion from the circle of those who, united by rank, can converse with ease. The content of the aside, its reference to the Festival of St Nicholas, represents the outer limit of the message's deformation by its context; the point at which the process we have been tracing finally transforms the herald's message bathetically from a declaration of hostility to a demonstration of clownishness. It is significant, then, that the game of St Nicholas is one of linguistic parody which depends on the insider's sensitivity to a confusion of linguistic registers, or miscontextualised speech.

The breakdown of the herald's utterance, then, is characterised by a fracturing of the continuity between the speaker and his speech and between the matter and manner of his message. Puttenham's other associated examples stress that it is the diplomat's confrontation with a foreign language which is the principal cause of his failures, as in the case of the Bohemian answering the French Princess's query about his Empress's taste for hunting: 'Par ma foy elle chevauche fort bien, et si en prend grand plaisir.' The laughter which meets this reply is explained by Puttenham as follows: 'This word Chevaucher in the French tongue hath a reprobate sense, specially being spoken of a womans riding' (p. 272). In examples like this Puttenham is at pains to stress that the lack of a specifically linguistic competence makes the Ambassador a special case; a case which he aligns with that of the translator, who is sharply distinguished at the beginning of the treatise from the 'original' native poet for whose use his translations are intended.

As I suggested earlier, this specification of the negative case – as a means of delimiting the area within which the rules of successful communication *can* be taught – is crucial in establishing the legitimacy and effectiveness of Puttenham's educational project. Accordingly, Puttenham characterises the return to the native tongue as a return to safe ground where communication can be brought back under control by being submitted to the government of method:

> In which respect it is to be wished, that none Ambassadour speake his principall comandements but in his own language, or in another as naturall to him as his owne, and so it is used in all places of the world saving in England. The Princes and their commissioners fearing least otherwise they might utter any thing to their disadvantage, or els to their disgrace . . . . (p. 271)

In the native language, according to Puttenham, there is a return of the simple communication model outlined earlier, in which the speaker is able to bring the contents of his mind into a continuous relationship with the words which are to express them, and so achieve a clear communication. It is this reintegration of language and, with it, the speaking subject which the Earl of Arundel invokes when explaining his persistence in English to a servant of the Prince of Orange: 'Quoth the Earle againe, tell my Lord the Prince, that I love to speake in that language, in which I can best utter my mind and not mistake.'

If we consider the cultural status of the Ambassador in sixteenth-century Europe, this exclusion of diplomatic activity from the social field cultivated by the arts of language itself seems eccentric. The sense of diplomacy as the epitome of humanist practice, as an active realisation of the ideal of enlightened civic service based in a specifically linguistic training, is pervasive in the period. It is to be found in More's account at the beginning of *Utopia* of the circle of learned and energetic men gathered in Antwerp from across Europe by their diplomatic vocation, and in the eponymous ambassadors of Holbein's painting, surrounded by the icons of the new learning.[3] It is also to be traced in the intertwining of literary production and high diplomatic service in the careers of such figures as Sir Thomas Hoby, Sir Thomas Wilson and Sir Philip Sidney. Indeed, for the ambitious writer in Elizabeth's reign there is a sense in which the purpose of a literary career was as preparation for the Queen's diplomatic service. Gascoigne, Harvey and Spenser are among the many who might have endorsed Fulke Greville's statement: '. . . having many times offered my fortune to the course of foreign employments as the properest forges to fashion a subject for the real services of his sovereign'.[4]

From this perspective, then, the activity of the ambassador appears as an exemplary employment of the arts of language and the educational ideal which they support; in short, of the Humanist tradition with which Puttenham's work so clearly aligns itself. When Puttenham pushes to the margin of his discourse what we might expect to find at the centre we might detect an effort of displacement – an attempt to externalise a disturbance (the fear of a constitutional ungovernability of communication) which in fact threatens the heart of the project. A closer examination reveals that this is precisely what is at stake in the marginalisation of the ambassadorial case.

If we consider again the example of the Imperial herald it is clear that the problem of incompetence in a foreign language is not in fact a principal reason for the incoherence of the communication. The problem is not linguistic in this global sense; the herald betrays if anything a disabling fluency in the French language, introducing an excess into his translation of the Emperor's message. The breakdown is rather at the level of *sociolect*, produced by the ambiguity of the speaker's position in terms of rank (he is the 'voice' of the Emperor and yet merely a servant) and by his unfamiliarity with the habitual forms of address specific to this Court and this particular Prince; an unfamiliarity which would be shared by any native French speaker entering the Court for the first time.

What occurs in this situation is a fracturing of the ideal model of communication which I outlined above, at each of the three principal points of its articulation: the speaker loses control over the message, the message itself is split between its intended and its realised meanings, and the addressee is the site not of a confirmation of meaning and intention, but their loss.

Despite Puttenham's attempt to marginalise this case under the special category of ambassadorial speech or translation between languages, what it actually reveals is a problem of translation between different fields of utterance *within the same language*. The sovereignty of the speaking subject in relation to the production and transmission of meaning is threatened not only by the special circumstance of a departure from the security of the native tongue, but by the multiple, divergent, often contradictory determinations exerted upon any speech-act by the contingencies of its social context.

As an acute and conscientious analyst of the speech-act, Puttenham is fully aware of this reallocation of power from the speaker to the multiple forces at play in the act's environment; indeed, the last third of his treatise confronts the student with a daunting array of examples. Despite this, however, the ideology of the speech-act which underpins the text, and its theoretical model of seamless semantic transfer, remain in place, apparently undisturbed by the contradictory implications of its specific pragmatic instances. It is this contradiction, and the effects which it produces in Puttenham's text, which I want to consider next.

* * *

... the first and principal point sought in every languadge is that wee maye expresse the meaning of our mindes aptlye each to other; next, that we may do it readilie without great adoo; then fullye, so as others may thoroughlie conceive us; and last of all handsomely, that those to whom we speake may take pleasure in hearing us . . . .
(Richard Carew, *The Excellencie of the English Tongue*, ?1595–6)[5]

... speech, which He hath made the instrument of our understanding, and key of conceptions, whereby we open the secrets of our hartes, and declare our thoughts to other . . . .
(Henry Peacham, *The Garden of Eloquence*, 1577)[6]

... that which we thinke let us speake, and that which we speake let us thinke; let our speache accorde with our life . . . .
(Thomas Nashe, *Preface to Greene's Menaphon*, 1589)[7]

The examples could be added to indefinitely; the view of language proposed in these statements amounts to a sixteenth-century orthodoxy overriding differences in philosophy, religion and politics, and acting as the fundamental support for the discourses of education, rhetoric, poetics, translation theory and homiletics. It is a position articulated upon three mutually implicated principles:

1. *Binary Division*: between an internal, non-material component and an external component available to the senses. In the examples I have quoted, that is an opposition between on the one hand 'meaning', 'conceptions' and 'thoughts', which are located in 'mind', 'understanding' or 'heart', and on the other their 'expression', 'speech' or 'declaration'.

2. *Subordination*: the external component is subordinated to the internal. The primary function of language is the preservation and transfer of meaning. Within that process, speech or expression is merely instrumental and secondary, analagous to matter in its subordination to spirit.

3. *Continuity or Unification*: The difference between the two components of an utterance is asserted, only to be negated by the subordination of one to the other – the word submits itself to the service of the thought, and so the thought received in the hearer's mind is identical to that conceived in the speaker's. This in-dividuality of the process of communication also determines another kind of individuality: that is the integrity of the speaking subject, which is declared by the absence of any 'divorce betwixt the tongue and the heart',[8] indicating the integration and proper hierarchical disposition of mind and body, of the spiritual and material components of man's mixed constitution.

   The dominance of such a conception of language can be explained by its conformity with the archetypal division between God – as Spirit, the Essential, the In-dividual, the One – and the Creation – as matter, the accidental, the dispersed and differing. The institution of these original oppositions and their hierarchical disposition into a relationship of continuity is the work of God as *Logos* or perfected Word:

   1. *Division*:

      3. And God said, Let there be light: and
         there was light.
      4. And God saw the light that it was good:
         and God divided the light from the darkness.

2. *Subordination*:

> 7. And God made the firmament, and divided the waters
>   which were under the firmament from the waters
>   which were above the firmament: and it was so.
> 8. And God called the firmament Heaven . . . .
>   And God said, Let the waters under the heaven be
>   gathered together unto one place, and let the dry
>   land appear: and it was so.

3. *Continuity*:

> In the beginning was the Word, and the Word was
> with God, and the Word was God.
> 2. The same was in the beginning with God.[9]

The Word creates by naming; at this moment of Creation word and thing are undivided, and the proliferating differences of matter are sustained by the singularity of the originating spiritual principle.

In so far as it conforms to Puttenham's theoretical model of seamless communication, the language of men has the privilege and responsibility of reconfirming in each utterance the foundational speech-act of the Logos: what is at stake in the ethics of human discourse is the affirmation or denial of the fundamental structure of the Christian cosmology. It is from such an assumption that the analogy between poetry – as the perfected form of human discourse – and the Logos, which we find in Sidney, and here in Puttenham, acquires its justification:

> A Poet is as much as to say a maker . . . such as (by way of resemblence and reverently) we may say of God who without any travail to his divine imagination, made all the world of naught . . . . Even so the very poet makes and contrives out of his owne braine both the verse and the matter of his poeme . . . and this science in his perfection, can not grow, but by some divine instinct, the Platonicks called it *furor* . . . . It is therefore of Poets thus to be conceived, that if they be able to devise and make all of these things of them selves, without any subiect of veritie, that they be (by manner of speech) as creating gods. (p. 4)

Puttenham supports the analogy between the poet and God when he describes the poets 'searching after the first mover, and from thence by degrees coming to know and consider of the substances separate and abstract', or when he asserts that they 'made the first differences between vertue and vice', or describes 'phantasy', the poet's distinguishing creative faculty, as:

> . . . very formall, and in his much multiformitie uniforme, that is well proportioned, and so passing cleare . . . [that it is] a representer of the best, most comely and bewtifull images or apparences of thinges to the soule and according to their very truth. (p. 19)

In these examples, the poet's claim to a quasi-divine status is justified by his inspiration (echoing the original infusion of spirit into matter), his recreation of fundamental identities and differences, and his alignment of the 'soul' – the perceiving and understanding subject – with things in their essence, their true appearance, and their faithful representation, or 'image'. In this portrayal of the poet's distinctive powers and activity, derived from the commonplaces of contemporary poetics, Puttenham creates an image which exemplifies the metaphysical principles of the ideology of language which I outlined earlier. Most importantly, the poet as demiurge represents a speaker with full authority in the government of his utterance. This sovereignty of the subject, in guaranteeing the conscious organisation of the chain of communication and the proportionality of its elements, is the cornerstone both of Puttenham's ideology of the speech-act, and of the educational status of his treatise.[10]

Puttenham's treatise is typical of the discourse of Humanist education in its conviction that if human speech is potentially a rearticulation of the Logos then its realisation of that potential need not be surrendered to the mysterious determinations of divine grace.[11] In the absence of inspiration or natural predisposition, education proposes a regime of rational self-determination, by which the gifts of grace may be worked towards and finally merited. Art, in other words, can redeem the deficiencies of post-lapsarian human nature:

> And this science in his perfection, can not grow, but by some divine instinct, the Platonicks call it *furor:* or by excellencie of nature and complexion: or by great subtiltie of the spirits and wit, or by much experience and observation of the world . . . . If

they do it by instinct divine or naturall, then surely much
favoured from above. If by their experience, then no doubt
very wise men. If by any president or paterne layd before
them, then truly the most excellent imitators and counterfaitors
of all others.

. . . If again Art be but a certaine order of rules prescribed
by reason, and gathered by experience, why should not poesie
be a vulgar Art with us as with the Greekes and Latines, our
language admitting no fewer rules and nice diversities than
theirs? (pp. 3–5)

With the shift here to the category of *experience* comes the transition
from a dependence upon metaphysical agencies to the process of
self-determination. Art, or method, serves that process by providing
a secular 'transcendence' of the individual's powers – it is a distillation
of the experience of many other individuals into a generalised form
which can supplement the student's own experience. Method, as
that reduction of general experience into 'a certaine order of rules
prescribed by reason' is thus established as the keystone of the
educational process:

. . . if Poesie be now an Art, and of al antiquitie hath bene
among the Greeks and Latines, and yet were none, untill by
studious persons fashioned and reduced into a method of
rules and precepts, then no doubt may there be the like with
us. (p. 283)

Without this distillation of historical experience, education would
be redundant – the student would be left to a protracted and hazardous
encounter with his own unique and unprecedented experiences. By the
force of its pre-scription, method allows the student to anticipate his
own experience, to exert a certain control over the specific eventuality
by referring it to an already constituted general category. In its content
and its structure Puttenham's treatise announces itself as such an
art, founded in such a method: an art by which the student may
triumph over contingency by pre-determining the language which
is appropriate to his conceptions, and so convey them without loss
or distortion to the mind of his reader or listener. In its implicit
ideology, and as both educational project and discourse on method,
the *Arte* necessarily installs the speaking subject as sovereign in its
determination of the communication process.

The orthodox model of communication constitutes utterance as the reproduction of the fundamental categories and relationships of Christian cosmology, a process by which things are known in their truth and in their authentic, divinely instituted relationships. The social articulation of this process is to be found in the discourse of Commonwealth, with its divinely authorised structure of vocation and degree. For Puttenham, accordingly, the decorum which ensures the proportionality of thing, image and concept in the speech-act is intimately related to that social decorum which fixes the subject in its divinely appointed category and allows this essential positioning to be read off from the appearance which the subject presents to the world:

> And in the use of apparell there is no little decencie and undecencie to be perceived, as well for the fashion as the stuffe, for it is comely that every estate and vocation should be knowen by the differences of their habit ... the chiefe of every degree from their inferiours, because in confusion and disorder there is no manner of decencie. (p. 283)

As with cosmic order, social order is sustained by that continuity between thing and sign which allows things to be seen unambiguously as they are, which is to say *in their places*; a continuity which, under the name of decency, Puttenham shows to be as much at stake in the regulation of apparel (indeed of all things which take on a semiotic function) as in the regulation of discourse.

The purpose of Puttenham's treatise, however, is not adapted to the world of immutable feudal hierarchy, but to one of unsettling social mobility; a world captured in the widely circulated sixteenth-century anecdote of an argument between the low-born Humanist Richard Pace and a traditionalist nobleman over the necessity of the 'new' education. Pace admonishes the nobleman with these words:

> ... if some foreigner, such as the ambassador of princes, comes to the king and an answer has to be given to him, your son, educated as you desire, may blow his horn, but it is the learned sons of mean men who are called to make the reply ... .[12]

As this suggests, Humanist education is a principal agent of social mobility, and as an advocate of the new educational methods, Puttenham clearly advertises his treatise's function as a manual of social advancement:

[We] have apparelled [the poet] to our seeming, in all his gorgious habilliments, and pulling him first from the carte to the schoole, and from thence to the Court, and preferred him to you Maiesties service, in that place of great honour and magnificence . . . being now lately become a Courtier [may] he show himself not a craftsman, and merit to be degraded, and with scorne sent back againe to the shop, or other place of his first facultie and calling, but that so wisely and discreetly he behave himselfe as he may worthily retaine the credite of his place, and profession of a very Courtier . . . . (p. 299)

The self-cancellation of Puttenham's text, its dismantling of the 'official' model of communication which underpins it, begins here. For the situation which Puttenham describes involves a systematic effacement of social origins, a deliberate uncoupling of the signs of current status from the ideal order of fixed social categories, so that the function of the sign becomes anything but to convey clearly the essence of the thing it represents:

And as we see in these great Madames of honour . . . if they want their courtly habilliments or at leastwise such other apparell as custome and civillitie have ordained to cover their naked bodies, would be half ashamed or greatly out of countenaunce to be seen in that sort, and perchance do then thinke themselves more amiable in every mans eye when they be in their richest attire, suppose of silkes or tyssues and costly embroideries, then when they go in cloth or in any other plaine or simple apparell. Even so cannot our vulgar poesie shew itself either gallant or gorgious, if any limme be left naked and bare and not clad in his kindly clothes and colours, such as may convey them somwhat out of sight, that is from the common course of ordinary speech and capacitie of the vulgar iudgement . . . . (pp. 137–8)

Here status is not to be read off from the 'naked' person's position in relation to any external hierarchy which is the ground of rank: apparel in such a scheme would be the transparent sign of a status determined by a 'natural' standard. As Puttenham describes it, however, the function of apparel is actively to prevent any reference to the 'reality' of the person that it ornaments. Instead, the sign itself becomes the ground upon which status is assessed: he/she is gorgeously dressed therefore he/she is of high status.[13]

Puttenham's assimilation of linguistic production to the rhetoric of apparel in this passage announces the alignment of his work with the emerging forces of social mobility and displacement, its 'counterfaiting'[14] of linguistic currency with which the novice may infiltrate and destabilise the economy of status-signification. As the purveyor of off-the-peg 'gorgious habilliments', however, Puttenham is wholly at odds with his role as the upholder of differences of 'habit'.[15] This contradiction derives ultimately from a larger disturbance within the discourse of Humanist education which I will consider more fully later. What should be stressed here is that the emerging contradiction in Puttenham's text between its theoretical paradigm and its pragmatic analyses indicates precisely a contradiction between the ideology of Commonwealth and the existing social relations which it seeks to organise.

Puttenham's linguistic paradigm is one in which communication flows without distortion along eternally established channels between firmly integrated and 'placed' subjects. In this it is fully adapted to the social paradigm of Commonwealth, a static order of rigid stratifications from which the valencies of power, internal mobility and historical development have been excluded. For the text to justify its functional claims as an educational manual, however, its pragmatic analyses are obliged to confront these excluded issues, because for the linguistic novice who is also a social climber, language is a medium through which power is articulated, negotiated, and, with skill, appropriated.[16]

Puttenham's text is delicately positioned at the point where the Elizabethan establishment of Crown and Court attempts to manage a regulated interaction with the forces of social mobility, represented by the ranks of 'new men' from which, increasingly, it draws its personnel. The contradictions of Puttenham's position are produced by this structural ambiguity and the requirement that his work should articulate the interests of both the *arriviste* and the Court. The process in which Puttenham's work intervenes extends beyond the issue of the recruitment of new men into government; it also involves the state's accommodation with emerging capitalist tendencies in its efforts to rationalise the bureaucracy and to maximise revenue – as I have shown in previous chapters, the disturbances and incongruencies which mark Puttenham's writing are also registered in the discourses which embrace these fields.[17] Puttenham's confrontation with the problematic relationship between communication and social power arises from his implication in this wider, precarious process of negotiation between the maintenance and the regeneration of the Elizabethan power-structure. It is here that Puttenham's work manifests at the level of rhetorical theory the contradictions which a writer such as Gascoigne confronts in the crises of his poetic career.

As the *Arte* itself makes clear, this relationship is evident at the most fundamental levels of linguistic organisation. Before considering the rules applicable to the rhetorical embellishment of language, Puttenham submits the poet's lexicon to a restriction which reveals the role which language plays in the process of political centralisation which has been under way since the reign of Henry VII:

> This part in our maker or Poet must be heedyly looked into, that [his language] be naturall, pure, and the most usuall of all his country: or for the same purpose rather that which is spoken in the Kings Court, or in the good townes and cities within this land, then in the marches or frontiers, or in porte townes . . . or finally in any uplandish village or corner of a Realme, where is no resort but of poore rusticall or uncivill people . . . . But he shall follow generally the better brought up sort, such as the Grekes call (charientes) men civill and graciously behavioured and bred . . . ye shall therefore take the usuall speech of the Court, and that of London and the shires lying about London within lx. miles, and not much above . . . herin we are already ruled by th'English Dictionaries and other bookes written by learned men, and therefore it needeth none other direction in that behalfe. (p. 145)

As we saw earlier, for Puttenham, the retreat of the Ambassador from the problems of translation implied a secure homogeneity of the native language. Here this is revealed to be an illusion or convenient fiction: English is many languages, and Puttenham is aware of the process by which the specific dialect of the powerful is being established as the standard of admissible speech, and formalised into the global prescriptions of 'dictionary' English.[18] From the beginning, then, the language of Puttenham's student is subject to a decisive external determination: the question of whether the words he uses are within the authorised English lexicon is decided by reference to the social power of those at the centre of the political nation.

When Puttenham moves beyond the question of vocabulary to that of the approved stylistic repertoire of the 'standard' dialect, he reveals a further stage in this implication of language with social and political power. If English is being brought increasingly under central regulation, this is because to control language is to have acquired the means of controlling people through the exercise of persuasion: those in power define what it is to speak well because to speak well is to secure power. In discussing 'the Courtly figure Allegoria' Puttenham states:

> The use of this figure is so large, and his vertue of so great efficacie as it is supposed no man can pleasantly utter and perswade without it, but in effect is sure never or very seldome to thrive and prosper in the world, that cannot skilfully put in use in so much as not only every common Courtier, but also the gravest Counsellor, yea and the most noble and wisest Prince of them all are many times enforced to use it, by example (say they) of the great Emperour who had it usually in his mouth to say, Quis nesce dissimulare nescit regnare. (p. 186)

The specific style of Court discourse, then, its deployment of the repertoire of rhetorical figures and tropes, is not merely an ornamentation of status, the production of a conspicuous, luxurious surplus to common sense – it is one of the means by which the social and economic power of the speaker is originally achieved and then maintained.

Puttenham's definition of language as the means of persuasion is of course one of the basic tenets of post-Aristotelian rhetoric, but by situating persuasion within the realities of contemporary social and political relations, Puttenham instigates a decisive separation of linguistic practice from his own theoretical paradigm. Communication appears now not as a seamless and undistorted transmission of concepts from mind to mind, but as a deliberate circumvention or disablement of the listener's understanding:

> As figures be the instruments of ornaments in every language so be they also in a sort abuses or rather trespasses in speache, because they passe the ordinary limits of common utterance, and be occupied of purpose to deceive the eare and also the minde, drawing it from plainnesse and simplicitie to a certaine doublenesse, wherby our talke is the more guilefull and abusing, for what else is your Metaphor but an inversion

> of sense by transport: your allegorie by a duplicitie of meaning
> or dissimulation under covert and dark intendments . . . then
> by periphrase or circumlocution when all might be said in a
> word or two . . . and many other waies seeking to inveigle and
> appassionate the mind . . . . (p. 154)

We should note here that the departure from the paradigm entails
an unsettling of the fundamental binary oppositions which inform
it: the abuseful is precisely what is of most use, the trespass
becomes the rule, the double is privileged over the single, darkness
over light, the superfluous over the simple, and the mind is
overcome by the passions. So it is that at the centre of Puttenham's
pragmatic discourse, which is to say at the pinnacle of linguistic and
political power, is the linguistic trespass par excellence, a speech act
which comprehensively violates the treatise's original paradigm of
communication:

> Of this figure therefore which for his duplicitie we call the figure
> of (false semblant or dissimulation) we will speake first as of the
> chiefe ringleader and captaine of all other figures, either in the
> poeticall or oratorie science. (p. 186)

Let me recapitulate: if Puttenham's reader is to take his lesson, he
will be obliged to commit himself to a language whose basic lexicon
is determined by the conventions of a restricted but powerful speech
community, and whose stylistic repertoire is dictated by the need of
that group to maintain and reproduce its power. And, most damaging
to the *Arte's* own theoretical premises, it is a language which, because
of these determinations, is based in the systematic corruption of any
ideal model of unambiguous communication:

> . . . thus, marshalling [words] in their comeliest construction
> and order, and as well by sometimes sparing, sometimes
> spending them more or lesse liberally, and carrying or trans-
> porting of them farther off or nearer, setting them with sundry
> relations, and variable formes, in the ministry and use of wordes,
> do breede no little alteration in man. For to say truely, what els
> is man but his minde? which, whosoever hath skil to compasse,
> and make yeelding and flexible, what may he not commaunde
> the body to performe? He therefore that hath vanquished the
> minde of man, hath made the greatest and most glorious
> conquest. (p. 197)

The reader of Puttenham's treatise is a novice in the exercise of this persuasive power of language. If the novice seeks to persuade, it is against the flow of the prevailing power, so that the will to conquest is accompanied by the need to advertise the speaker's deference; in Puttenham's words, the necessity of being a 'creeper, and a curry favell with his superiors' (p. 293). The doubleness of this position is another reason why the discourse of the courtier is itself double, relying upon the splitting of the sign in figural language and its powers of dissimulation. Clearly the act of subverting the judgement of one's superiors while declaring at once their omnipotence and one's own worthlessness is not to be accomplished by plain speaking. The character of the utterance, far from being governed solely by the intention of the speaker, is the result of a complex tactical negotiation, whose character in turn depends upon the positions of speaker and addressee within the prevailing disposition of power.

What the *Arte* pursues, then, is a redistribution of discursive control from the sovereign speaker of the idealist paradigm to the context of the utterance – a context which is as complex and unstable as the relationships of power which constitute it. This redistribution can be seen most clearly in the shifting emphases of Puttenham's discussion of style:

> And because this continuall course and manner of writing or speech sheweth the matter and disposition of the writers minde, more than one or few words or sentences can shew, therfore there be those that have called stile, the image of man . . . for man is but his minde, and as his minde is tempered and qualified, so are his speeches and language at large, and his inward conceits be the metall of his minde, and his manner of utterance the very warp and woofe of his conceits . . . . (p. 148)

Here style is a continuity of discourse by which the integrity of the communication and of the speaking subject is secured. The maintenance of this stylistic continuity is the role of decorum, which as we have seen regulates the proportionality of elements within the utterance. By the time Puttenham comes to discuss in detail this 'line and levell for all good makers to do their busines by' (p. 261), however, decorum and the stylistic integrity which it underwrites have begun to disintegrate:

> But by reason of this sundry circumstances, that mans affaires are as it were wrapt in, this (decencie) comes to be very much

alterable and subiect to varietie, in so much as our speech
asketh one maner of decencie, in respect of the persone who
speakes; another, of his to whom it is spoken: another of whom
we speake: another of what we speake, and in what place and
time and to what purpose. And as it is of speach, so of al other
our behaviours. (p. 261)

Decorum here has become a matter of negotiating such a complexity
of determinations that we might ask whether it is still to be considered
a rule capable of governing situations in advance, or more accurately
as a mobile, improvisational and reactive practice. Before considering
this question in more detail, I will reproduce one of Puttenham's own
examples where the decorousness of a communication is in question.
The communication is non-verbal – an act of giving and receiving –
but as we have just seen Puttenham has by this stage subsumed all
signifying behaviour within negotiations of power under the category
of communication:

> Therefore we say that it might become King Alexander to give
> a hundreth talentes to Anaxagoras the Philosopher, but not
> for a beggarly Philosopher to accept so great a gift, for such
> a prince could not be impoverished by that expence, but the
> Philosopher was by it exessively to be enriched, so was the
> kings action proportionable to his estate and therfore decent,
> the Philosophers, disproportionable both to his profession and
> calling and therefore indecent.
>
> And yet if we shall examine the same point with a clearer
> discretion, it may be said that whatsoever it might become
> King Alexander of his regal largesse to bestow upon a poor
> Philosopher unasked, that might as well become the Philosopher
> to receive at his hands without refusal, and had otherwise been
> some empeachement of the kinges abilitie or wisdome, which
> had not been decent in the philosopher, nor the immoderatnesse
> of the kinges gift in respecte of the Philosophers meane
> estate made his acceptance the lesse decent, since princes
> liberalities are not measured by merite nor by other mens
> estimations, but by their owne appetits and according to their
> greatnesse .... But peradventure if any such immoderat gift
> had bene craved by the Philosopher and not voluntarliy offred
> by the king it had been undecent to have taken it. Even so
> if one that standeth upon his merite, and spares to crave the

princes liberalitie in that which is moderate and fit for him, doth as undecently. For men should not expect till the Prince remembered it of himselfe and began as it were the gratification, but ought to put in remembrance by humble solicitations, and that is duetifull and decent . . . . And yet peradventure in both these cases, the undecencie for too much craving or sparing to crave, might be easily holpen by a decent magnificence in the Prince . . . . (pp. 277–8)

The crisis of competence and judgement which such a situation creates for the 'speaker' clearly also signals a crisis for Puttenham's text in its claim to educational effectiveness. What is at stake in the necessarily improvisational nature of the speech-act, as it appears in examples such as this, is precisely the prescriptive force of the text over action – the power of writing to govern behaviour before the fact – which is the guiding premise of Puttenham's work and of the Humanist educational tradition which it represents.[19] The disturbance which this produces in the text's conceptual framework can be traced in an erosion of one of the treatise's central terms – the *example*.

As we have just seen, the status of decorum as a general principle for the government of discourse has been undermined by Puttenham's elaboration of the unprecedented nature of each specific speech-act and its determining context. It is as a means of shoring up this subsidence in the treatise's educational function that Puttenham produces the example:

But since the actions of men with their circumstances be infinite, and the world likewise replenished with many iudgements, it maybe a question who shall have the determination of such controversie as may arise whether this or that action or speach be decent or undecent: and verely it seems to go all by discretion, not perchaunce of everyone, but by a learned experienced discretion, for otherwise seems the decorum to a weake and ignorant iudgement, then it doth to one of better knowledge and experience . . . . The case then standing that discretion must chiefly guide all those businesse, since there be sundry sortes of discretion all unlike, even as there be men of action or art, I see no way so fit to enable a man truly to estimate of (decencie) as example, by whose veritie we may deeme the differences of things and their proportions, and by particular discussions come at length to sentence of it generally, and also in our behaviours the more easily to put it in execution. (pp. 263–4)

This shift from the promulgation of a rule to the proffering of examples marks an abrogation of the authority and priority which Puttenham's text claims in its relation to experience. Whereas the rule claims to exercise a prior government of experience, and retains an ideality and unity in relation to the fissile, multiplicitous nature of the experience which it governs, the example claims merely to supplement a quantitive deficiency in experience itself. Rather than articulating the rule of decorum by which experience may be mastered, the text now provides instances of unmediated experience from which the nature of decorum has to be inferred. Puttenham's discourse undergoes an erosion of the self-consistent ideality which characterises the sovereignty of *method* and begins to manifest the fragmentation and particularity of the material which it claims to organise. Instead of a generally prescriptive text standing in opposition to the flux of experience, the *Arte* now appears as a discourse which seeks to pre-empt the ungovernable speech-act instance by instance, and so threatens to become as interminable as actuality itself. As a result, Puttenham increasingly characterises the function of his text as recreational rather than educational:

It were too busye a peece of worke for me to tell you of all the partes of decencie and indecency which have been observed in the speaches of man and in his writings, and this that I tell you is rather to solace your eares with pretie conceits after a sort of long scholasticall preceptes which may happen have doubled them, rather then for any other purpose of institution or doctrine, which to any Courtier of experience, is not necessarie in this behalfe. (p. 274)

This redefinition is accompanied by a radical shift in the address of the text, in its implied reader. The relegation of the text to the status of a mere supplement to experience is epitomised in a tautology: those who benefit by experience are the experienced, and mastery of the speech-act is achieved by the linguistically masterful.[20] The final sections of Puttenham's treatise become, accordingly, a familiar address to the initiated rather than a guide to the 'rude rimer' of earlier chapters:

> To tell you the decencie of a number of other behaviours, one
> might do it to please you with pretie reportes, but to the
> skilfull Courtiers it shalbe nothing necessary, for they know
> all by experience without learning. (p. 292)

The hapless novice, having taken up a text which offered a means
of access to linguistic and social power, has been left instead with a
double-bind: what gets you 'in' is knowledge which is only available
– such is the pragmatic, contextual nature of linguistic and social
competence – on the inside:

> Nor in speaches with [Kings] to be too long, or too much
> affected, for th'one is tedious th'other irksome, nor with lowde
> acclamations to applaude them, for that is too popular and rude
> and betokens either ignoraunce, or seldome accesse to their
> presence, or little frequenting their Courts . . . . (p. 294)

In its final stages, then, Puttenham's treatise manifests a disabling
uncertainty about its own educational status and function. This
relates to a more general uncertainty about the status of the
pedagogical text within the discourse of Humanist education. Such
texts make two essential claims: to rationality and to prescriptiveness.
Rationality, because in serving a regime of self-determination they
plot a course between the supra-rational sphere of grace and divine
intervention on one hand, and the sub-rational determinations of
appetite and circumstantiality on the other. Prescriptiveness, because
self-determination depends upon the consolidation of reason and will
before their embroilment with the seductive texture of experience. The
two claims come together in the power of writing to impose clarity
and coherence upon the experiential material which it organises –
a function which distinguishes it equally from the unworldliness
of metaphysical principle and the chaotic disorder of unmediated
experience. As a rationally ordered representation of the world, the
text operates as a map whose perusal may keep its reader one saving
step ahead of the unfolding contingencies of social reality.

This textual rationality and orderliness serves the Humanist
ideology of personal reformation, in which the exercise of reason
may secure a gradual amelioration of the subject's fallen human
condition. That ideology is realised in the educational treatises as
a characteristic structure of pedagogical 'narrative': a structure in
which truth emerges dialectically out of the encounter between the

understanding and worldly experience, and in which the ethical antitheses of prophetic and homiletic discourse are dissolved into a temporal *process*: where the categorically opposed terms of Evil and Good, Damnation and Salvation, Falsehood and Truth, become the termini of a journey, marked out by transitional stages, which the rational man may travel.

However, the prophetic and the pedagogical models cannot simply be placed in opposition. The discourse of Humanist education, as it develops in Northern Europe, is articulated within the conceptual framework of Christian ethical judgement, and its melioristic strategies acquire their meaning precisely in relation to that framework's absolute ethical distinctions. This static juridical structure of antitheses is always potentially in contradiction with Humanism's model of graduated ethical states traversed by the mediating agency of reason.

That latent contradiction emerges in a variety of ways in the major educational treatises of the century. It appears, for example, in *The Education of a Christian Prince*, in the tendency of Erasmus's discourse to congeal into a static opposition between the absolute types of the Good Prince and the Tyrant; a fixation which contradicts the treatise's educational 'narrative', in which the prince gradually progresses from a state of common sinfulness to the rational virtue of the learned ruler.[21] More's *Utopia* displaces the same contradiction between educational moderation and judicial absolutism into a virtuoso juggling of oppositions: between the principled inflexibility of Hithloday and the pragmatism of 'More', between the painstaking verisimilitude of the first part of the book and the equivocal fictionality of the second, and between the mandarin playfulness of the book's framing devices and the urgency of its social and economic criticism. Among its other effects, this play of oppositions produces a generic evasiveness, a refusal of the text to declare itself either as fiction or reportage, as pedagogical or merely recreational in its intentions. The question of philosophical and ethical 'purity' with which Hithloday challenges 'More' – how can truth remain truth if it engages with the realities of secular power and the persuasive strategies of fiction and rhetoric? – is put in suspension by this complex play of textual potentialities. The result is that a profound anxiety about the text's own ethical status and pedagogical effectiveness is transmuted into metadiscursive energy and 'writerly' pleasure.[22]

More creates a peculiarly ingenious and brilliant strategy to circumvent the fundamental problem which troubles Erasmus and his fellow Humanist educators; the question of how to reconcile the absolute values of Christian ethical discourse with a pragmatic engagement with the secular circumstantiality within which personal and social reformation is acted out.

In fact, it is in its discourse on language that Humanism develops its most effective techniques for engaging with the prodigality of the world while sustaining the authority of established ideological categories and systems. The art of rhetoric establishes such a method of *dynamic conservation* upon the basis of the duality of the sign. The fundamental structure of a work like Erasmus's *De Copia* is to be found in the systematic elaboration of a stable semantic core, which is 'found' within the table of 'places' or categories. In this way the expenditure of the signifier is licensed because it always begins with a return to the fund of settled categorical meanings. As Marion Trousdale writes of Erasmian copiousness:

> To see artistic detail in such a way suggests that the redundant and the commonplace . . . is the primary matter (*res*) of the artist and the efficacious expression of forms of common knowledge the definition of his artistry.[23]

The 'matter' of the rhetoricians – whether it be an ethical commonplace, a proverb, or an axiom of natural philosophy – is named as having the same status as material things (*res*). This conflation of discursive categories and natural objects is encouraged by the tendency of sixteenth-century rhetoric to subsume the theory of logic.[24] The fulcrum of this process is the *place*: place logic differentiates and names the contents of reality, and it is these categories which comprise the system of places or 'topics' out of which rhetoric elaborates its regulation of 'scheme' and 'figure'. It is through such a system of linkages that the ornamentation of language can be anchored to the stable disposition of things in their natural order, so that the copiousness of the word appears as only the final realisation of a divinely originated organic fecundity.

As we have seen, Puttenham's theoretical premises are entirely congruent with this tradition. Where his work makes a difference is in its introduction of the dynamics of worldly power and social contradiction into the theoretical consideration of the production of discourse. As a result his treatise confronts the fact that the resources of language are not the universally distributed gift of nature, but are generated and disposed within constraints set by the established framework of social hierarchy and authority.

The conflict between this account of language and the logocentric account enshrined in the rhetorical tradition is focused in the equivocal nature of the term 'decorum' in Puttenham's discourse. In the *Arte*, decorum represents both the anchoring of the word in the 'places' of natural order and the vigilance by which the speaker conforms his discourse to the shifting circumstantiality of power in the social environment of the speech-act. The conventional paradigm of copiousness locates the ostentation of the signifier within an organic economy, a vision of Golden Age fecundity; Puttenham's theory of the speech-act assumes a Fall into worldliness which has submitted language to an economy of calculation, profit and loss – a Fall, as it were, from the *De Copia* of Erasmus into the world of another of the period's rhetorical treatises, Johann Sturm's *Ritch Storehouse or Treasure for Nobility*.[25]

5

Mortality and the Utility of Courtship: Castiglione's *Book of the Courtier*

Mortality is Change's proper stage:
States have degrees, as human bodies have,
Spring, Summer, Autumn, Winter, and the grave.
Fulke Greville, 'A Treatise of Wars'.

Machiavelli and Aretino knew the lessons by heart and were not to seek how to use the wicked world, the flesh, and the Devil. They had learned cunning enough: and had seen fashions enough: and could and would use both, with advantage enough. Two courtesan politicians.
Gabriel Harvey, *Marginalia*.[1]

Book Four of Castiglione's *Book of the Courtier*[2] interrupts the treatise's 'discourse of reason' with a rumination upon the mortality of gentlemen and its implications for the life and death of the state:

> ... not long after these reasonings were had, cruell death bereaved our house of three most rare gentlemen .... These men ... had they lived ... woulde have showed a manifest proofe, how much the Court of Urbin was worthie to be commended, and how furnished it was with noble knights .... Therefore (mee thinke) whether it be by happe, or through the favour of the starres, the same cause that so long a time hath granted unto Urbin very good governors, doth still continue and bringeth forth the like effects. And therefore it is to be hoped, that prosperous fortune will still encrease these so vertuous doinges, that the happinesse of the house, and of the state, shall not only not diminish, but rather dayly encrease .... (pp. 257–9)

This chapter will discuss the relationship foreshadowed in this passage between the rational discussion of the ends of courtship, the ravages of fortune, and the perpetuation of gentlemanly and political 'virtue'.

The context for Castiglione's meditation on mortality and the ends of human existence is to be found in a process of political and ideological rupture which has been described by Quentin Skinner and J. G. A. Pocock.[3] It is a process in which the Italian republics and principates of the late medieval period and the Renaissance attempted to free themselves – in fact and in jurisdiction – from the contending powers of the Empire and the Papacy. Both these institutions founded their hegemonic pretensions in a claim to be the agency through which the eternal order of Divine providence is articulated within secular time. As Pocock's remarkable work has suggested, in their opposition to this claim, the Italian states severed themselves from the primary conceptual and imaginative structure through which medieval political thought rendered the flux of earthly time and the purpose of the earthly city intelligible. The political rupture opened up a new ideological space in which

> the republic was seen as confronting its own temporal finitude, as attempting to remain morally and politically stable in a stream of irrational events conceived as essentially destructive of all systems of secular stability.[4]

In the late fifteenth and early sixteenth centuries this consciousness of the incoherence of secular time and the radical instability of political structures was exacerbated by the experience of the French invasions of the Italian peninsula and the resulting internal political turmoil. Felix Gilbert's account of Italian historiography in this period reveals a shift from the stable cyclical schemes and moral categories of medieval historical writing to a mode in which the mere succession of events resists the imposition of any explanatory model, and in which the moral intelligibility of action is denied by the operation of contingency or *fortuna*; a shift into a mode of ironic narrative whose most distinguished practitioner is Gucciardini.[5]

Pocock's analysis of Florentine republicanism centres on this problem of conceptualising secular time, and on the associated development of a theory of politics as

> the art of dealing with the contingent event . . . with *fortuna* as the force which directs such events and thus symbolises pure, uncontrolled and unlegitimated contingency. In proportion as

the political system ceases to be a universal and is seen as a particular, it becomes difficult for it to do this.[6]

Principates such as Castiglione's Urbino confront this problem alongside the republics, and their writers and theorists take advantage of the new republican discourse on temporality and political structure – enlisting, for example, the republican concepts of 'balanced government' and 'dynamic *virtù*' as defences against *fortuna*. In retaining monarchical rule, however, the principates also retained a central element of Imperial ideology, which enabled secular authority to claim a metaphysical legitimation by analogy with the unitary rule of God. A work such as Castiglione's, then – and this is also the basis of its pertinence, in Hoby's translation, to the English situation – proposes a double response to the threat of a chaotic secular time. Elements derived from republican theory work as if in the absence of any metaphysical authority, seeking to govern the field of contingency or *fortuna* through a rational management of immanent forces. At the same time the analogical potency of the idea of the monarch sustains the possibility of linking the political order to the eternal order of Providence. For Castiglione, then, time is, contradictorily, both a recalcitrant material to be shaped by the unaided rational initiatives of men and a transparent medium in which is represented the redeeming operation of Grace. Time as the arena of mortality, in which stasis or equilibrium is the greatest attainable good; or time as the theatre of salvation, where the promised end is a beatific release from the condition of temporality itself. It is as a means of negotiating between these antithetical visions that Castiglione devises the doubled, mediating strategies of courtiership.

By opening with a lament for the dead heroes of Urbino, Book Four situates itself squarely within the problematic (and the pathos) of secular time, in which:

> Fortune many times in the very middest of our race, otherwhile nigh the ende disapointeth our fraile and vaine purposes . . . .
> (p. 257)

The rule of fortune over the corruptible bodies of individual and state links them in a common mortality, but also, because of fortune's radical unpredictability, in the possibility of reversal and regeneration:

> And therefore it is to be hoped, that prosperous fortune will still encrease these so virtuous doinges, that the happinesse of the

house, and of the state shall not onely not diminish, but rather
daily increase. (pp. 258–9)

The first three books of Castiglione's treatise have described the
rational arts by which the individual courtier may restrain the chaotic
potential of his own mortal body and fallible nature within an order
dictated by reason. Through the mediating figure of the Prince – at
once an individual and the incarnation of the power of the state –
Book Four shows how this discipline may be reproduced within the
body politic.

Chief among the courtier's gifts to his Prince is temperance, a
rational restraint of those immoderate drives and desires which are
the inheritance of fallen humanity, and whose site is the body:

> . . . evermore the thing whereby greedy desire overcommeth
> reason, is ignorance, neither can true knowledge bee overcome
> by affection, that proceedeth from the bodie and not from the
> minde, and in case that it be well ruled and governed by reason,
> it becommeth a vertue: if not, it becommeth a vice.
>
> But such force reason hath, that she maketh the sense alwaies
> to obey, and by wondrous meanes and waies perceth, lest
> ignorance should possesse that which she ought to have . . . .
> (p. 270)

The exercise of rational discipline upon the body of the Prince is
the means by which a shape and a value are imposed upon the
incoherence of secular time, converting the rule of contingency into
a redemptive teleology:

> But in case our Courtier will doe as we have saide . . . he shall
> feele very great contention within himself, when he remembreth
> that he hath given him [i.e. the Prince], not ye things which
> foolish persons give . . . but that vertue, which perhaps among
> all the matters which belong unto man is the chiefest and rarest,
> that is to say, the manner and way to rule and to raigne in the
> right kinde. Which alone were sufficient to make men happie,
> and to bring once againe into the world the golden age, which
> is written to have been when Saturnus raigned in the olde
> time . . . . (p. 273)

Temperance operates as a principle of economy, organising the
potentially divergent forces of the affects around 'the meane of

reason'. The idea of the rational mean derives primarily from Aristotelian ethics, but for Castiglione its particular force arises from its use within a Christian Humanist tradition which stresses the mixed nature of man, poised between exaltation and depravity. The *Courtier* aligns itself from the beginning with the educational writing of this tradition whose first major work is Erasmus's *Education of a Christian Prince* (1519):[7]

> I say, that between this excellent grace, and that fond foolishnes, there is yet a meane, and they that are not by nature so perfectly furnished, with studie and diligence may polish and correct a great part of the defaults of nature . . . . (p. 33)

If it is the nature of humanity precisely to be undetermined by nature, then human nature is malleable, and the work of reason is to contrive a balanced constitution of the subject in which opposed potentialities are in equilibrium. It is upon this basis that the *Courtier* grounds itself as a manual in self-fashioning, and from which it derives its characteristic terminology of craftsmanship and aesthetic technique, its vision of the self as a work of art:

> So in like case this vertue not enforcing the mind, but pouring thereinto through most quiet waies a vehement perswasion that may incline him to honestie, maketh him quiet and full of rest, in every part equall and of good proportion: and on every side framed of a certaine agreement with himself . . . . (p. 271)

An art, then, which achieves its effects of harmonious stability precisely through a determined engagement with the recalcitrant material of the body and its affects: an art not of transcendence and denial ('meete for some Monke or Hermite' (p. 272)) but of a certain calculated worldliness:

> I have not said that temperance should thoroughly rid and root out of mens mindes affections: neither should it bee well so to doe, because there bee yet in affections some parts good: but that which in affections is corrupt and striving against honestie, she bringeth to obey unto reason.
> Therefore it is not meete, to ridde the troublesom disquietnesse of the minde, to roote up affections, cleane, for this were as if to avoid dronkennesse, there should be an acte established, that no man should drinke wine: or because

> otherwhile in running a man taketh a fall, every man shoulde
> bee forbid running . . . . (p. 272)

According to Lord Octavian, temperance opens up a middle way
between the opposed alternatives of contemplative withdrawal and
a compromising embroilment with the world. This opposition is at
the basis of Humanist educational theory; its classical statement is in
the debate between Hithloday and 'More' in the first book of More's
Utopia.[8]

Hithloday insists upon the radical incompatibility between philosophy – an agency of truth and reality – and the normal conditions of
human existence, which he characterises as built upon falsehood, self-
interest and sensuality. 'More' meets this Platonic position with the
idea of a 'civil' philosophy which secretes its burden of truth beneath
an artful mimicry of worldliness, converting the corrupt materials
that lie to hand into vehicles of virtuous doctrine. 'More's', then,
is a philosophy of devious persuasion and strategic dissimulation;
a philosophy which – embracing the qualities which Hithloday's
Platonic discourse would define precisely as anti-philosophical – is
rhetorical, pragmatic, performative: 'What part soever you have taken
upon you, playe that as wel you can and make the best of it . . . .'[9]

It is this context – the polemical opposition between a corrupt
worldliness and an alienated idealism – which accounts for Lord
Octavian's decisive reorientation of the *Courtier*'s analysis of courtly
accomplishments at the beginning of Book Four.[10] After the quanti-
fication in the first three books of those attributes which are to
grace the courtier, Octavian begins by proposing a redefinition of
excellence, a shift from the enumeration of skills to a consideration
of purpose and context:

> For doubtlesse if the Courtier with his nobleness of birth,
> comely behaviour, pleasantnesse and practise in so many
> exercises, shoulde bring foorth no fruite, but to be such a
> one for himselfe . . . I woulde say that many of the qualities
> appointed him, as dauncing, singing and sporting, were lightnes
> and vanitie, and in a man of estimation rather to be dispraised
> than commended. (p. 260)

This opening draws the discussion of the courtier's worldly accomplishments squarely into the ideological framework which I have

discussed in earlier chapters, and particularly into alignment with the discourse on Narcissus. The primary association of self-dedication and 'vanity' in that discourse returns here, with its associated tropes of flower and fruit, which carry the critique of the subject whose talents and abilities are not dedicated to the uses of the Commonwealth:

> But in case the Courtiers doings be directed to the goode ende they ought to be, and which I meane: me thinke then they should not only not be hurtful or vaine, but most profitable, and deserve infinite prayse.
>
> The ende therefore of a perfect Courtier ... I believe is to purchase him, by the meanes of the qualities which these Lordes have given him, in such wise the good will and favour of the Prince ... that he may breake his minde to him, and alwaies, enforme him franckly of the truth of every matter meete for him to understande, without feare or perill to displease him .....
>
> And therefore in mine opinion, as musicke, sportes, pastimes, and other pleasant fashions are (as a man woulde say) the floure of Courtlinesse, even so is the training and helping forward of the prince to goodnesse, and the fearing him from evil, the fruite of it. (p. 261)

The subordination of pleasure to truth, of artifice to goodness, is here revealed to be as fundamental a rule of courtiership as it is of making fictions. What Octavian's argument also makes clear as it continues is that the duplicitous strategies of the writer and the courtier are also alike in being responses to a crisis in the metaphysical legitimation of secular power.

As in the case of writing, the question of courtiership involves a chain of paired positive and negative terms, with the possibility of disruption at each point in the chain. We have just seen Octavian's demand for the regulation of the courtier's skills by the 'deep' requirements of the truth; this regulation is itself called for by the danger of a similar diseconomy in the prince:

> Of this it commeth, that great men, beside that they never understand the truth of anything, drunken with the licentious libertie that rule bringeth with it, and with aboundance of delicats drowned in pleasures, are so farre out of the way, and their minde is so corrupted with seeing themselves always obeyed, and (as it were) worshipped ... that through this

> ignorance they wade to an extreme self-liking . . . thinking it
> the true happiness to do what a man lusteth. (p. 262)

Here, in the delineation of the figure who is (for Protestant
England) the primary mediator of metaphysical authority, there
is also the epitome of earthly vanity; a type constitutionally and
circumstantially disposed to a blind indulgence of pleasure and
Narcissistic irresponsibility. The possibilities which this paradox holds
for an undoing of the priority and dominance of the metaphysical
are focused in Octavian's concept of idolatry, in which metaphysical
authority is usurped by the material forms of worldly power:

> . . . therefore taking these principles for a president, and
> suffering themselves to be led with self-liking, they waxe
> lofty, and with a stately countenance, with sharp and crule
> conditions, with pompous garments, golde and jewels, and with
> comming (in a manner) never abroade to be seene, they thinke
> to get estimation and authoritie among men, and to be counted
> (almost) Gods. (p. 263)

Octavian identifies the possibility of an analogous short-circuiting of
metaphysical authority in the equivocal potential of the counsellor,
who exemplifies the political and ethical culture out of which the
abberations of princely conduct arise. Octavian's discussion of counsel
is structured around an opposition between flattery and philosophy
which is parallel to the opposition represented by Hithloday and
'More' in the *Utopia*:

> And the root . . . is nothing els but lying . . . which vice
> is . . . more hurtfull to Princes than any other, because they
> have more scarcitie than of any thing els, of that which they
> neede to have more plentie of, than any other thing: namely,
> of such as should tell them the truth, and put them in mind
> of goodnesse, for enemies bee not driven of love to do these
> offices . . . [and] As for friends . . . many times to currie favour
> and to purchase good will, they give themselves to nothing els
> but to feede them with matters that may delight and content
> their mind, though they be foul and dishonest. So that of friends
> they become flatterers. (p. 262)

The analysis of flattery repeats the earlier analysis of the prince as the
meeting place of dangerously contradictory potentials: here the king,

who is ideally a primary conveyer of truth, is in fact at the centre of a culture of falsehood. As before, this contradiction represents an undoing of essential oppositions (truth/lies) upon which a whole system of metaphysical authority and hierarchical discriminations is constructed. Flattery itself accordingly performs its own disruption of binary order through a retailing of 'matters that may delight and content the mind, though they be foul and dishonest'. From this stress on the failure of an ideal reconciliation between pleasure and virtue, sensual appeal and moral teaching, it would seem that flattery manifests the same violation of semiotic economy as does delinquent poetising or fiction-making.

As Octavian describes it, flattery represents a political and ethical culture which is a closed circuit where secular power interacts with the field of contingency without reference to any metaphysical framework of value or truth. *Philosophy*, on the other hand, represents for Octavian the redundancy of a metaphysics which refuses worldly mediations:

> But in case a grave Philosopher should come before any of our Princes, or whoever beside, that would shew them plainly and without anie circumstance the horrible face of true vertue, and teach them good manners, and what the life of a good Prince ought to be, I am assured they would abhorre him at the first sight, as a most venemous serpent, or els they woulde make him a laughing stocke, as a most vile matter. (p. 264)

The possibilities of political persuasion are suspended then, it seems, between two fruitless extremes: a total embroilment in the false order of worldly contingencies, or a truth which is alienated in its ideality.

It is as a means of mediating between these antithetical positions that the two-faced strategies of courtiership are produced by Octavian. The 'pleasant fashions' which the courtier shares with the flatterer are positively valorised by becoming the surfaces or pleasing enclosures of a truth which is their proper 'end'.[11] Their exercise allows the superficies of pleasantness to remain undisturbed while the otherwise rebarbative truth is insinuated beneath them:

> ... the Courtier by the meane of those honest qualities that Count Lewis and Sir Fredericke have given him, may soone, and ought to goe about so to purchase him the good will, and

> allure unto him ye mind of his Prince, that he may make him
> a free and safe passage to commune with him in every matter
> without troubling him. And if he bee such a one as is saide, hee
> shall compasse it with small paine, and so may he alwaies open
> unto him the trueth of every matter at ease. (p. 265)

The double nature of courtly strategy allows for a commutation of
values where before there was antithesis:

> Beside this, by litle and litle distil into his mind goodnesse,
> and teach him continencie, stoutnesse of courage, justice,
> temperance, making him to taste what sweetnesse is hid under
> that litle bitternesse, which at the first sight appeareth unto him
> that withstandeth vices, which are always hurtfull, displeasant,
> and accompanied with ill report and shame, even as vertues are
> profitable, pleasant and prayseable . . . . (p. 265)

The deferred disclosure of meaning which is implied by the binary
nature of the sign becomes here the basis of moral discipline. Truth
and goodness secrete themselves beneath the 'pleasant fashions' of
the courtier, becoming visible as the prince is enticed into seeing
through the alluring surface; this is also the model for the process
of seeing through the immediate pleasantness of vice to the 'deep'
pleasures of virtue. The reconciliation of truth and delight in the
skills of the courtier foreshadows the union of virtue and pleasure
in a dimension beyond the antinomies of experience: the narrative
structure of hermeneutic disclosure implies the Humanistic model
of ethical reform.

It is this grounding of interpretation and ethics in the binary
structure of the sign which makes Gascoigne's discourse on allegory,
for example, an exercise in courtiership and moral casuistry as well
as in literary theory. It is not surprising, then, to find that Lord
Octavian's summing up of the courtier's duties and methods deploys
the same repertoire of tropes – the rough way of duty and the flowers
of pleasure, the secreting of the 'wholesome' under the 'flickering
provocation', the veil of pleasure – as appears in the literary defences
that I have discussed:

> In this wise may hee leade him through the rough way of
> vertue . . . decking it aboute with boughes to shadow it, and
> strowing it over with sightly flowers . . . . And sometime
> with musicke, sometime with armes and horses, sometime

with rymes, and meeter, otherwhile with communications of love ... continually keepe that minde of his occupied in honest pleasure: imprinting notwithstanding therein alwaies besides ... in company with these flickering provocations some vertuous condition, and beguiling him with a wholesom craft . . . .

The Courtier therefore applying to such a purpose this veile of pleasure, in every time, in every place, and in everie exercise he shall attain to his end, and deserve much more praise and recompence, than for any other good worke that he can doe in the world. (p. 265)

The art of the courtier (like that of the 'legitimate' writer) is justified as a means of mediating between the contradictory imperatives of metaphysical principle and secular engagement, truth and pleasure, dialectic and rhetoric, righteousness and pragmatism. It is, in other words, an elaborated form of what 'More' describes in the *Utopia* as a 'civil' philosophy; a philosophy which dissimulates in order to secure the truth, and saves the soul by indulging the body. Octavian sums up the case for such a strategy of mediation in his portrait of Aristotle as the exemplary courtier. Octavian's Aristotle *activates* truth by accommodating it to the specific circumstances of Alexander's Court. In doing so, Octavian implies, he dissolves the Platonic antinomy between philosophy and rhetoric by realising philosophy rhetorically:

And because it is the office of a good Courtier to know the nature and inclination of his Prince, and so *according to the businesse, and as occasion serveth* with slightnesse to enter in favour with him (as we have saide) by those waies that make him a sure entrie, and afterwarde bind him to vertue. Aristotle so well knew the nature of Alexander, and *with slightnesse framed him selfe so well thereafter* that he was beloved and honoured of him more than a father . . . And of these thinges in Alexander, the author was Aristotle, in practising the waies of a good Courtier: the which Calisthenes coulde not do, for all Aristotle shewed him the way of it, who because he was a right philosopher, and so sharpe a minister of the bare truth without mingling it with courtlinesse, hee lost his life and profited not, but rather gave a slander to Alexander. (pp. 299–300, my emphases)

The 'bare truth' fails and profits not; it is only in so far as it is incarnated in the rhetorical body of courtliness that the spirit of truth comes to life; indeed the uncourtly truth-bearer dies because of his inability to accommodate his words to the environment of secular authority, in which the naked truth translates as bare-faced slander. Equally, however, it is only as the corporeal form of truth that the rhetorical strategies of courtliness find their legitimation.[12]

If the courtier fails to subordinate his worldly skills to this justifying end, he abandons not only himself but the prince to an interminable wandering in worldliness. If this happens, the chain of delinquency and disorder will acquire another link; without the restraint of reason, administered by the arts of the courtier, the prince is capable of delivering the entire polity up to the temporal logic of sensuality, with its endless proliferation of desire across an infinity of transient gratifications. For Castiglione this literally endless process is epitomised by war, in which the tyrant's desire for total power confronts but violently disavows the impossibility of its temporal gratification:

> And all these thinges and many moe, were invented to make men
> warlike, onely to bring others in subjection, which was a matter
> (almost) unpossible, because it is an infinite peece of worke,
> until all the worlde be brought under obeisance . . . . (p. 281)

The preference expressed by Bembo in Book Four for democracy over the rule of kings is based precisely in a fear of the desires of one man exposing the polity as a whole to the ravages of *fortuna*:

> Beside that, both in judgements and in avisements it happeneth
> oftener that the opinion of one alone is false, than the opinion
> of many, because troublesome affection either through anger, or
> through spite, or through lust, sooner entreth into the minde
> of one alone than into the multitudes . . . . (p. 274)

Octavian's answer to Bembo is that the educational strategy of the courtier, while ministering to the sensual gratification of the prince, secures the predominance of reason in his decisions and actions. In addition, Octavian makes some concession to Bembo's principle of the greater inherent rationality of the many over the individual with his proposal for the creation of counsels of the nobility and the commons to advise the prince.

This version of the mixed constitution (one of course which, in Hoby's translation, would have a clear application to contentions over the constitutional balance of the English polity) serves not only to regulate the desire of the ruler in the interests of the people, but also, conversely, to regulate the body of the populace. This is the function of the mixed constitution as it appears in Italian republican theory: to stabilise the polity by the balanced gratification of the desires – for security and for power – of its component classes.[13]

This management of the volatile immanent forces of the polity, the production of a generalised reason from the equalisation of singular desires, is aided by another agency of 'quietness', derived again from republican theory. This is the moderation and equalisation of wealth among the populace, which, Octavian states, is necessary because it is in the gap between the extremities of poverty and ostentation that the spark of intemperate desire is generated:

> Therefore the best way were, to have the greater part of the Citizens, neither verie wealthie, nor verye poore: because the overwealthie many time waxe stiffe necked and recklesse, the poore, desperate and picking. But the meane sorte lye not in waite for others, and live with a quiet mind that none lye in waite for them . . . . (p. 286)

The establishment of this balanced state is to be reinforced by sumptuary regulations and the encouragement of trade, and by a more equal distribution of gifts, offices, liberties and justice. It is through such an organisation of appetites around a rational mean, Octavian claims, that the polity is stabilised and secured from the turbulent rule of *fortuna*, so that the people may '. . . injoy peacably this ende of their practises and actions, which ought to be quietnesse . . .' (p.280).

Octavian's analysis has moved from the body of the courtier to that of the prince, to that of the polity. In each case, he recommends a rational discipline based in the organisation of affects around a median point; in each, there intervenes a certain 'politicke usage' or art which achieves its virtuous effects precisely through an orchestration of appetites and pleasures; in each, there is the establishment of a mixed constitution, be it in the courtier's balanced qualities, the prince's fusion of action and contemplation, or the organisation of the social and political 'estates'; in each, an end is proposed which secures a meaning for the protracted work of reason and art – the end of quietness, or stability in the face of the incoherence of secular time.

What Octavian's redefinition of the courtier and his accomplishments aims at is a stabilisation of the polity which avoids the democratic and levelling implications of the republican discourse articulated by Bembo. The problem of monarchy is met by a practice which exerts the rational control of the politically enfranchised 'many' upon the prince while maintaining established systems of subordination and deference. As a consequence the cosmological relations which legitimate monarchy and the hierarchical society are reinforced; indeed they are exemplified in the distinction between worldly accomplishment and rational 'end' which distinguishes the courtier from those whose 'graces' are dedicated to vanity and self-adornment; a distinction which preserves the metaphysically grounded economy of the sign from which it is derived.

In turning to the next chapter's discussion of Jonson's masques and his courtly play *Cynthia's Revels*, we should bear in mind the following points in particular from Castiglione's treatise. That the discipline of courtship demands a double inscription: no imprint of 'flickering provocation' without its subtext of 'holesom craft'. That this implies a discipline of vision; the eye must be led to see behind the 'veil of pleasure' which constitutes the dazzling surface of courtly culture. That these disciplines are peculiarly at risk from the very circumstances which elicit them; the circumstances of earthly power, concentrated and displayed in the royal Court.

6

The Radiant and the Reflective:
Courtly Authority and Crisis
in Jonson's Masques and
Cynthia's Revels

... for the truth of being and the truth of knowing are one,
differing no more than the direct beam and the beam reflected.
Francis Bacon, *The Advancement of Learning*[1]

In Jonson's masque, *Oberon. The Faery Prince*, Silenus confronts his
band of unruly satyrs with the following vision:

There the whole scene opened, and within was discouer'd the
Frontispiece of a bright and glorious Palace, whose gates and
walls are transparent. (ll. 138–40)[2]

Silenus exclaims 'Looke! Do's not his Palace show/ Like another Skie
of lights?' (ll. 143–4). This second sky is the Court of Oberon, and its
light, emanating from the Faery Prince himself, is later figured as the
invigorating sunlight of a second Nature:

He makes it euer day, and euer spring,
Where he doth shine, and quickens euery thing
Like a new nature. (ll. 354–6)

At the end of the masque, however, this second sun is replaced by
its natural counterpart, and the usual diurnal rhythm is reaffirmed:

Lest, taken with the brightnesse of this night,
The world should wish it last, and never miss
[the sun's] light. (ll. 454–5)

This dream of a perpetual light recurs in *Love Freed from Ignorance
and Folly*, in which the Graces pursue the Sun in his course,
'Grieuing, that they might not euer/ See him' (l. 81). After being

waylaid and confined to darkness by Ignorance, they are at last granted their view of the Sun in his western palace, the illumination occurring at the place and time of his setting: 'Thus should the Muses PRIESTS, and GRACES goe to rest,/ Bowing to the Sunne, throned in the West' (ll. 377–8). As in *Oberon*, the dream of endless light is followed by a reassertion of the natural cycle of day and night.

What precisely is this extraordinary light, at once superior, analogous and deferential to natural sunlight? What gift is foreshadowed in the dream of its perpetual reign? And what constitutes the special nature of the illumination by which it confounds Ignorance? These questions can be approached through considering the imagery of light in the Neoplatonic discourse of erotic knowledge, and its implications for sixteenth-century practices of allegorical writing. By pursuing the relationship between the luminosity of knowledge and the radiance of political power, the function of Jonson's allegorical masques at the Court of a self-styled philosopher-king will be illuminated.

* * *

The Neoplatonic vision of the cosmos, as it appears in the authoritative statements of Ficino,[3] is of a series of mutually enclosing spheres beyond whose outer circumference rests their originator, the One beyond being, or God. The hierarchy of the spheres is based on their relative proximity to this external source of all being: the nearest, that of Cosmic Mind, is the most nearly perfect, and the most distant, that of recalcitrant matter, the most degraded:

> For all men assert . . . that this thing does not exist at all, that that thing exists in an imperfect way, and that another thing exists in a more perfect way. Such gradation in existence does not happen, nor can it be known except by proximity to the highest Being, which is God himself, and likewise by distance from it.[4]

This definition of the existence of any particular entity by the degree of its differentiation from the undifferentiated unity of the One is also conceived as the extent to which each receives the progressively mediated influence of that 'splendour of Divine goodness' (l. 98) which penetrates and sustains the cosmos. Here the One is figured as the external source of a generative radiation which is increasingly refracted by its passage through the spheres. The usual image for this process is the operation of sunlight:

> . . . the sun, being the first among light-bearing things, lacks no degree of light, whereas the other light-bearing things beneath it, such as the stars and the elements, do not receive the whole fullness of light.[5]

Ficino expands upon this image in his tract *De comparatione solis ad Deum*, in which God appears as the 'father of lights'. In the terms of this image-repertoire, particular entities in the lower spheres now appear as more or less partial reflectors of the divine radiance, or, when the perspective of the perceiving subject is introduced, as more or less impenetrable veils masking that radiance. It is at this point, as Edgar Wind has shown, that the language of light becomes a discourse on knowledge.[6] The human mind (that part of the soul whose natural tendency is held to be towards reunion with the One from which it emanated) is confronted by a knowable universe populated by entities each of which bears a trace of that originary light which is itself beyond knowledge. The typical mode of Neoplatonic knowledge is therefore characterised by nostalgic suspense: a partial recognition of an unknowable origin in a plethora of inscrutable or evasive signs. This situation is poignantly evoked by Maximus of Tyre:

> God himself, the father and fashioner of all that is . . . is unnameable by any law-giver, unutterable by any voice, not to be seen by any eye. But we, being unable to apprehend his essence, use the help of sounds and names and pictures . . . yearning for the knowledge of Him, and in our weakness naming all that is beautiful in the world after his nature – just as happens to earthly lovers.[7]

The divine light which is only available to human eyes through its partial mundane reflections is therefore equivalent to an unknowable transcendental Signified which suffers dispersal among the multitude of earthly signifiers: as Cusanus baldly puts it, 'The signs vary, but not the signified'.[8] (In this mythology, the bar in Saussure's seminal formulation – S/s – becomes the sickle with which Uranus was castrated, dispersing his seed upon the waters – for Pico della Mirandola, an inevitable dismemberment if the One is to be expressed in the Many, the Ideal to infuse matter.[9]) The condition of knowledge in this system is then one of a perpetual yearning: the mind being constantly aroused by intimations of a divine totality of meaning beyond signification, but at every turn reminded of its embroilment in the shadowy order of the earthly signifier. It is this inevitable lack which casts knowledge as a form of desire, a deferment of erotic satisfaction in which the signifier is placed in suspension, and the subject is revealed as indeed subjected, suspended in anticipation of the always deferred gift of a higher, ineffable power:

> Hence the impulse of the lover is not extinguished by the sight or touch of any body. For he does not desire this or that body, but admires, yearns for, and wonders at the spleandour of the higher light shining over all bodies. The lovers do not know what they wish or desire, because they do not know God himself, whose secret flavour infused some sweet odour of himself in his works.[10]

Knowledge, then, always involves a realisation of one's subordination to, and desire towards, a greater power; a power which has in its gift the revelation of an Ideal order beyond the earthly order of partial and occluded signs. A passage from Pico's *Heptaplus* will demonstrate how, using the imagery of divine illumination, this discourse of knowledge as a relation of power can be articulated in terms of social and political authority. Pico refers to

> the tailors, cooks, butchers, shepherds, servants, maids, to all of whom the written law was given. Would these have been able to carry the burden of the entire Mosaic or Divine understanding? Moses, however, on the height of the mountain . . . was so illuminated by the rays of the Divine sun that his whole face shone in a miraculous manner; but because the people with their dim and owlish eyes could not bear the light, he addressed them with his face veiled. [11]

Clearly Moses is here both inspired prophet and earthly ruler, and his unmediated access to the Divine light is also the ground of his authority over those subject to the written signs of the Law. Pico's fiction anticipates the appropriation of Neoplatonic myth by State Protestantism, in which another figure is added to the list of exalted persons – the mystic, the poet, the lover – who are marked by a special illumination from the Godhead, their souls rendered sensitive to the light by a rejection of matter and its dubious significations. This new figure is the godly ruler, and it is in him or her that the interaction of light, knowledge, power and desire articulated in Neoplatonic theory finds its most productive political realisation. Before considering this development in relation to Jonson's masques, I want first to look at the metaphysics of the sign in allegorical writing of the period.

* * *

For Ficino, as we have seen, the lover is not satisfied with the sight of the loved one's body, but rather looks beyond it for intimations of a more exalted glamour. The body typifies the earthly sign: the lover or seeker after knowledge is enjoined to a constant suspicion, a discipline whereby he must discard the signs presented to his senses and see through them to the fitfully illuminated order of the Signified. In this system, then, subjective experience is a prolonged exercise in allegorical reading,[12] a disciplining of mind and vision to apprehend intimations of an original, totalised meaning beyond the dubieties of signification. Spenser articulates a characteristically Protestant internalisation of this process in which the Ideal order becomes that of the mind and its images. The proem to Book Six of *The Faerie Queene* complains that in the present age 'true curtesie' is

> nought but forgerie,
> Fashioned to please the eies of them, that
> pass,
> Which see not perfect things but in a glass,
> Yet is that glass so gay, that it can blynd
> The wisest sight, to think gold that is bras.
> But vertues seat is deep within the mind,
> And not in outward shows, but inward thoughts
> defynd.

> (St.5)[13]

The hierarchy of value implicit in the transparency of the allegorical sign is demonstrated by Spenser's image: the order presented by reflection is also one of falsely inflated value in relation to the true gold of the spiritual order. The surplus – of light, of knowledge – which is in reserve beyond the allegorical sign is also one of value, and the discipline of vision which Spenser recommends is also an ethical regime, a pilgrimage towards absolute value, beyond the seductive but treacherous economy of sensual appetites. This double purification, of vision and value, is enacted in Guyon's journey to the Bower of Bliss in Book 2, Canto XII.

Guyon's progress is guided by the Palmer, an exemplary allegorical pilgrim whose function is to redirect his charge's attention from the play of appearances to the real significance that they veil. This rigorous reading of an allegorised Nature is at the same time an education in the rashness of sensual expenditure and the transience of what the world deems valuable:

> The Palmer seeing them in safety past,
> Thus said; behold th'ensamples in our sights,
> Of lustfull luxurie and thriftlesse waste:
> What now is left of miserable wights,
> Which spent their looser daies in lewd
> delights,
> But shame and sad reproch, here to be red,
> By these rent reliques, speaking their ill
> plights?
> (St.9)

The Palmer's explication of the Wandering Islands reveals them as exemplars of the insubstantial, dangerously truant signifier:

> For those same Islands, seeming now and than,
> Are not firme lande, nor any certaine wonne,
> But straggling plots, which to and fro do ronne
> In the wide waters . . .
> (St.11)

As such, they expose the risk inherent in vision when, undisciplined, it aligns itself with those senses which are more thoroughly implicated in materiality, most notoriously that of touch:

> [The island] seemd so sweet and pleasant to the
> eye,
> That it would tempt a man to touchen there.
> . . . . .
> But whosoeuer once hath fastened
> His foot thereon, may neuer it recure,
> But wandreth euer more uncertain and
> unsure.
> (St.12)

Sailing between the quicksand of Unthriftyhed – where the mariners and merchants of a wrecked ship 'Labour'd in vain, to have reccur'd their prize' (St.21) – and the Whirlepool of Decay, Guyon appears as a moral merchant-adventurer whose prize will transcend the groundlessness and transience of mundane value; a value which is transmitted by those treacherous significations whose power of obfuscation is figured as the 'grosse fog' which

> overspred
> With his dull vapour all that desert has,
> And heaven's chearfull face enveloped,
> That all things one, and one as nothing was,
> And this great universe seemd one confusd
> mass.
>
> (St.34)

The darkness of earthly confusion is here a parodic inversion of that gathering of the many into the luminous One which is the Neoplatonic image of eternal order.

The arrival at the Bower reveals it to be a triumph of wrongful expenditure, an extravagant investment in transient material effects:

> In which what ever in this worldly state
> Is sweet, and pleasing unto living sense,
> Or that may daintiest fantasie aggrate,
> Was poured forth with plentiful dispence,
> And made there to abound with lavish
> affluence.
>
> (St.42)

It is also the most powerful of challenges to Guyon's 'sober eye', a challenge which reaches its height in the vision of the maids in the fountain, two specialists in specifically visual enticement who call forth all the Palmer's defensive powers:

> He much rebuk't those wandring eyes of his,
> And counseld well, him forward thence to
> draw.
>
> (St.69)

In the Bower of Acrasia is displayed the fate which Guyon has escaped through the Palmer's censoring of his vision. While an attendant sings of the transience of human pleasures, Acrasia hangs over her entranced lover:

> With her false eyes fast fixed in his sight . . .
> And through his humid eyes did suck his
> spright,
> Quite molten into lust and pleasure lewd.
> (St.73)

Here the undisciplined eye is the channel for an expense of spirit which delivers up the lover to decay; the play of appearances soliciting a vision which is equivalent to blindness:

> But in lewd loves, and wastefull luxuree,
> His dayes, his goods, his bodie he did spend:
> O horrible enchantment, that him so did blend.
> (St.80)

Guyon's destruction of the Bower of Bliss is then a victory of the disciplined eye over the seductive play of the earthly signifier, a triumph of allegorical elucidation. It is at the same time a refusal of an earthly economy of rash expenditure, fruitless investment and ineluctible decay. The two processes are inseparable, and each tends towards a deferred but potent absolute: on the one hand a total, luminous knowledge beyond the dubieties of the sign, and on the other a place of plenary value, beyond lack, loss and exhaustion.[14] For Spenser, the location of both these possibilities is in the mind in so far as it turns towards and participates in the radiations of the mind of God.

The eroticism of inflaming looks and unveilings which Guyon avoids in the Bower of Bliss is an earthly parody of the erotic and visual dialectic which informs the Neoplatonic discourse on knowledge. For a summary restatement of that dialectic we can turn to Drayton's *Endymion and Phoebe*, which recounts the education of Endymion's 'eyes not yet of perfect sight' (l. 531)[15] until he is capable of a knowledge beyond the sensual, and is initiated into the hierarchies of divine 'government':

> Into his soul the goddess doth infuse
> The fiery nature of a heavenly muse,
> Which in the spirit labouring, by the mind
> Partaketh of celestial things by kind:

For why the soul being divine alone,
Exempt from vile and gross corruption,
Of heavenly secrets comprehensible,
Of which the dull flesh is not sensible;
And by one only powerful faculty
Yet governeth a multiplicity,
Being essential, uniform in all;
Not to be sever'd nor dividual,
But in her function holdeth her estate,
By powers divine in her ingenerate.
                              (ll. 507–20)

The soul is here the medium of both the 'heavenly secrets' and divine power: in a necessarily double movement, revelation lays bare two aspects of the transcendental One – an absolute knowledge and the power which asserts the authority of the uniform over the multiplicity of the body's corrupted elements. The point of rest beyond the severed and dividual order of earthly signs and sensual desire, beyond imperfect vision and the ravages of decay, is the seat of universal government. The gift foreshadowed by Neoplatonic knowledge and the perennial surplus promised by the allegorical sign both amount to this revelation of absolute order and the ineffable authority of the One. The very ground and goal of true knowledge is the acknowledgement of one's own absolute subjection.

* * *

In the masques of Jonson and Inigo Jones this mythology of light, love and knowledge is adapted to the articulation of royal power. By an identification of the King (or, as occasion demands, his consort or children) with the Neoplatonic deity, the masque is able to dramatise configurations of power (within the Court, between the Court and the nation) under the appearance of a natural or indeed cosmic order.

The characteristic movement enacted by the masques is one from darkness to light, from ignorance to knowledge, from erotic frustration to the gift of love. So *Love Freed from Ignorance* shows the three Graces, moved by love, in pursuit of the Sun, but arrested in their progress by the umbrageous Ignorance, figured as a sphinx. The frustration of their pursuit of light and erotic satisfaction is ended through the solving of the sphinx's riddle. The sphinx

> Then, to prison of the night,
> Did condemne those sisters bright,
> There for euer to remaine,
> 'Lesse they could the knot un-straine
> Of a riddle, which shee put
> Darker, then where they are shut.
>
> (ll. 113–18)

Should the riddle not be solved, the price of the Graces' release will be the sacrifice of their associate, Love. This makes the solution of the riddle a means of salvaging unity from the threat of fragmentation, of overcoming the contradiction through which Love would be dissociated from the Graces. The liberating effect of knowledge involves, then, a release from the antinomial order of the signifier – the realm of Ignorance, in which Love and Grace are incompatible categories – into the unitary order of the Signified, the One beyond contradiction.

The solution of the riddle is effected by an effusion of light from 'the brightest face here shining' (l. 280); that is, in the words of Jonson's marginal note, 'The Maiestie, and wisdom of the King, figur'd in the Sunne' (l. 94). By this elucidation, Love and the Graces are united (Love being 'absold' from the appearance of a merely sensual eroticism) and the Graces are released into light and the satisfaction of their love:

> Appeare then you, my brighter charge,
> And to light your selues enlarge,
> To behold that glorious starre,
> For whose love you came so farre.
>
> (ll. 306–10)

The Graces' love of Light – the sun-king – is shown to have been justified by the saving power it has now exercised in their behalf; its primacy has not been merely asserted, but proven dramatically. In a similarly reflexive movement, the answer to the riddle which is revealed by the illuminating power of the King is that

> The King's the eye, as we do call
> The sunne the eye of this great all.
> And is the light and treasure too;
> For 'tis his wisdome all doth doo.
>
> (ll. 286–9)

The truth of this claim to power is endorsed by the fact that it has been released into meaning from the obscurity of the riddle by the very elucidatory power which it acclaims. The circularity of this process, whereby the knowledge that the King imparts is that he is indeed all-knowing, the illumination which he grants is of his own light-radiating nature, and the love which he imparts saves and confirms the love that he receives, is further proof that the King partakes of the divine attributes of the One, who, extended through the *circuitus spiritualis* of the cosmos, is at once the source and the object of love, illumination and knowledge.[16]

The masque, then, contrives actively to produce and demonstrate the royal omnipotence which it declares, indeed to make its own progress as a fiction (in this case over the impasse of the riddle) depend on the truth of the claim that it makes for the King's power. This is made possible by its articulation of power as illumination/knowledge, so that the fiction's progress towards the clarity of its meaning is also a discovery of the truth of royal authority. This double movement is confirmed at the masque's conclusion, when the revelation of the Graces' virtuous beauty by the luminous power of the King produces a variation of the Neoplatonic theme in which the perception of beauty arouses a desire for the good, which is in turn a mode of worship of the One:

> How neere to good is what is faire!
> Which we no sooner see,
> But with the lines, and outward aire
> Our senses taken be.
> We wish to see it still, and proue,
> What waies wee may deserue,
> We court, we praise, we more then loue,
> We are not grieu'd to serue.
>
> (ll. 348–55)

By clarifying the beautiful, the King has initiated a progression through a hierarchy of terms – Beauty>Good>God/Delight>Desire>Worship – which terminates in the worship of the King. Political submission appears under the guise of a natural appetite – the willed subservience of the Neoplatonic lover.

The double presence of the King at the masque, as both its chief spectator and the agent of a crucial intervention within the performance, reproduces the dual nature of the Neoplatonic deity, who both presides over a static ideal order beyond the earthly, and rearticulates some measure of that order in the chaotic domain of matter.[17] The desire of the lover for the static order of the Ideal is sustained by this partial mundane reproduction of it.

The movement from the confusion of the antimasque, through the intervention of the external ordering power of the King, to the harmonious configurations of the climactic revels, is a dramatic representation of this double existence of divine authority. The King is displayed as both the guarantor of a Utopian order – in the structure of the performance this appears as the Court enclosing the stage-world of the masque – and as the agent of that order's constant reproduction in the world. It is this entry of power into the mundane which accounts for its periodic submission, in the form of light, to the natural diurnal rhythm. Both poles of the process are necessary: Utopian stasis being the reward promised for submission to authority, and authority constantly re-presenting within the secular domain the reality of the promised state of rest. It is in the space between these two poles that the courtier rehearses the desire for his own subjection.

So, in *Love Restored*, the antimasque presents a state of disorder ruled by the god of money, Plutus. Plutus is disguised as Cupid, a subterfuge in which his creation of false monetary values is compounded by a resort to false signification. Bribery and false seeming are also exercised in Robin Goodfellow's attempts to trick his way through an unruly crowd of attendants to see the masque at Court. At this point in the action the false Cupid is exposed and the authentic God of Love is released from his frozen cell by:

> the virtue of his Maiestie, who projecteth so powerful beams of
> light and heat through this Hemispheare, thaw his icie fetters,
> and scattered the darkness that obscures him. (ll. 194–7)

On being thus restored to light, Love rewards the Majesty which released him by uniting with it. In doing so, he dispels the chaotic struggle for admission to the Court which was shown in the antimasque, and replaces it with a display of harmoniously orchestrated courtly qualities:

> Nor will they rudely strive for place,
> One to precede the other; but,
> As musique them in forms shall put,
> So will they keep their measures true,

And make still their proportions new,
Till all become one harmonie.

> (ll. 260–4)

This dance of love demonstrates the dual nature of divine (and monarchical) power, being a static configuration which reproduces itself in motion. The courtiers have this impressed upon them when the dance is arrested and their configuration is held, waiting to be set in motion again by an impulse from the *primum mobile*, which is represented by the King and his party:

And now like earth themselues they fixe,
Till greater powers vouchsafe to mixe
Their motions with them.

> (ll. 284–6)

Once again, a relation of power is figured in the guise of a natural process; in this case the effusion of love from the Godhead which gives the lower spheres their motion. The courtiers, moreover, have literally asked for it; in appealing to the potent light of the King for the release of Love, which allows their performance to proceed, they request the elucidation of an order which places them as subjects. In this willed submission they are analogous to the Neoplatonic lovers depicted in one of the masque's final songs, who would rather 'die a destin'd sacrifice, then live at home, and free' (ll. 290–1).

The restoration of Love is also a penetration of Plutus' illusions, an access of knowledge parallel to that through which Guyon overcomes false evaluations and dubious signs in the Bower of Bliss. As we saw in the case of Spenser, this defeat of the signifier is also a transcendence of sensual desire and its transient satisfactions, and an escape from the ravages of Time. In its intimations of an absolute order beyond signification, the masque also foreshadows the gift with which that order rewards its willing subjects – a Utopian dream of Time arrested, the transcendence of decay, and the perpetual gratification of the spectator-subject:

Whose breath or beams, have got proud earth
with child,
Of all the treasures that great Nature's worth,
And make it every minute to bring forth?

> . . . Behold a King

Whose presence maketh this perpetual Spring,

> The glories of which Spring grow in that Bower,
> And are the marks and beauties of his power.[18]

It is in visions such as this, in which the visual and substantial magnificence of the Court is rearticulated as the mark of a metaphysical authenticity and authority, that the masque makes its distinctive contribution to the legitimation of courtly power. In turning to *Cynthia's Revels*, however, we will be looking at a drama which, by unsettling the formal integrity of the masque, also puts into question the dialectics of illumination and power which it performs.

Cynthia's Revels: Narcissus and the courtly image

> . . . the mother of falsity is the semblance of things which reaches the eyes.
>
> *St Augustine*

> Representation mingles with what it represents to the point where one speaks as one writes, one thinks as if the represented were nothing more than the shadow or reflection of the representer. A dangerous promiscuity and nefarious complicity between the reflection and the reflected which lets itself be seduced narcissistically. In this play of representation, the point of origin becomes ungraspable. There are things like reflecting pools, and images, an infinite reference from one to the other, but no longer a source, a spring. There is no longer a simple origin . . . . What can look at itself is not one.
>
> Jacques Derrida, *Of Grammatology*[19]

The ethical choice which confronts Guyon in the Bower of Bliss is dramatised by Spenser as a conflict between ways of seeing, between a vision which allows itself to become fixated upon the objects presented to sense, and a disciplined seeing-through of object and surface to the immaterial reality which they veil. This antithetical structure is also that of the masques which I have considered. The pivotal moment in the masque is one in which the carnal spectacle of the antimasque literally vanishes, dispelled by a radiance in which a new regime of the visible is disclosed as here, in *Mercury Vindicated*:

> Vanish, I say, that all who have but their senses may see and

judge the difference between thy ridiculous monsters and his absolute features.[20]

The light emanating from the royal presence opens a visual field in which appearances are subordinated to the invisible harmonies and structures which dispose and orchestrate them, so that what is seen is not the mere spectacle of the Court at play, but the animated image of the cosmic order which the Court represents.

What the masque rehearses, then, are the visual and metaphysical implications of the distinction insisted upon by Castiglione in Book Four of *The Book of the Courtier*: between the éclat of courtly accomplishments and their proper understanding as the sensible lineaments of virtue. Where *Cynthia's Revels* exceeds and interrogates the masque structure which it incorporates is in pursuing the danger identified by Lord Octavian at the beginning of his discourse – that of an exclusive investment in the sensible, a Narcissistic indulgence of the courtly image.

Jonson's suspicion of courtly entertainments emerges on stage in the very production with which, as Joseph Loewenstein has noted, he makes a bid to succeed Lyly as Master of the Revels. Jonson's coming career as court masque writer will involve a constant effort to secure the predominance of the written, learned, metaphysical and pedagogical 'soul' of the masque over its physically spectacular and glamorously staged 'body'. The struggle between these elements becomes explicit at a textual level in the prefatory material to 'Hymenaei',[21] with its linked oppositions between the 'shew' and 'inward parts', 'bodies' and 'soules' of masques, and their appeal to, respectively, the 'sense' and 'understanding'. Jonson's insistence on an aesthetic (and conceptual) economy which places the sensual elements of these pairings under the regulation of the metaphysical represents a principle of government within the domain of courtly entertainment which reproduces the structure proposed for the Royal Household as a whole in the Ordinance of Edward IV, which I discussed earlier.[22]

As this parallel suggests, the struggle over the aesthetic economy of the masque which develops between Jonson and Inigo Jones is intimately related to the broader struggle over royal income and expenditure, courtly extravagance, and the relationship between image and morality at Court which develops as James's reign progresses. Staged at the end of a reign in which royal authority was exercised to an unprecedented degree through the 'theatrical' manipulation of image and audience, *Cynthia's Revels* foreshadows this Stuart process by exposing (reluctantly) a crisis in the authority of courtly representations which is linked to an evacuation of the metaphysical bases of courtly, and so too royal, authority.

As my quotation from *Mercury Vindicated* suggests, the masque ends in a triumphal enforcement of differences, in the celebration of the integrity of the Court and the banishment of its disorderly Other. *Cynthia's Revels* puts the security of this process in question from its beginning.[23] It opens with a questioning of its own identity, an introduction of difference into the propriety of its own name – *Cynthia's Revels, or the Fountain of Self-Love*. The revels or masque element in the title appears to have priority, but this is ceded in the possibility of the secondary title standing as an alternative or equivalent. Masque implies a work of integration, of the uniformity of the proper; the fountain of self-love counters this with the alienating reflex of a perverse self-mirroring, identity disabled by self-difference. If the work's second title is read as being subordinated to the governing uniformity implied in the first, then it must be asked whether the uniform can dominate difference when it seems to admit a potential equivalence with the differing/different in its own self-entitlement. The implied priority of the monological form of the masque is, then, already undermined by the dialogical play of the title: if the drama is to incite its audience to a categorical choice between the Same and the Different then the choice will be made in the light of this initial self-differing of the play's proper title.

The dubiety of the play's title introduces its fundamental uncertainty: the question of whether the ideal Court can indeed be distinguished from and be seen to justify its Narcissistic Other. This troubling of the secure discriminations enforced by the masque is taken further in the play's prefatory address:

TO THE SPECIAL
FOUNTAIN OF
MANNERS:

Thou art a bountiful and brave spring: and waterest all the noblest plants of this island. In thee the whole kingdom dresseth itself, and is ambitious to use thee as her glass. Beware, then, thou render men's figures truly, and teach them no less to hate their deformities than to love their forms: for, to grace there

should come reverence; and no man can call that lovely which
is not also venerable . . . . (p. 33)

This courtly fountain, as a fructifying source, is a figure of depth, and
as such is placed in initial opposition to the static reflective surface
of the Narcissus pool. As we have already seen, this opposition of
surface and depth around the figure of Narcissus involves certain
other conceptual oppositions: between on the one hand the linked
delinquencies of the signifier and the socially unintegrated subject,
and on the other the 'deep' structures of the integrated sign and of
social order.[24] Against the deep structural dynamism of those forces of
opposition which bind subjects (of discourse, of state) into order, the
pool of Narcissus is imaged as still water, undisturbed by any motion
from the depths. The redundant reflectiveness of its surface, then, is
the result of this stagnant stillness.

What occurs in Jonson's preface is a seepage of connotation between
these opposed terms so that the clarity of their opposition is eroded.
The process is already at work in the decision to name the source
of self-love as a 'fountain' rather than a 'pool'. The connotations of
isolation, self-enclosure and sterility which gather about the pool of
Narcissus are joined here by those of copiousness, irrigation and
fertilisation which appeared to be the particular properties of its
courtly antithesis. The transfer of connotation implies the anxiety
which haunts the play: that the crime of Narcissus is not merely
an abdication or standing aside from meaning and socialisation, but
rather a dynamic principle which animates and indeed originates
society itself, establishing it as a mere congeries of auto-affective
fixations and vacuous 'images' without structural anchorage.

The transfer of meaning between Court and Narcissus proceeds,
this time in the other direction:

. . . in thee, the whole kingdom dresseth itself, and is ambitious
to use thee as her glass. (p. 33)

The moral discourse on vanity which is conventionally articulated
through the mirror of Narcissus here shadows the Court and its
relation to the kingdom, which appears, in the terms of that discourse,
as the female in thrall to the mirror and superfluous dressing. If
the pool of Narcissus has assumed some of the dynamic generative
potential of the fountain of manners, the Court is shifted here towards

the connotative field of paralysed repetition, specious ornamentation, and the barren duplication of surface, image and manner.

The use of the mirror of Narcissus here is particularly pointed given the conventional uses of the trope of the court as mirror:

> Therefore, even as in the firmament the sunne and the moone and the other starres shew to the worlde (as it were) in a glasse, a certain likenesse of God: So upon the earth a much more liker image of God are those good Princes that love and worship him, and shew unto the people the cleare light of his justice, accompanied with a shadow of the heavenly reason and understanding.[25]

Here Castiglione shows how the image of the mirror can deploy the Neoplatonic epistemology of light[26] as a specifically inflected articulation of the Humanist discourse on the necessity of just and rationally informed rule, as stated here by Erasmus:

> The common people imitate nothing with more pleasure than what they see their prince do . . . you will find the life of the prince mirrored in the morals of his people . . . . A beneficent prince . . . is a living likeness of God, who is at once good and powerful. His goodness wants him to help all; his power makes him able to do so.[27]

Through this relay of reflections – God–Prince–People – the discourse of the mirror articulates an injunction to justice and responsibility which bears (as always) upon the people, but also on the Prince. Moreover, the congruence of the Neoplatonic structure of hierophantic initiation with that of Humanistic educational development means that the discourse offers scope for the influence of counsellors in bringing the Prince nearer the state of divine reflection, as the context of the last quotation, in Erasmus's *Education of a Christian Prince*, suggests. The godly mirror is at the heart of the tradition of courtly counsel and education which feeds into the Jonsonian masque, and it appears again here, in Jonson's exhortation to the Court to embody that exalted mode of reflection, even as his terminology suggests that what is actually taking place is a merely sensual, fashionable and 'ambitious' mirroring of the Court in the habits of the people.[28]

The warning which Jonson addresses to the Court-as-mirror opens further the potential divergence between visual image and ethical propriety. Jonson's language attempts to hold these two levels in play at once, but the tension between the Court as a display of merely physical glamour, and as the incarnation of sublime faculties, is persistent

> Beware, then, thou render men's figure truly, and teach them
> no less to hate their deformities than to love their forms: for,
> to grace there should come reverence; and no man can call that
> lovely which is not also venerable . . . . (p. 33)

The congruence between the lovely and the venerable which is asserted here is precisely what the play has begun to put in question. There is also the question of how the reproduction of visual images by the mirror can be said to be a kind of teaching; of how the reproduction of form in the sense of visual or physical figure is also to encompass the delineation of deformities understood morally. If the Court, mirror-like, is to reproduce its image in the manners of the nation, how is that process to be kept from being a vacuous reiteration of mere image and manner? If imitation takes purchase upon externals, is the interior or depth of the image also capable of transmission? In other words, is the truth which underwrites courtly accomplishments transferred to those who fashion themselves in the image of the Court, or is the dissemination of courtliness precisely a displacement of truth by fashionable images?

These questions, which centre upon the Court's exemplary function, are fundamentally about pedagogy, about the possibility and danger of teaching courtliness. As we have seen in our discussions of Gascoigne, Elyot and Puttenham, the extension and consolidation of the Elizabethan State involves the Court as a primary agency of recruitment and acculturation for personnel from hitherto excluded social groups.[29] The danger of this process from the point of view of the State is that the influx of 'new men' threatens a disintegration of the ethos of the political elite, its 'natural' cohesion around commonplaces of attitude, assumption and ideology. The educational dissemination of courtliness, from this point of view, risks a promulgation of courtly manners which fails to carry with it the preserved 'essence' of ideological orthodoxy. So, in the case of Gascoigne, the assumption of courtly literary manner by the aspiring writer is deemed impertinent until underwritten by a demonstration of allegiance to those codes of discretion and discursive propriety by which the elite sustains its cohesion and legitimacy. Similarly,

Puttenham's treatise is suspended between the necessity of teaching the manners of the powerful, and the ideological requirement that power should continue to be defined as a natural, genetic endowment. In both cases the core of established power relations which is to be preserved and rearticulated is readily described as a mysterious 'essence' of courtliness which constitutes its truth and the authenticity of its proponents, and which risks degradation in the process of communication.[30]

The masque, as practised by Jonson and Inigo Jones, emerges as a powerful device for the confirmation of the courtier in the metaphysics of courtliness. By absorbing the act of looking and the posture of spectatorship into its Platonic thematics of visual discipline and semiotic integrity, the masque incorporates its audience and makes their registration of courtly manner a crux in the action's unveiling of truth and power. This formal self-enclosure – a legitimation, or *subliming,* of the entrancement with which the Court regards itself – is a dramatisation of the desired insularity and exclusivity of court culture.

It also indicates the circularity of the process by which the masque enacts the essential and inimitable nature of courtly power. If the agents of chaos and delinquency who people the antimasque are known by the *uncourtliness* of their behaviour – antic gesture, slovenly speech, cacophonous song – then the forms of courtly discipline and recreation are clearly also the forms of order. By producing Evil as the uncourtly, the masque produces the Court, antithetically, as necessarily grounded in the Good. The look of the Court, apparently reaching out to confront alien opposition, turns in fact upon its own inverted self-image and returns in self-confirmation. It is this circularity which produces spontaneous assent to the masque's climactic metaphysical claims, and allows the relation of the earthly Court and monarch to their ideal forms to appear as simply visible, simply *there*.

The masque, then, is a closed form. Its production of the essence of courtliness is in opposition to all that it defines as uncourtly, and it is this which leads to the exclusion of a citizen audience from courtly performances being incorporated as a dramatic element in several of Jonson's masques.[31] Excluded from the circular process by which the masque sublimes the courtier's self-regard, the look of the citizen spectator has no place within the Platonic dialectics of vision. The confinement of the excluded spectator to a merely corporeal plane of vision and apprehension is forcefully confirmed in the practice of breaking up the physical machinery and costumes at the conclusion of the performance and dispersing them among the citizens gathered outside.[32] This discarding of the masque's 'body' is a public confirmation of the hierarchies of matter/spirit, and of social and political power which inform the masque, reserving to the courtly elite the consumption of its 'inventive part' or incorporeal essence.[33]

The peculiarity and difficulty of *Cynthia's Revels* is that it relocates the self-enclosed form and transcendentalist ideology of the masque within the open and empiricising form of the Jonsonian comedy.[34] The comedy's commitment to education and the reformation of manners encloses the masque and its denial of the problems of courtly instruction. The play's hybrid structure reinstates the question of the dissemination of courtliness by exposing the closed circuits of the masque to the heterogeneous audience of the public theatre, and by testing the educational claims of the public play against the theory of the incommunicability of truth built into the masque.

It is this mutual interrogation of the play's two generic components which gives it its profoundly unsettled and unsettling character, and which accounts for its problematic early performance and textual history.[35] If the play deals centrally with the dangers of a pedagogical representation of courtliness, it also finds those dangers in its own educational representation of a Court which has become the mere (pedagogically reproduced) image of courtliness. This fear that the satirical representation of courtly imitation will serve only to reiterate the image, arresting the gaze of the audience in a confirmation of the visible, becomes one of the play's themes. It is posed antithetically against the danger (also articulated as part of the play's 'content') that the masque's 'escape' from the problems of representation implies a paralysis of courtly culture, a self-confirmation achieved at the expense of a disabling isolation and introversion.

*   *   *

The play sets its representation of the Court and courtliness in a frame derived from the mythical narratives of Echo and Narcissus, and Actaeon and Cynthia. Together these stories are used to articulate the play's central cluster of themes: the opposition between self-regard and mutuality, social integration and vanity, and the relationship between different kinds of seeing, truth and power.

The lament of Echo over Narcissus traces his self-destruction to the inversion of an essential opposition of terms:

> Why did the gods give thee a heavenly form
> And earthy thoughts to make thee proud of it?
> (I.ii.40–1)

Form, in this corporeal sense, is properly earthy; thought, correspondingly, should be heavenly. Narcissus, in embodying a disruption of the essential relation between the material and the spiritual, is a 'spoil of nature' (I.ii.25), and as such constitutionally alienated from the truth:

> But self-love never yet could look on truth
> But with bleared beams.
> (I.ii.36–7)

Echo represents the possibility of a re-engagement with truth through the restoration of a heterosexual mutuality which stands for all forms of 'natural' relationship:

> She would have dropped away herself in tears
> Till she had all turned water, that in her,
> As in a truer glass, thou mightst have gazed,
> And seen thy beauties by more kind reflection.
> (I.ii.32–5)

'Kindness' links the healing and proper care of the self to the consolidation of 'normal' sexual relations; the emphasis on reflection links this process in turn to a righting of the epistemological relation between perception and truth.

The focus of Echo's speech now broadens to place this discourse on subjective economy in a context of social integration and delinquency. The terms of this passage are those of stewardship, 'use', husbandry and hospitality which were central to my discussion of economic theory and, in particular, the discourse on usury:

> Oh, hadst thou known the worth of heaven's rich
> gift,
> Thou wouldst have turned it to a truer use,
> And not, with starved and covetous ignorance,
> Pined in continual eyeing that bright gem,
> The glance whereof to others had been more

> Than to thy famished mind the wide world's
> store:
> 'So wretched is it to be merely rich.'
>
> (I.ii.95–101)

This is entirely characteristic of the discourse of Commonwealth and stewardship which opposes economic 'singularity'. The true origin of wealth is not the industry of the usurer (the word 'use' here places the usurer as a special type of the miser represented in the following lines) but the beneficence of God; the miser/usurer is not then the owner but the custodian of a divine resource; the proper destiny of wealth is not self-enrichment but its circulation through the social body. So the passage opposes at each of these points an account of the 'true' relationship between wealth, the wealthy and the social order, and the illusory, 'singular' version of those relations which is invested in by the miser. This double perspective sustains the connection between economic delinquency and epistemological/perceptual disorder which we have considered in our discussion of usury; a connection focused here in the image of the miser's 'continual eyeing that bright gem'. This fixation upon the dazzling surface of the valuable is named as a kind of ignorance: the miser, like Narcissus, is alienated from the truth because his perception (and so his consciousness of *relationship*) fails to penetrate surfaces to the depths in which their truth is located. The relationship between subjective and social disorders is developed from Echo's metaphorical linkage of riches and beauty; so the *sentence* with which she concludes – 'So wretched is it to be merely rich' – implies that the hollowing out of a dimension of authentic value beneath the superficies of earthly wealth is also the assertion of a primary dimension of the visible beneath the seductive play of earthly appearances.

If Narcissus represents the dangers of an occluded vision, the virtues of relationality are articulated through Echo's association with the audible. The song with which she ends her lament for Narcissus represents a transition from the eye to the ear, from the blindness of singularity to the harmoniousness of integration:

> Slow, slow, fresh fount, keep time with my salt
> tears;
> Yet slower yet, oh faintly gentle springs:
> List to the heavy part the music bears,
> 'Woe weeps out her division when she sings.'

Droop herbs and flowers;
Fall grief in showers,
'Our beauties are not ours.'

(I.ii.65–8)

The Pythagorean theory which underlies this passage also informs the use of music in the masque or revels more generally. The harmonious interrelation of voice and natural melody is based in the resonant structure of intervals, proportions and analogies which comprises cosmic order. This intimacy between the integration of self and of cosmos is focused in a pun: 'Woe weeps out her *division* when she sings.' Division is the technical term for a descant or musical variation: to weep out division unites the participation in musical – and so in cosmological – harmony with the expulsion or salving of alienation and self-estrangement. The opposition of Echo's version of self-integration and the account of Narcissus' 'disease' amounts to a paradoxical theory of subjectivity which will inform the play's account of courtliness: the independent self-involvement of Narcissus is in fact a model of subjective disintegration, while the integration of the subject is based in an abnegation of self, a submission of individuality to external authority: 'Our beauties are not ours'.

The fatality of the fountain of self-love derives from an association not only with Narcissus, but also with the death of Actaeon. The killing of Actaeon by Cynthia's hounds is taken up as an element of the play's dramatic frame; Cynthia's promised return during the revels is in order to dispel the slanders which have been aimed at her motives in punishing Actaeon so violently. The Actaeon theme picks up the issue of illicit or irresponsible looking from the discussion of Narcissus, and opens within it the question of power and its relation to visibility. As we have seen from our discussion of Jonson's masques, the Platonic theory of vision which they draw upon is also a theory concerning eroticism and the grounds of power. The devotion of the subject to his monarch involves a seeing-through of the monarch's physical presence to the idea of kingship which it represents, and which legitimated this particular king's power. This affection of the subject towards the king's ideal body is only one manifestation of that erotic yearning which, in Neoplatonic theory, directs the subject towards its lost origin in the Ideal, and through which it participates in the circulation of divine love which animates the cosmos.

The proper relation of subject to monarch, in which monarchical power is divinely legitimated, involves, then, the same discipline of vision which is implied by the discourse on Narcissus. The crime of Actaeon is a voyeuristic fixation upon the Queen's corporeal nakedness, rather than the unveiled monarchical Idea. It is the curtailment or partiality of Actaeon's look, its indifference to the integration of image and idea in the double person of the Queen, which is answered in the violent tearing into pieces of his own body. The erotic scandal which is implied by Actaeon's irreverent look is emphasised if we consider that in *Cynthia's Revels* the crime of Actaeon veils a reference to the Earl of Essex's intrusion into the royal chambers, surprising the Queen in her privacy.[36]

The exercise and negotiation of power by means of the Platonised eroticism which we have discussed assumes a particular force and precariousness in the circumstances of Elizabeth's rule. The maintenance of the metaphysicality of these transactions, of their transcendence of the participants' corporeal selves, is a fundamental and inviolable rule. Essex's transgression is at once impious and impolitic, a reduction of the complex dialectic of deference and empowerment to an attempted seizure of person and authority.

This curtailment of the metaphysical dimension of monarchical and courtly authority is further indicated in the name of the last mythical participant in the fatality of Narcissus' fountain, Niobe, whose crime it was to challenge the gods on the ground of their intangibility, claiming her own superiority to them was proven by her unambiguous sensory visibility. That this challenge also involves the taunting of the goddess Leto for her childlessness only increases Niobe's pertinence to a questioning of the bases of the ageing and heirless Elizabeth's power, and to the sexual aggression of the rejected consort Essex.

The Actaeon and Niobe elements of the play's opening contribute, then, to the establishment of a political context – veiled by mythological allusion – which encompasses mutually implicated disturbances of the legitimation of courtly appearances, the regulation of the metaphysically encoded power relations between male courtiers and female monarch, and the authority and charisma of the monarch herself in her declining years. It is this sense of a destabilised and precariously legitimated Court which frames Jonson's correspondingly unstable play.

With the appearance of the chief courtier Amorphus, the play initiates its critique of Cynthia's Court as an arena of shifting shapes and ungrounded images. Echo's rejection of Amorphus provokes him to a self-assessment whose terms locate personal essence in elaborated surfaces and externals:

> What should I infer? If my behaviours had been of a cheap or customary garb; my accent or phrase vulgar; my garments trite; my countenance illiterate; or unpractised in the encounter of a beautiful and brave-attired piece; then I might, with some change of colour, have suspected my faculties: but, knowing myself an essence so sublimated and refined by travel; of so studied and well exercised a gesture; so alone in fashion; able to tender the face of any statesman living . . . one that hath now made the sixth return upon venture . . . whose optics have drunk the spirit of beauty in some eight score and eighteen prince's courts where I have resided and been there fortunate in the amours of three hundred forty and five ladies . . . whose names I have in catalogue . . . certes, I do neither see, nor feel, nor taste, nor savour the least steam or fume of a reason that should invite this foolish fastidious nymph so peevishly to abandon me. (I.iii.23–41)

'Essence' here is embedded within an accumulating terminology of garb, garment, attire, gesture, fashion and face; categories which are properly subordinated to essence in any metaphysical account of subjectivity and substance. This process of insubordination is centred in the self-congratulatory 'knowing myself an essence so sublimated and refined by travel', in which the sublimation of matter into spirit is reversed, and self-knowledge is grounded in the 'perfection' of spirit by the processes of physical motion and change.

The account of the self which is implied in this first speech is one in which experience is conceived in the material terms of quantity (the 'catalogue' of seductions), and profit (the 'return upon venture', in which the traveller bets upon his own prompt and safe return from a journey abroad). It is a subjectivity in which essence is dispersed into surfaces contrived through 'practise', 'exercise' and 'study', and in which the primary 'faculties' are imitation ('able to tender the face of any statesman living') and gesture. The self-fashioning of the courtier is vilified here as mere *bricolage*: a piecing together of ready-made or off-the-peg components:

> *Crites*: . . . yourself can best inform him of yourself, sir; except
>   you had some catalogue or list of your faculties ready

drawn, which you would request me to show him for
you . . . . (I.iv.36–9)

In the image of the catalogue, Crites locates the inauthenticity of
the courtier in a prior textualisation of the self. The spontaneity of the
spirit is replaced by the secondariness of writing: in the conception of
a self derived from a *script*, Jonson fuses a critique of the courtship
manual and the principle of imitative performance – of acting – as
the two principal 'sources' of the self-fashioning subject.[37]

The emergence of courtliness as a species of delinquent writing is
confirmed when Amorphus' drinking at the fountain of Narcissus is
linked parodically to the drawing of inspiration from the fount of the
Muses:

Amorphus: Sir, your muses have no such water, I assure you,
your nectar is nothing to it; 'tis above your metheglin,
believe it.

Asotus: Metheglin! What's that, sir? May I be so audacious to
demand?

Amorphus: A kind of Greek wine I have met with, sir, in my
travels: it is the same that Demosthenes usually drunk,
in the composure of all his exquisite and mellifluous
orations.

Crites: That's to be argued, Amorphus, if we may credit
Lucian, who in his Encomio Demosthenis affirms he
never drunk but water in any of his compositions.
(I.iv.8–18)

Narcissus is here the source of a counter-poetic, a watery rhetoric
whose opponent is the vinous Lucianic/Horatian principle invoked by
Crites. As so often in Jonson, Latin satire is here the reference-point
for a writing in which critical directness and principled classicism
are enclosed by a certain bluffly convivial masculinity. The virility
of the wine-drinking truth-teller opposes the effeminate fanciness of
Demosthenean rhetoric; the association of femininity with vacuous
surfaces which informs the discourse on vanity and which recurs in
the play's satire on courtly posturing is also central to the critique
of delinquent writing.[38]

If courtliness is a species of bad writing, it is manifested not only
in the vaporous extravagances of the courtiers' speech, but also in
the imitative, formulaic nature of their social interaction. The central
instance of this is the training of Asotus by Amorphus.

Amorphus' first approach is through that formal selection of an ingratiating subject which the rhetoricians term *inventio*:

> Since I trod on this side the Alps, I was not so frozen in my invention. Let me see: to accost him with some choice remnant of Spanish or Italiean? . . . . Step into some *ragioni del stato*, and so make my induction? . . . . No, it must be a more quaint and collateral device. As – stay: to frame some encomiastic speech upon this our metropolis, or the wise magistrates thereof, in which politic number, 'tis odds but his father filled up a room? (I.iv.69–80)

The ensuing exchange upon Asotus' headwear associates the ingenuities of fashion with the terminology of rhetorical composition and sophistication:

> *Amorphus*: 'Tis a most curious and neatly-wrought band, this same, as I have seen, sir . . . . I have not seen a young gentleman, generally, put on his clothes, with more judgement . . . . A very pretty fashion, believe me, and a most novel kind of trim: your band is conceited too! (I.iv.112–16)

The *conceited* is the category in which the vanity of self-image joins with that of an evacuated rhetoric. Self-fashioning is here a subordination of subjectivity to fashionable forms which derive ultimately from the prescriptions of the courtly manual. So the fashioning of Asotus in the image of Amorphus represents the reproduction of courtliness as a mirroring which is also a reiteration:

> He that is with him is Amorphus . . . one so made out of the mixture and shreds of forms that himself is truly deformed . . . he is the very mint of compliment, all his behaviours are printed, his face is another volume of essays; and his beard an Aristarchus . . . . The other gallant is his zany, and doth most of these tricks after him; sweats to imitate him in every thing . . . is in all as if he were moulded of him. (II.iii.76–96)

It is this reiteration of prescribed forms which Amorphus teaches as the secret of courtship. The theoretical basis of the lesson is an explicit undoing of the hierarchical integration of mind and body which is characterised as a disruption of semiotic economy – as, that is, a subversion of *indexicality*:

You shall now as well be the ocular as the ear witness how
clearly I can refel that paradox, or rather pseudodox, of those
which hold the face to be the index of the mind, which I assure
you, is not so, in any politic creature. (II.iii.10–13)

Amorphus' rehearsal of the repertoire of faces condenses a vision
of social being in which reference to the 'truth' of the subject
('my most proper and genuine aspect') is replaced by the play of
'politic' imitation. It is important to note, however, that Amorphus'
performance of the faces is also an opportunity for the actor who plays
him to display his own technique, and that the audience which is being
offered a critique of systematic gestural imitation is also here to take
pleasure in a virtuoso 'turn' of mimicry. This realisation of a critique
of imitation through satirical mimesis is central to *Cynthia's Revels*
– it is the source of both the play's metadramatic sophistication and
of its uneasy self-interrogation; or rather of the difficulty of deciding
which of these is the play's own 'most proper and genuine aspect'.
The rhetorical question with which Mercury anticipates Amorphus'
performance is consequently also one posed seriously on behalf of
the audience of the play: 'Oh, what a mass of benefit shall we
possess in being the invisible spectators of this strange show now
to be acted?' (II.iii.8–9)

If Mercury opens the question of the profits of spectating, it is also
through him and Cupid that a questioning of the value of performing
is produced. It is this pair of Gods, in association with Crites, who
carry the play's mimetic commentary on fatuous courtliness in a
series of verbal portraits which are clearly to be underscored by
impersonation and mimicry:

Nay, Cupid, leave to speak improperly, since we are turned
cracks, let's study to be like cracks; practise their language and
behaviours, and not with a dead imitation: act freely, carelessly,
and capriciously, as if our veins ran with quicksilver, and not
utter a phrase but what shall come forth steeped in the very
brine of conceit, and sparkle like salt in fire. (II.i.3–8)

If the play, as its critics have often complained, is static and verbose,
it is largely due to this staging of the prose 'Character' in a sequence
of verbal and gestural portraits where the emphasis is on accurate
delineation and the capturing of visual detail:

Mercury: Oh, for some excellent painter, to have ta'en the copy of all these faces! (II.iii.62)

Cupid: Stay, and see the ladies now, they'll come presently. I'll help to paint them.

Mercury: What! Lay colour upon colour? That affords but an ill blazon. (II.iii.139–42)

The question posed in this last line is clearly whether the satirical portrait ('That was pretty and sharply noted, Cupid' (II.iv.17)) risks compounding the fixation upon image, surface and gestural style which it aims to expose. Can the contagiousness of *cosmesis* be remedied by a species of painting? If 'it is with your young grammatical courtier, as with your neophyte player' (III.i.2–3), is dramatic art the medium in which to counter the arts of courtship?

*   *   *

What Mercury, Crites and Cupid expose to the eyes of the audience is, as I have already indicated, a courtly society in which being and social exchange are prefabricated from a repertoire of commonplace formulas:

Hedon: ... sirrah, I have devised one or two of the prettiest oaths, this morning in my bed, as ever thou heard'st, to protest withal in the presence.

Anaides: Pray thee, let's hear them.

Hedon: Soft, thou'lt use 'em afore me.

Anaides: No, damn me then, I have more oaths than I know how to utter, by this air. (II.ii.10–16)

This retailing of formulas leads to the fear of plagiarism which Hedon expresses, or, given the hectic rhythm of Courtly fashion, of the formula's instantaneous obsolescence:

Philautia: ... What! Have you changed your head-tire?

Phantaste: Yes, faith, the other was so near the common .... I cannot abide anything that savours the poor overworn cut, that has any kindred with it; I must have variety, I: this mixing in fashion I hate it worse than to burn juniper in my chamber ...

Philautia: And yet we cannot have a new peculiar court-tire but

these retainers will have it; these suburb-Sunday-
waiters; these courtiers for high days . . .
Phantaste: Oh, aye, they do most pitifully imitate . . . .
(II.iv.57–71)

The competition for status and precedence is founded in imitation,
but it is the compulsion to imitate which renders the signs of status
instantly redundant. As a result, social being and interaction take on
the restlessness and insatiability which, as I have shown elsewhere,
characterise the culture of vanity. If the Court distinguishes itself by
its mastery of a rhetoric of verbal and visual forms, then that rhetoric
is inherently vulnerable to reproduction and dissemination, so that to
preserve its distinction the Court is obliged to enter upon a perpetual
generation of new signs of distinction and exclusivity.[39] It is in this
constantly recuperated novelty that the play locates the inauthenticity
of the Court and the groundlessness or merely self-constituted nature
of its authority. The Court then epitomises the self-constituting and
proliferating order of worldliness whose patron is Narcissus; Crites
sums up the indictment by visualising a Court which has become its
own dramatic representation:

> . . . I have seen, most honoured Arete,
> The strangest pageant, fashioned like a
> court . . .
>
> There stands a neophyte glazing of his face,
> Pruning his clothes, perfuming of his hair,
> Against his idol enters; and repeats
> Like an unperfect prologue, at third music,
> His part of speeches and confederate jests,
> In passion to himself. Another swears
> His scene of courtship over . . . .
> Then walks off melancholic, and stands
> wreathed,
> As he were pinned up to the arras, thus . . . .
> A fourth, he only comes in for a mute:
> Divides the act with a dumb show, and
> exit. (III.iv.3–4; 55–72)

Enclosed within the reflex of a narcissistic self- and mutual scrutiny,
the sharpest revenge which the courtiers can devise against their chief
critic is to refuse him visual recognition:

Anaides:	This hath discountenanced our scholaris most richly.
Hedon:	Out of all emphasis. The monsieur sees we regard him not.
Amorphus:	Hold on: make it known how bitter a thing it is not to be looked on in court. (V.iv.64–7)

However, the force of Crites' stoical self-containment lies precisely in his refusal of the reiterative and reflective principles which animate the courtiers, his indifference to the rhetoric of face and apparel:

> *Hedon*: . . . By this heaven, I wonder at nothing more than our gentlemen ushers, that will suffer a piece of serge or perpetuana [i.e. Crites] to come into the presence: methinks they should, out of their experience, better distinguish the silken dispositions of courtiers than to let such terrible coarse rags mix with us . . . . (III.ii.25–30)

As the terms of this counter-critique imply, the opposed subjectivities of Crites and the courtier also entail opposed accounts of the relationship between authority and presence. Hedon's hierarchy of apparel parodies a metaphysics of presence, articulating identity and difference, incorporation and exclusion around the central organising presence of the monarch. What is actually orchestrated here is of course the interaction between a rhetoric of surfaces and the conditions of mundane power – as we have seen, the authority of the Court in *Cynthia's Revels* is self-constituting and involves a constant displacement or evacuation of presence. What Crites represents is a grounding of subjectivity not in its own self-constituted forms – not, that is, in the self-confirming reflexivity of the Narcissist – but in a paradoxical abandonment of the self, a submission to external authority. As Arete tells Cynthia:

> Thy favour's gain is his ambition's most,
> And labour's best: who, humble in his height,
> Stands fixed silent in thy glorious sight . . . .

Cynthia:	Our eye doth read thee, now enstyled our Crites;

> Whom learning, virtue, and our favour last,
> Exempteth from the gloomy multitude.
> 'With common eye the supreme should not see.'
> Henceforth be ours, the more thyself to be.

Crites:　Heaven's purest light, whose orb may be eclipsed,
　　　　　But not thy praise, divinest Cynthia,
　　　　　How much too narrow for so high a grace
　　　　　Thine, save therein, the most unworthy Crites
　　　　　Doth find himself! (V.viii.26–8; 31–40)

The refusal of worldly visibility which is Crites' defence against the
culture of vanity is here rewarded by his recognition within a new
regime of vision. By remaining obscure, Crites has prepared a 'fixing'
of subjectivity in the light of a vision which excludes and exceeds that
of the 'gloomy multitude'. It is this authoritative vision which reads
Crites in his truth, a reading which follows upon the reading of his
work, in the masque which has just been performed. The occluded
truth of the subject is articulated in the obscure forms of the masque,
and the recognition of both in Cynthia's penetrating reading confirms
her as the reference-point and guarantor of the discourse of truth. The
circularity of this process, by which the writer and his work elicit
the authority which confirms them, which is in turn confirmed by
their representation of it, is repeated in the relationship of authority
to subjectivity. The posture of submission becomes the ground of
the writer/subject's self-immediacy, thus releasing the 'powers' by
which the subject creates the work in which the liberating force of
the authority to which he submits is celebrated.

　　The evacuation of the forms of subjectivity and courtly authority by
the courtiers is answered by a process which begins with a movement
beyond empirical vision into a new dimension of the visible; the
dramatic occasion for this shifting of perspectives is the performance
of the masque or revels. The necessity for a redefinition of looking if
the Narcissistic regime of courtliness is to be opposed is articulated
in Crites' earlier analysis of courtly vice:

Tut, [Vice] is stale, rank, foul, and were it not
That those that woo her greet her with locked eyes,
In spite of all the impostures, paintings, drugs,
Which her bawd custom daubs her cheeks withal,
She would betray her loathed and leprous face,
And fright the enamoured dotards from themselves:
But such is the perverseness of our nature
That if we once but fancy levity,
How antic and ridiculous so e'er
It suit with us, yet will our muffled thought

Choose rather not to see it than avoid it:
And if we can but banish our own sense,
We act our mimic tricks with that free licence,
That lust, that pleasure, that security
As if we practised in a pasteboard case,
And no one saw the motion but the
motion. (I.v.46–61)

Addiction to vice is here the result of a fixated looking, an
enthralment by the painted features of a whore. At the same
time, however, the gazers after vice are characterised as blinded:
their 'locked eyes' are both fixed upon the object and shut up, as
Crites' proposal that what they need is to *really see* the face of vice
implies. If the truth of Vice's foulness would declare itself visually in
this way, he implies, the viewers would be shocked into their true
selves, and the acting out of 'mimic tricks' in the puppet-theatre of
Narcissism would be halted: 'As if we practised in a pasteboard case/
And no one saw the motion but the motion'. Again, the restoration
of truth is located by Crites in an intensification or supplementation
of a restricted looking.

There is a contradiction in this account of the relation between
vice and vision. What is characterised as a suppression of vision is
in fact a dubiety within vision: Crites proposes that Vice be defeated
by her servants opening their eyes, but his syntax obscures the fact
that their eyes have been open from the beginning. Similarly, the
metaphor of the puppet-play involves naming the deficiency of the
puppet as blindness, but then redefining it as the illusion that only
the puppets can see. Consequently the possibility of authentic vision is
projected beyond the frame of the stage to the audience of this play of
courtly puppets, which is able to see the failure of the puppet's vision.
What is implied in both these cases is some second order of the look
which illuminates the blindness of a first-order empirical vision.

As we have seen, the Platonic dialectic of vision in the masque
supplies just such a regime of the look, but at this early point in
the play, the context for these issues is still that of the empiricising
comedy with its reliance on 'hitting off' the visual and charactero-
logical lineaments of vice. As long as it remains within this regime
of satirical mimesis, with its appeal to recognition as the means
of placing and undoing the forms of vice, the play is kept from
any progression into that other dimension in which visual forms

evaporate before the ideal reality which they disclose. Consequently the resolution of the contradictory binding of blindness and sight which is offered at this early stage of the play is one which remains within the dimension of empirical vision. The second order of the look at this stage, then, is to be found in the audience's observation of the play; it is through that doubling of the look, by which the audience looks knowingly at characters looking blindly, that the self-subversion of vision is to be overcome without exceeding the regime of empirical representations.[40]

So, immediately after this speech of Crites', Mercury and Cupid prepare to expose the folly of the Court by acting it out:

> . . . since we are turned cracks, let's study to be like cracks; practise their language and behaviours, and not with a dead imitation . . . . (II.i.3–5)

It is this possibility of a live imitation, which will oppose the moribund order of Courtly imitation, that we have seen coming under question in the exchange about 'painting'. The idea that acting can counter the performative inauthenticity of the Court by exposing the truth is immediately challenged by the ambiguous impact of Amorphus' performance of the faces, which Cupid and Mercury observe. As we have seen at the beginning of the play, Amorphus asserts the usefulness of acting as a technology of insincerity, a politic undoing of propriety and truth, and this fact is exposed in the performance of an actor who appeals to the audience's pleasure in imitation. The nature of that pleasure is inflected by the presence of Mercury and Cupid as an avowedly critical audience within the representation, so that the possibility of a disillusioned looking is presented to the gaze of the audience. This possibility would seem to be reinforced by the fact that Mercury and Cupid appear as page-boys, but are known by the audience to be in fact gods; a disguising which asserts the presence of a dimension beneath appearances, and offers the prospect of a restoration of truth and identity in a dimension of revealed divinity. It could be argued that this possibility is sufficient to ground the play of representations and looks in the scene and to assure the eventual emergence of a perspective in which truth will be disclosed beyond the ambiguities of earthly vision. It seems to me, however, that the play does not proceed with any confidence that its audience will enter into such a resolution: an insecurity which can be ascribed to the fact that if the page-boys are known to be played by gods, the audience can also see that the gods are played by boy actors whose imitative virtuosity is well known to be the target of godly critics of the theatre.

In other words, the critique of imitation through dramatic mimesis is prevented from resting itself upon some ground beyond the play of imitation, returning instead to a constantly intensified complexity of the imitative.[41] So, in the long 'duel' between Amorphus and the disguised Mercury, the critical representation of bad courtship risks becoming indistinguishable from its target:

> *Amorphus*: I say you are fair, lady, let your choice be as fit as you are fair.
> *Mercury*: I say ladies do never believe they are fair until some fool begins to dote upon'em.
> *Philautia*: You play too rough, gentlemen.
>
> . . . . .
>
> *Mercury*: Buzz . . . How heartily they applaud this, Crites!
> *Crites*: You suffer'em too long.
> *Mercury*: I'll take off their edge instantly. (V.iv.413–26)

The problem, then, is that the inauthentic Court is too insistently visible, its embossed surfaces being reinscribed rather than abolished by the play's critique.

This egregious visibility of the inauthentic has its counterpart in the persistent invisibility of the 'authentic' Court. The play repeatedly asserts the presence of those in whose name judgement is passed on the bad courtiers, but at no point are they actually *represented*:

> *Crites*: . . . It is a crown to me
> That the best judgements can report me
> wronged . . .
> What can his censure hurt whom the world
> Hath censured vile before me? If good Chrestus,
> Euthus, or Phronimus, had spoke the words,
> They would have moved me . . . (III.i.9–20)

Throughout the play Crites invokes the presence of this other Court of 'the best judgements', but from a position of isolation: he is the only verse speaker and soliloquiser in a society of contagious prose posturings. His only verse dialogue is with Mercury when the latter has resumed his divine status; but it is precisely that shift to another level of reality – a metaphysical level which is held in reserve through most of the play – which raises the question of how the society of the good is to be incarnated at the same level of reality and representation as the one inhabited by the delinquent courtiers:

Crites: . . . though Mercury can warrant out
           His undertakings, and make all things good,
           Out of the powers of his divinity,
           The offence will be returned with weight on me,
           That am a creature so despised and poor;
           When the whole Court shall take itself abused
           By our ironical confederacy.
Mercury: You are deceived. The better race in
           Court
           That have the true nobility, called virtue,
           Will apprehend it as a grateful right
           Done to their separate merit . . .
Crites: Well, since my leader on is Mercury,
           I shall not fear to follow. If I fall,
           My proper virtue shall be my relief,
           That followed such a cause, and such a chief.
                                         (V.i.23–43)

Crites here asserts the difficulty of distinguishing between the forms of authentic and delinquent courtship: the isolation which he fears is in relation to the *whole* Court. Mercury maintains the distinction which separates out 'the better race in Court', but the difficulty of locating this 'true nobility' returns in Crites apprehension that his failure would be relieved only by his 'proper [i.e. his own] virtue'. The alliance with Mercury (the patron of Humanistic and esoteric learning, as well as the arts of writing) has, in other words, no social articulation within the world of the actually visible Court. True nobility, it seems, is held in abeyance, in a 'space' outside the terms of representation which the play initially sets for itself.

The play is suspended, then, between an empirical order of representation which risks the reiteration of inauthenticity and the absence of a dramatic mode for the representation of ideality. The play's initial attempt to resolve this problem is by removing itself from the circuits of reiteration and imitation through an act of self-origination. It is that function that the play's metadramatic 'frame' of Prologue and Induction are intended to fulfil.

The reiterative forms of literary imitation which the play seeks to

insulate itself from are at the root of delinquent courtship. Asotus'
initiation into the arts of courtly love, for example, consists of a
bricolage of quotations from fashionable romances and familiar plays
such as Kyd's *Spanish Tragedy*:

> *Asotus*:   Well, sir, I'll enter again: her title shall be, 'My dear
>   Lindabrides'.
> *Amorphus*: Lindabrides?
> *Asotus*:   Aye, sir, the Emperor Alicandro's daughter . . . in *The
>   Knight of the Sun* . . .
> *Amorphus*: Oh, you betray your reading.
> *Asotus*:   Nay, sir, I have read history, I am a little humanitian.
>   (III.v.24–31)

Amorphus' praise of this parroting aligns the principles of *scripting*
with those of superfluous apparel:

> Oh, that piece was excellent! If you could pick out more of these
> play-particles, and as occasion shall salute you, embroider or
> damask your discourse with them, persuade your soul it would
> most judiciously commend you. (III.v.104–8)

The discourse on extravagant apparel which we considered earlier
characterises the excess of clothing as one instance of the revolt of
matter over spirit, of the artificial and the supplementary against the
natural and the essential. The piecing of discourse together from
already constituted textual elements is portrayed here in similar
terms, because it replaces the proper government of the production
of discourse by the mind, with determination by the pre-text. A process
which is properly a government of matter - *res* – by spirit becomes an
ungoverned self-reproduction of matter.

It is for this reason that Jonson's play declares itself as un-
contaminatedly original:

> In this alone, his Muse her sweetness hath,
> She shuns the print of any beaten path.
>   (Prologue, 9–11)

Jonson, the Prologue asserts, is untouched by the 'disease' that is
described by one of the Induction's children in the guise of a
gentleman critic:

> It is in the general behalf of this fair society here that I am
> to speak . . . they could wish your poets would leave to be

promoters of other men's jests, and to waylay all the stale
apothegms or old books they can hear of (in print, or otherwise)
to farce their scenes withal. That they would not so penuriously
glean wit from every laundress or hackney-man, or derive their
best grace, with servile imitation, from common stages, or
observation of the company they converse with; as if their
invention lived wholly upon another man's trencher. (Induction,
158–68)

In a paradoxical formulation which we have encountered before,[42] the
insubordinate materiality of this process is figured as vaporous; the
solidity of reality being lodged in another, metaphysical dimension:

Oh . . . they say the *umbrae* or ghosts of some three or four
plays, departed a dozen years since, have been seen walking
on the stage here: take heed, boy, if your house be haunted
with such hobgoblins, 'twill fright away all your spectators
quickly. (Induction, 177–81)

Reiteration is a generation of shadows; in the ghostliness of the
reiterated text there is a return of the vocabulary (*'umbrae'*) which
is associated with the fruitlessness of Narcissus.[43] In this way the
possibility is opened up that the play itself may be criticised as
another instance of that Narcissistic redundancy of the sign which
is its own central target.

It is in order to reinforce the claim to originality that the play
opens with a particularly complex example of the metadramatic
framing that Jonson uses in other works. By absorbing its immediate
extra-dramatic context into its own order of representation, the play
aims to ensure that its action issues not from a contaminating
intertextuality, but from a space which is already, and exclusively,
ordered by its own writing. As well as attempting to insulate the
play from the disseminating force of literary influence, the Induction
is also intended to curtail in advance the associated dangers of
misinterpretation and unilluminated reading. By *showing* the risks
of inept reading the Induction aims to educate the responses of the
play's audience: this is an instance of that remedial doubling of the
look which, as we have seen, is proposed in Crites' discourse on Vice
and the image.

So, the Induction represents a critic of the drama whose reading
is relentlessly reductive and fixated upon its material 'body':

> By this light, I wonder that any man is so mad to come to see
> these rascally tits play here . . . not the fifth part of a good face
> amongst them all – and then their music is abominable . . . and
> their ditties – most lamentable things . . . By this vapour, and
> 'twere not for tobacco – I think – the very stench of 'em would
> poison me . . . . (Induction, 104–11)

The fixation of reading upon the drama's material surfaces submits
it to the logic of Narcissism which it exists to refute. Similarly, the
next critic judges the play in terms of the rhetoric of apparel:

> As some one civit-wit among you that knows no other learning
> than the price of satins and velvets; nor other perfection that
> the wearing of a neat suit; and yet will censure as desperately
> as the most professed critic in the house: presuming his clothes
> should bear him out in't. (Induction, 184–8)

Through critical representations of its critics, the Induction attempts
to perform a benign doubling which, far from furthering the
generation of redundant imitations, will arrest it by presenting
an image of reiteration at work which is placed and enfolded by
the play's own critical perspective.

However, if the play seeks to exert this control over the forces
of imitation by enclosing its own context, the figure of the gallant
critic ensconced 'in state on the stage' (Induction, 131) represents
a disabling encroachment of the context into the play. This member
of the audience, who displays from his seat on the stage the latest
fashions and accomplishments, is already constituted within the relays
of courtly representation which the play would guard him from. In
this image of an extra-literary actuality which is already textualised
and imitative, the play confronts the redundancy of its educational
and discriminating intentions. Rather than functioning as a cordon
sanitaire, the Induction is an ambiguous space where the forces
of monological regulation meet and cross with those of imitative
contagion, so that finally it is difficult to distinguish between them.

The failure of the play's frame to enforce the required discriminations means that the task has to be taken up by the play's
double structure. This structural division of the drama is anticipated
in the Prologue's opening up of a division between two possible modes
in which the play may be apprehended:

> If gracious silence, sweet attention,

Quick sight, and quicker apprehension,
(The light of judgement's throne) shine
anywhere;
Our doubtful author hopes this is their sphere.
And therefore opens he himself to those;
To other weaker beams his labours close:
As loth to prostitute their virgin strain
To every vulgar and adulterate brain . . .
Nor hunts [his Muse] after popular applause,
Or foamy praise that drops from common jaws,
The garland that she wears, their hands must
twine
Who can both censure, understand, define
What merit is: then cast those piercing rays,
Round as a crown, instead of honoured bays,
About his poesy; which, he knows, affords
Words above action, matter above words.
　　　　　　　　(Prologue, 1–8,13–20)

What is prepared here is the movement of exclusion by which the masque restricts its audience to those who are already disposed to accept that there is another dimension beneath its material surface. The Prologue asserts that the play in its truth will be validated and indeed realised through its recognition by those who already perceive the nature of 'merit'. It is in the ideal sphere of understanding that the play has its true existence. By granting custody of the play's 'truth' to those who are already in the know, the Prologue prepares a decisive abdication of the educational intentions which are written into the prose comedy element of the play. Let the corporeally-fixated 'vulgar' consume the body of the drama, so releasing its soul or 'inventive part' into its proper sphere; that occupied by the audience of 'true judges'.

This act of discrimination is enforced in structural terms by the location of the masquing or revels at the end of the play. As a result the prose comedy and its compromised mode of representation are defined retrospectively as elements of an antimasque. The climax of illumination, in which the authentic Court becomes visible, involves then a dismissal not only of the forms of inauthentic courtliness, but also of the mimetic form which has failed to stage decisively the difference between the proper and the imitative. The comedy has worked by confirming the audience in a recognition of the delinquent forms of courtliness: the pleasure which it offers to the audience is that of an acknowledgement, a recognition, that the Court is in truth like this. The treacherous implication that the Court is indeed what it appears to be renders the comedy radically incompatible with any discourse – like that of the masque – which insists that the Court is precisely other than its appearance.

In the transition to the masque, the nature of the play's theatricality is accordingly redefined, and in the same movement the play turns itself towards a radically different audience to that represented in the Induction:

> *Crites*: Phoebus Apollo: If with ancient rites
> And due devotion I have ever hung
> Elaborate paeans on thy golden shrine,
> Or sung thy triumphs in a lofty strain,
> Fit for a theatre of gods to hear . . .
> Now thrive invention in this glorious court,
> That not of bounty but of right,
> Cynthia may grace, and give it life by sight.
> (V.v.59–72)

The dedication to the sun-god announces the 'subliming' of the play from its public corporeality into a mode dominated by invention: the 'incorporeal part' of the theatre's double nature. The shift into a new regime of illumination is accompanied by a turning towards a new class of spectator – a 'theatre of gods'. It will be their – and specifically Cynthia's – sight which vivifies the play by understanding it; an understanding which will, it is implied, transcend the problematic play of imitations which has constituted the drama so far.

The movement of discrimination and exclusion which begins here continues in the hymn which opens the next scene. This is sung by a group of characters who 'exist' on a radically different plane of representation to the comedic order of recognition which addresses the public audience:

> Enter Hesperus, Cynthia, Arete, Time, Phronesis, Thauma.
> (V.vi. s.d.)

The relationship between these figures and what they represent is crucially distinct from the relation of recognition which grounds the play's earlier satirical discourse. There the representation of the courtiers elicited a reference on the part of the audience from the stage images to a publicly circulating 'knowledge' or set of representations of the Court and courtliness which allowed the recognition of courtly mannerisms to function. Here the 'realisation' of the figures demands a reference to a restricted body of knowledge; a departure into erudition which restricts the play's address to that part of the audience which is already initiated into specialised mythological and philosophical discourses. It is this restriction which the play figures as a rarefaction of light:

> Hesperus entreate thy light,
> Goddess, excellently bright.
> Earth, let not thy envious shade,
> Dare itself to interpose;
> Cynthia's shining orb was made
> Heaven to clear, when day did close.
>   (V.vi.5–10)

The obstructive materiality of earth is banished, and with it that worldly audience whose consumption of the drama is restricted to its material 'body'.

The masque now begins with the procession of Perfection's maids. They are introduced by Cupid, who now appears as Anteros. The redefinition of the God of Love in terms of a recondite philosophical discourse epitomises the strategy of the masque; the figure of playful eroticism who figures in the 'popular' comedy is discarded, and with him that part of the audience which is unfamiliar with Neoplatonic theories of love.

The maids bear with them an orb in which is visible 'Whatsoever the world hath excellent, howsoever remote and various' (V.vii.17). In offering this to the perusal of Cynthia's 'irradiate judgement' (l.18) they enact within the stage picture that purification of vision which will allow the forms of Goodness to be perceived within the indiscriminate, obscuring forms of worldliness. The maids themselves embody this appeal to a restricted order of vision by disclosing their own significance through the coded visual signs of their apparel, a hieroglyphic order of dress which opposes the elaborated clothing of the courtiers:

> Themselves, to appear more plainly, because they know nothing more odious than false pretexts, have chosen to express their several qualities thus, in several colours. (V.vii.19–22)

This pictographic display is contemptuous of *pretexts* because it aims to move beyond the contaminated order of textuality and into a domain of 'plain' and self-declarative meaning. This differentiation of levels within signification is then followed by a passage in which the false forms of courtship are discriminated from their authentic counterparts. The central example is that in which Narcissism is separated out from its virtuous antithesis, 'this handmaid of reason, allowable self-love' (V.vii.25).

The problem of discrimination which the play has defined precisely in terms of a public *extroversion* of courtliness – the definition of authentic courtliness as against its disseminated, reiterated, publicly circulated forms – is 'solved' here behind the closed doors of the masque's 'mysteries' and hieroglyphic signs. Those who will appreciate the subtle distinctions between the forms of virtue and of vanity are those whose perceptions are already organised by the recondite discourses of virtuous knowledge.

However, *Cynthia's Revels* is a play which necessarily takes place (at least in its initial performances) in the public theatre, because its origin is precisely in the relationship between a 'closed' courtliness and the public domain. Because of this unavoidably double address, the drama is not able at this late stage to take its departure into obscurity to its logical conclusion. The solution of the play's self-disabling problem of discrimination may demand the abolition of the compromising significations of the *pretext* – the (antimasque) text which precedes the revels, the text which intrudes itself before the self-declarations of meaning – but it is precisely a series of pretexts which Cupid/Anteros now produces in the form of the elucidatory commentary on the figures of the masque which he speaks for the benefit of the audience.

With this, even as it retreats into the obscurity of true courtliness and addresses itself to an audience already knowledgeable in courtly mysteries, the play hesitates – and continues to *explain*. What it reveals in this final equivocation – despite itself – is the fundamental confusion of the forms of true and false courtliness which the masque is designed to cover up with its obscure discriminations. For if the play is finally unable to disavow its educational, or explanatory, intentions, it is because it cannot discard its prior representation of the Court as an arena of vanity and still remain a play, a drama which addresses an audience beyond the closed circuits of courtly self-legitimation. That prior representation of the Court implies that the education in true courtliness must operate *within* the Court before it can take effect (be 'mirrored') among the public audience which consumes the courtly image. The masque's attempt to enforce a difference between the Court and a contaminated exterior masks the insistence of that difference as a self-division within courtliness, and the fact of the Court's fixation upon its own external forms of manner, apparel, style and display.

So the declaration of the difference between the masque personages and the delinquent courtiers is not the play's final disclosure. This arrives when the masque personifications are revealed as veiling not the abstract forms of ideal courtliness, but Amorphus and his crew, who have assumed the lineaments of authenticity as a politic disguise. It appears from this revelation that the legitimation of the Court by an appeal to another ideal dimension beyond appearances may be merely the last subterfuge of the politic and inauthentic, a final refinement of devious representation.

Once discovered, the masked delinquents are banished to drink of the 'well of knowledge, Helicon' (V.vii.153): precisely the educational injunction which the masque attempts to turn away from the Court on to those excluded from courtly *gnosis*. With this, the stage is evacuated of any representation of the Court, whether true, false or equivocal. Those who are left in view are the isolated Crites and his associate Arete – representatives not of any Court, but of a critical discourse *on* courtliness – and Cynthia, a goddess now clearly bereft of earthly representatives, a Queen without a Court.

Cynthia's last attempt to reconstitute authentic courtliness is through an act of disinterested patronage. She rewards as her one true courtier the critic who has revealed that the hidden truth of courtliness is that the Court is constitutionally false:

> We do approve thy censure, beloved Crites . . .
> And for this service of discovery
> Performed by thee, in honour of our name,
> We vow to guerdon it with such due grace,
> As shall become our bounty, and thy place.
> 'Princes that would their people should do well
> Must at themselves begin, as at the head;
> For men, by their example, pattern out
> Their imitation, and regard of laws:
> A virtuous court a world to virtue draws.'
>
> (V.xi.161–73)

This declaration of the grounding of courtly authority and of social order in the *image* of courtliness is made precisely at the point where all representations of the Court have had to be abolished. If, as Cynthia states, the law which founds society is articulated through imitation, it is also imitation whose disseminating and deconstituting force undoes the difference between legality and the forms of delinquency. At the play's end, when the revealed lineaments of Divine authority are intended to make their appearance, staged in a 'theatre of gods', there remains to be seen, instead, only a 'courting of puppets'.[44]

Afterword

When Thomas Harman opens his treatise on vagrancy by praising the Countess of Shrewsbury's 'vigilant and merciful eye', he identifies an aristocratic regime of the gaze which is framed and secured by the natural order of Commonwealth.[1] It is a gaze, therefore, which establishes a clear and metaphysically grounded order of differentiation within the social field which it surveys: between the mastered and the vagrant, the dutiful and the delinquent, the authorised and the illegitimate, the true and the false, authority and its others.

Jan. 2, 1619: [The king] has made seventeen knights, men of no note.[2]

The discourse on vagrancy identifies a counter-order of social being which is originated by the vagrant's undoing of differentiation, by his assumption of the signifiers of states and conditions not 'properly' his own. This mimetic delinquency opens a social field of theatricality where the signification of degree is unfixed and social identity becomes metamorphic and exchangeable.

June 4, 1617: So many knights are made that there is scarce a Yorkshire esquire left to uphold the race, and the order has descended even to the Earl of Montgomery's barber and the husband of the Queen's laundress.

The semiotic vagrancy initiated by the cony-catcher or counterfeit crank is met by the judicial theatre of the pillory, procession and banner, which reasserts the power of authority to reveal and fix the 'truth' of identity and degree; a reassertion too of the security of that regime of knowledge and vision within which truth is captured and the sign secured.

May 13, 1605 . . . : Arguments in favour of the King's absolute right to confer knighthood on whomsoever he pleases, irrespective of rank, with examples from history, English and foreign, and confutations of the arguments of 'Advocate' or Censurer on the other side, dated March 1, 1605.

The theatrical genre which reproduces the security of the aristocratic gaze which Harman's eulogy celebrates is the Jonsonian masque. Here the loving but severe gaze of the monarch opens a regime of vision within which, once again, a natural security of differentiation – between the courtly and the uncourtly, the gracious and the grotesque, masque and antimasque – reigns. The masque secures the identification of the Court with what I have referred to, in my discussion of Gascoigne, as the *ideal* economy of natural reciprocations, while in the same gesture differentiating itself from the sphere of degraded *mundane* transactions.

Wm. Bruce to Queen Anne, 1603 (?): Prays her interest with the King that he may have the profits of making four knights or two Serjeants-at-Law.

The masque secures the metaphysical endorsement of courtly authority by discarding and negating the 'fallen' world of secular worldliness, in the jettisoned grotesque and superogatory forms of antimasque 'reality'. A crucial complement to that action is the set of strategies by which the material magnificence of the masque itself – its sensually palpable 'body' – is rendered subordinate and transparent to the radiance of the 'idea' which it discloses. In this light, the exemplary Jonsonian masque is *Love Restored* in which, as we have seen, the god of money is thwarted in his attempt to impersonate Cupid in his role as the binding spirit of the courtly community. The unmasking and ejection of Plutus is a triumph over the powers of monetary affiliation and false-seeming which, we have already seen, come together elsewhere in the figure of the usurer. Plutus's defeat is accompanied by a purging of competition from the Court, so that the scramble for material gain and status which characterised his false 'reign' is replaced by a spontaneous cohesion and harmony which issues from the ideal order incarnated by the King.

Nov. 11, 1613: The King has made six new knights, though he has of late been sparing of the dignity, wishing to raise the price to 500 l.

Cynthia's Revels confronts the self-confirming and idealising gaze of the Court with a scrutiny from outside, from that discarded exteriority in which the secular processes of monetary destabilisation and social imitation are at work, a world of which the Jonsonian comedy itself – as a commodity within the marketplace of the public theatre – is both product and critique. In doing so, *Cynthia's Revels* announces the infiltration of the precincts of courtly ideality by the commercial logic of the usurer and the semiotic promiscuity of the vagrant. The agent of 'contamination' is identified as the courtship manual, which, with its commercial re-presentation of courtliness, its fuelling of a contagious imitative self-fashioning of 'courtiers', renders the Ideal, original or proper form of the courtly impossible to distinguish.

Jan. 29, 1606: The King to the Lord Chancellor. To enforce the payment of such fees and duties as are appointed by Letters Patent to be paid to certain officers and servants, by parties receiving the honour of knighthood.

The disappearance of any metaphysical ground of courtly authority in the endless relays of narcissistic reflection/imitation may initially be ascribed to the courtship manual's breaching of the membrane which seals off the Court from a 'fallen' secular exteriority, but as the play progresses this seems an increasingly untenable attempt to maintain the founding differentiation of an entire system of power and knowledge. The courtly order exposed by the end of the play is one in which the existence of an ideal Court beyond the play of imitation may still be asserted, but cannot be represented; one where the banishment of the inauthentic courtier leaves the courtly stage empty.

It is onto this stage that one imagines a final figure making an entrance; that of the 'right mineral man' and newly minted knight, Sir Bevis Bulmer;[3] projector and self-styled 'hasserd adventurer', a 'gamester playing at dice' who piously submits himself and his enterprises to Providence, true courtier and – the distinction is difficult to draw in this arena of prefabricated courtly subjects – Jonsonian fiction:

In the first year of [James's] reign, Bulmer had an audience with the King, in which a 'plott' was hatched for providing capital for a search for gold in Scotland ... The plan was to secure a contribution of £300 sterling from each of 24 gentlemen, who should each be worth

£10,000, or £500 a year, and in return each should be knighted, and be known forever as the 'Knight of the Golden Mynes or the Golden Knight'.

The Earl of Salisbury, however, managed to cross the plan, and only one knight was made . . . . The King probably paid the expenses of the abortive company-promoting. Bulmer himself took the disappointment philosophically: 'Well, [said he,] God giveth, and God taketh away; blessed be the name of the Lord from this time forth for evermore . . . .

Notes

Introduction

1. Barthes (1973), p. 155; St Jerome, cited in Gascoigne (1907/1910), Vol. II, p. 409.
2. All quotations are from Salgado (1972). The question of the factual status of the vagabond pamphlets, and so of the vagrancy 'problem' itself, is not pertinent to my own discussion, which concerns the imaginative power of the vagrant within a certain predominating ideological and signifying framework. That vagrant is both real and imaginary. For the historical evidence, see Beier (1985).
3. Cited in *Shakespeare's England* (1916), p. 240.
4. 'A letter from the Lord Mayor and Aldermen to the Privy Council', 28 July 1597; cited in Dover Wilson (1944), pp. 231–2.
5. Ibid., p. 230.
6. Cited in Edwards (1979), p. 20.
7. Ibid., pp. 20–1.
8. Ibid., p. 21.
9. Ibid., p. 21.
10. On the perceived relationship between the social mobility of actors off stage and their representation of their social superiors on stage, see Stallybrass (1987), p. 126.
11. Ibid., p. 23. In a period of rapid social mobility and of a fixed, complex codification of the signs of status, there is a conservative fear that those signs are too readily reproduced and appropriated; an encroachment of the powers of performance over those of hierarchical being:

    > . . . who can live idly and without manuall labour, and will beare the port, charge and countenance of a gentleman, he shall be called master . . . and shall be taken for a gentleman. (Sir Thomas Smith, *De Republica Anglorum* (1583), cited in Montrose (1983), p. 429)

    The instability of performative identity (and we might note from Smith's fulminations that the vagrant is already well on the way to a convincing imitation of gentlemanliness, being another who 'live[s] idly and without manuall labour') is a theme of many different sixteenth-century discourses of social analysis and complaint, some of which will be addressed in the following pages. That material and ideological context encloses and inflects the antitheatrical discourses of the period in historically specific ways, a fact which needs to be stressed in contrast to the trans-historical perspective of Jonas A. Barish's valuable *The Antitheatrical Prejudice* (see Barish, 1981). For the connections between social mobility and the mobility of the actor's identity see also Stallybrass (1987), p. 126.

12. Stephen Greenblatt discusses the printer's role, and Harman's treatise more generally, in 'Invisible Bullets' (Greenblatt, 1985), pp. 37–8.
13. Cited in Jean E. Howard 'Renaissance antitheatricality and the politics of gender and rank in *Much Ado about Nothing*', in Howard and O'Connor (1987), pp. 163–87. This reference, p. 166.
14. Ibid., p. 166.
15. For the importance of this ideology of plainness to the theory, practice and apologetics of literary language, see below, Chapters 3 and 4, particularly pp. 168–78 and 208–13.
16. Harman's work is drawn at this point into the contemporary debate on linguistic imports or 'inkpot' terms. For more on this debate, see Smith (1904), Vol. 1, p. lvi.
17. *Certain Sermons* (1890): Homily XXX 'Of the state of matrimony', pp. 510–24; this reference, p. 510.
18. Compare the paradigm of the inevitable failure of rebellion – derived, as Wyatt himself indicates, from the chronicles – which underlies the address attributed to Sir Thomas Wyatt, from the scaffold, where he stood for his part in the abortive rising of 1554:

> Lo here and se in me the same end which all other commonly had, which haue attempted like enterprice from the begynning. For persue the Chronicles through, and you shall see that neuer rebellion attempted by subiectes against their prince and countrye from the begynning did euer prosper or had better success . . . . For the loue of God all you Gentlemen that be here present, remember and be taught as well by examples past as also by this my present infelicity and most wretched case. (Cited in L. B. Campbell (1938), pp. 49–50).

Chapter 1

1. Cited in Tawney (1926), p. 34.
2. For the ideological and political context of Hooker's work, see Collinson (1967), Cross (1969), Haller (1963) and Lake (1988). I retain the terms Anglican and Puritan here, despite their problematic nature; 'Puritan' for want of a better ('presbyterian' is too narrowly focussed for my purposes), 'Anglican' to stress Hooker's defence of a break with Catholic Universalism, and because the alternative ('conformist') distracts from

the innovativeness of Hooker's position. On terminology, see Collinson (1967), pp. 26–8 and Lake (1988), pp. 7–8. On Hooker's innovativeness, see Lake (1988), pp. 145–230.

3. On Elizabethan historiography, see Campbell (1938) and (1947). For Foxe and the *Actes*, see Haller (1963).

4. Hooker's emphasis is as much on the necessity of 'wearisome labour to know' as on 'the painfulness of knowledge': in this he shows his indebtedness to the epistemology and ethics of Humanist educational theory. For further discussion of the Humanist educational tradition, see below, Chapters 4 and 5, particularly pp. 147–50 and 155–6.

5. See the debate between the fundamentalist preacher and the humanistic civilian in Wilson's *Discourse upon Usury*, which I discuss below, pp. 83–4. Greenblatt (1980) discusses an earlier version of this dispute, played out between the Catholic More and the Protestant Tyndale (pp. 99–102). Tyndale's insistence on the availability to the godly reader of a 'literal sense' of Scripture is, as Greenblatt says, a democratising gesture, which undermines the authority over Scriptural meaning claimed by the Church and defended by More. The point is elaborated by Whigham (1984): '. . . obscurantism is the code of the religious and courtly elites; disruptive literalism is that of the unruly oppressed, ambitious for social and religious mobility' (p. 41). These statements need qualification according to the context of the hermeneutic/epistemological debate: the literalism which is democratic in relation to the Church's institutional regulation of meaning is at the same time deployed fiercely against the literary and theatrical pleasures of the common people; the traditional and consensual model of language is used to legitimate the emergence of a regulated and restricted credit economy (economically, a 'progressive' stance) against the opposition of the Puritan literalists. In the context of Hooker's work, the specific nature of his attack on an 'inspirational' literalism is another means of articulating a *measured* defence of hierarchy and established order.

6. The discourse which articulates that perspective most powerfully, centring on a vision of political chaos which is particularly germane to Hooker's immediate concerns, is the Guicciardinian/Machiavellian one which I will consider in relation to Castiglione's *Book of the Courtier* in Chapter 5.

7. See above, p. 32.

8. *Op.cit.*, Book II, p. 218.

9. Ibid., Book II, p. 239.

10. Ibid., Book I, p. 39.

11. Ibid., Book III, pp. 361ff.

12. For an equivalent metaphysical regulation of the ostentatious significations of *secular* authority, see my discussion of the Household Ordinance of Edward IV in Chapter 2 below, pp. 41–3. See also Baker (1952), pp. 200–2.

13. For the Old Testament prophet's disavowal of any supplementation of the Word in his own discourse, see Murrin (1969), p. 29. Murrin's references are to Deuteronomy 18: 20, Isaiah 6, Jeremiah 1: 4–10, Galatians 1: 11–17. We can compare the Puritan Thomas Wilson supporting his call

for an uncompromising policy against usury by citing the Emperor Leo, who

> fearing to blaunche the wrytynge of god, and for policye to deprave a veritie, folowethe the playne woordes of god, neither adding therto, nor diminyshing any iot thereof, as by the lawes he was commanded. (Wilson, 1925, p. 283)

The refusal to supplement 'the wrytynge of god' is invoked here in a challenge within another political sphere where the policy of state and church were marked by a hesitant and wavering accommodation with the forces of innovation, which in this case are economic. For an extended discussion of usury and its semiotic import, see Chapter 2 below.

14. See Pico della Mirandola's articulation of this position through the figure of Moses, below, p. 168.

Chapter 2

1. Cited in Tawney and Power (1924), Vol. III, p. 98.
2. Gordon Kipling, 'Henry VII and the origins of Tudor patronage', in Lytle and Orgel (1981), pp. 117–64; this reference, p. 119.
3. Ibid., p. 119.
4. Ibid., p. 120.
5. For Augustine's early involvement with the Neoplatonism of Plotinus, and its influence on his later thought, see Armstrong (1967), Callahan (1967) and Chadwick (1986), pp. 1–29, especially pp. 17–25.
6. On the confirmation of the Church's power through the machinery of Thomist realism, see Baker (1952), pp. 145ff.
   On Aquinas, Ockham and Scotus, see Copleston, Vol. II (1950), Chapters 31–40, pp. 302–422; and Vol. III (1953), Chapters 3–4, pp. 43–152; on Cusanus and negative theology, see Wind (1968), pp. 218–35; Cassirer (1963), pp. 7–45 and 46–72; and Copleston, Vol. III (1953), Chapter 15, pp. 231–47.
7. See Todorov (1982), Chapter 1, 'The Birth of Western Semiotics', pp. 15–59.
8. See Curtius (1953), Chapter 16, 'The Book As Symbol', section 7, 'The Book of Nature', pp. 319–26. On allegory and the symbolic media in the Renaissance more generally, see Allen (1970).
9. Kipling, *op.cit.*, pp. 121–62.
10. Cited in Knights (1968), p. 142.
11. Collected in Tawney and Power (1924), Vol. III, pp. 90–114 ('A Treatise concerning the staple . . .'), and 115–29 ('How to reform the realme . . .'). All references are to this edition. As my own argument will shortly suggest, there are significant continuities of style, imagery and ideological preoccupation between the two treatises which suggest they may be from the same pen: Tawney and Power's suggestion is that of Clement Armstrong.
12. See below, pp. 59–63.

13. See Wind (1968), p. 219.
14. Compare Hooker's discussion of the Church as reproducing Christ's mediation between the metaphysical and earthly dimensions, above, p. 56.
15. For the mechanism of seals operated by the Clerks of the Market, see William Harrison, *The Description of England* (1570), [Harrison (1897)], pp. 300ff. For a description of the function of the Norwich Clerk of the Market, see Tawney and Power, *op.cit.*, Vol. I, p. 127.
16. For a general discussion of these issues, see Allen (1970).
17. For the concept of husbandry in sixteenth-century economic theory and polemic, see the discussion in Tawney and Power, *op.cit.*, Vol. III, pp. 90ff.
18. Cited in Tawney (1926), p. 153.
19. A fictional version of this fantasy of a restoration of unmediated personal fealty between subject and monarch can be found in Thomas Deloney's novel *Jack of Newbury* (Deloney, 1961), Chapter 3, pp. 35–50.
20. One of the ironies of this critique is of course that governments of the period are equally adherents of the ideology which anathematises the middleman. For statutes and other measures which articulate this position see Ramsey (1963), p. 153; Knights (1968), pp. 149–50; and Tawney (1926), p. 48.
21. For a discussion of this suspicion in relation to literary writing, see Chapter 3 below.
22. Hunt and Sherman (1972), p. 10.
23. Quoted in Tawney and Power, *op.cit.*, p. 86.
24. See Tawney's introduction to Wilson (1925), pp. 25–58.
25. Tawney and Power, *op.cit.*, Vol. III, pp. 57–8.
26. Ibid., Vol. I, p. 325.
27. Ibid., Vol. I, p. 57.
28. Bacon (1985), 'Of riches', pp. 109–12; this reference, p. 110.
29. For an account of 'Evil May Day' 1517, and the riots against 'Genowayes, Frenchemen and other straungers', see Tawney and Power, *op.cit.*, Vol. III, pp. 82ff.
30. Ibid., Vol. I, pp. 308–10.
31. Great Britain (1786), '1&2 Phil. and Mar.c. 4', pp. 469–70.
32. Ibid., p. 242.
33. Gascoigne (1910), Vol. II, pp. 402–3.
34. Elyot (1967), Vol. 1, p. 276 and p. 283. All references are to this edition.
35. For overviews of this process, see Caspari (1968), Hunter (1967), and the first chapter of Whigham (1984).
36. See Elyot, *op.cit.*, Vol. 1, p. 243.
37. Marginal précis to 'An Acte for the Reformacion of Excesse in Apparaile', 1&2 Philip and Mary, 1554–5.
38. Cited in Tawney and Power, *op.cit.*, Vol. III. pp. 326–7.
39. Great Britain (1786), '1 Henry VIII c. 14', p. 8. See also Baldwin (1926), Stone (1976), Cressy (1976) and Whigham (1984), pp. 155–69.
40. 'The Sermon against Excess of Apparel', cited in Welsby (1970), pp. 59–62.

41. For the developing importance of the broker and money-lender in the growing credit economy of the period, see Tawney's introduction to Wilson, *op.cit.*, pp. 33–41.
42. John Hoskins, 'Sermon Preached at Paul's Cross', in Welsby, *op.cit.*, pp. 99–101; this reference, p. 100.
43. The *Shorter Oxford English Dictionary* derives *economy* from the Greek *oikovoμoς*: the manager of a household (*oikovoμia*), or steward. Della Casa's *Galateo* (1558), cited in Whigham (1984), p. 116, describes the painted woman in a way which, by associating her with the monetarised sexuality of the harlot, places her in strict opposition to the dutiful husbandry of the housewife: the painted woman, like 'any harlot' is 'anxious to hawk her wares and sell them at a good price'.
44. 'The Discourse of Corporations', in Tawney and Power, *op.cit.*, Vol. III, p. 267.
45. *Certain Sermons*, *op.cit.*, p. 131.
46. For attacks on the 'protean' nature of the female play-goer, see Stallybrass (1987), p. 127.
47. See Stallybrass, *ibid.*, pp. 127–8, on woman as both that which is most threatened by theatrical 'metamorphosis', and its exemplar. See also Rose (1984) on cross-dressing as a scandalous troubling of the binary economy of social appearances. The *fatality* of this binary 'logic' is, of course, the tragic subject of *Othello*.
48. Wilson, *op.cit.*, p. 290.
49. See Robertson (1962), pp. 143–4 for the iconology of the mermaid.
50. Fulke Greville (1973), 'A Treatie of Humane Learning', stanza 107.
51. See below, pp. 109–12.
52. See above, pp. 45–7.
53. Welsby, *op.cit.*, p. 110.
54. Thomas Adams, 'The White Devil, or the Hypocrite Uncovered', in Welsby, *op.cit.*, pp. 109–15.
55. Compare the critique of aristocratic entertainment of actors in the second *Parnassus* play, discussed above, pp. 7–9.
56. On sixteenth century attitudes to inflation, see *A Discourse of the Common Weal* [Dewar (1969)], pp. 33–48 and 95–102. See also Ramsey (1965), Chapter 4, 'Prices and Social Change', pp. 113–45.
57. See Dewar (1969). All references are to this edition.
58. Compare the following section on luxury imports with the discussion of the debate about linguistic importations in the Introduction, above, pp. 15–18.
59. Compare Burghley's 'Considerations' of 1559, in Tawney and Power, *op.cit.*, Vol. I, pp. 325–30: '#11 . . . that no merchant . . . bring into the realm caps, pins, points, dice, gilt stirrups, etc . . . . for they are not only false and deceitful wares, *rather serving for the gaze than any good use*, but for such trifles they filch from us the chief and substantial staple wares of the realm' (my emphasis).
    For a discussion of the analogous intoxications of the shop window at a later stage of capitalist development, see Bowlby (1985), pp. 32–4.
60. See Baudrillard (1981), Chapter 2, 'The Ideological Genesis of Needs', pp. 64–9.

61. The conduct book is a crucial participant – both product and producer – in this new situation of social mobility and contestation. For an important discussion of its social and semiotic effects, see Whigham (1984).
62. Cited in Tawney and Power, *op.cit.*, Vol. III, p. 165.
63. Wilson (1925). All references are to this edition.
64. Public Record Office (1978), SPD Eliz.LXXV, p. 54.
65. Cited in Knights (1968), p. 150.
66. Compare Thomas Adams, cited in Welsby, *op.cit.*, p. 114: 'The poet exclaims against this sin – Hinc usura vorax, avidumque, in tempore foenus, etc. – describing in that one line the names and nature of usury, *Foenus quasi foetus*. It is a teeming thing, ever with child pregnant, and multiplying. Money is an unfruitful thing by nature, made only for commutation; it is a preternatural thing it should engender money; this is *monstrosus partus*, a prodigious birth.'
67. Cited in Tawney's introduction to Wilson, *op.cit.*, p. 73.
68. Cited in Fraser (1970), p. 98.
69. Compare Nicholas Sander, *A Briefe Treatise of Usurie* (1568), cited in Robertson (1933), p. 131: 'And for as much as the authoritie of the Church being once called into question, the Scriptures also (whiche were given only to the Churche, and are knowen by their tradition and by her unwritten witnesse) can not keepe their creditte, but are expounded accordinge to everie mans lust and phantasie; I must also be forced to resort unto natural reason, and thereby to show also that usurie is of itself naught and uniust.'
70. See, for example, Wilson, *op.cit.*, p. 99.
71. See above, pp. 37–8.
72. See Wilson, *op.cit.*, p. 98.
73. As the channel through which unauthorised manuscripts find their way illicitly to the stationers, the scrivener (or copier) is often in the same 'dangerous' intermediate position in the processes of *literary* communication. See Miller (1959), p. 141.
74. Cited in Tawney's introduction to Wilson, *op.cit.*, p. 99.
75. Compare the extracts from Elizabethan Parliamentary debates on usury cited in Tawney and Power, *op.cit.*, Vol. II, p. 155 and p. 158.
76. The pragmatic economic pressure for the acceptance of some degree of usurious activity is registered in the 1571 Usury Act, which repealed the measure of 1552, which had prohibited all taking of interest, the later statute allowing an upper limit of 10 per cent. In a similarly pragmatic spirit, the Convocation of 1586 distributed Bullinger's *Decades*, which counselled the consideration of each specific case of usurious lending on its merits.
77. Compare the Puritan position on the immediacy of the Word outlined above, pp. 25–9. See also Murrin (1969) on the absolutism of prophetic discourse, pp. 27–30 and p. 32.
78. Lisa Jardine (1983, p. 163) comments: 'Gambling is symbolic, as almost nothing can be, of the random allocation of wealth and therefore power. For a society pledged to the equivalent of 'value' and social rank, the

acquiring of large sums of money by pure chance at the gaming-tables is the ultimate subversion of order . . . . Female gamblers epitomise the disorder attendant for such a society on the severing of authority from birth, and its association with cash and ready money.' This chapter of Jardine's book – 'Dress Codes, Sumptuary Law and "Natural Order"; – illuminates several of the present chapter's central concerns.

79. *Ovide Moralisé*, cited in Goldin (1967), pp. 64–5. Compare 5&6 Edward VI c. 20, 'Against Usury', on 'divers persons blynded with inordinat love of themselves', cited in Tawney and Power, *op.cit.*, Vol. II, p. 142.
80. Donne, Sermon XIV, cited in Haydn (1946), p. 365.
81. The following section is substantially indebted to the invaluable work of Vinge, *op.cit.*
82. Vinge, *op.cit.*, p. 147.
83. Ibid., p. 36.
84. Ibid., p. 183.
85. Ibid., p. 147.
86. For the scrivener, see above, pp. 81–2; for *Cynthia's Revels*, see below, pp. 178ff.
87. Vinge, *op.cit.*, p. 195.
88. Ibid., p. 148.
89. Ibid., p. 38. For flowers as images of transience and inutility, see Isa. 40:6–7; 1 Pet. 1–24; Job 14:2. For shadows, see 1 Chr. 29:15; Job 8:9 and 14:2; Eccles. 8:13 and 6:12.
90. Ibid., p. 72.
91. Goldin, *op.cit.*, pp. 64–5.
92. Wilson, *op.cit.*, p. 207.
93. The insatiable nature of the usurer's desire returns us to Hooker's vision of chaos as an infinite tracking of unsatisfied desire across its insufficient worldly objects (see above, pp. 30–1). The usurer and the Narcissist are exemplary protagonists of that other, non-metaphysical, unpunctuated and unlegitimated history which Hooker's work implies.
94. Wilson, *op.cit.*, p. 176.

Chapter 3

1. Richard Mulcaster *Positions* (1581), cited in Whigham (1984), p. 15.
2. All references are to Prouty (1966).
3. For a discussion of arguments around the idea of a dissociation of sensibility, see Ricks (1963), Chapter 1, 'The Milton Controversy', pp. 1–21.
4. See Richard Carew, *The Excellencie of the English Tongue* (?1595–6), in Smith (1904), Vol. II, pp. 291 and 293 on imported terms as a necessary reinforcement of the linguistic trading 'stock' of the native language. The idea that language, and literature, are as much media of international competition as is trade is constantly betrayed in the metaphors, as well as the explicit statements, of the period's literary polemic. See also above, pp. 15–18, and Introduction, n. 15.

5. See Matthiessen (1965), especially pp. 25ff. For Elizabethan translation generally, see Wright (1932), Yates (1934), Rosenberg (1955), especially pp. 55–60, and Miller (1959), p. 103.

6. Just as translation is the area where the maximisation of the Commonwealth's resources is most loyally declared, so it is the area where a fear of contamination and dangerous innovation is most pronounced. Ovid and the modern Italians were the most 'dangerous' sources, requiring an array of prophylactic measures to render them safe for consumption by the godly English reader: see Taylor (1982), on the dangers of Englishing Ovid, and the apologetic, allegorising preface written by Golding for his 1586 translation of the *Metamorphoses*; also Rosenberg (1955), pp. 159 and 178. On translation from the Italian, see Yates (1934), especially pp. 36, 50, 53, 117, 136–7; Eliot (1968), especially p. 4. on the 'empoysoning' of 'our English nation with the bookes of Nicholas Machiavell, and Peter Aretine, replenished with all filthinesse and villanie'; and Einstein (1902), particularly p. 113 on Anne Cooke's 1550 translation of Bernadino Ochino's *Sermones*, intended to demonstrate that Italian was not necessarily a godless study.

7. On the Elizabethan national economy and economic policy, see Ramsey (1965), Hill (1979), and Knights (1968).

8. See Tawney's introduction to Wilson (1925), pp. 64–8.

9. See Ramsey, *op.cit.*, Chapter 5, 'The Role of Government', pp. 146–79; also Unwin (1904) on the Statute of Apprentices as an attempt 'to regulate all classes of the working population . . . by assigning to each class its proper place in the framework of a uniform system . . . a vain endeavour to give fixity and permanence to a condition of things which already, in great part, belonged to the past'. Cited in Knights, *op.cit.* p. 161.

10. On writers and government employment, see Lytle and Orgel (1981), Chapter 7, Jan van Dorsten's 'Literary Patronage in Elizabethan England: The early phase', pp. 191–206, and Chapter 8, Arthur F. Marotti's, 'John Donne and the Rewards of Patronage', pp. 207–34.

11. See Prouty, *op.cit.*, pp. 193–4 for this episode.

12. For Spenser's career as another case study in this process, see Bradbrook (1960).

13. Prouty, *op.cit.*, Chapter II, 'The Worldling', pp. 22–48.

14. Ibid., p. 61.

15. All references are to Gascoigne (1907), *The Poetry and Plays*, and Gascoigne (1910), *The Prose Works*.

16. More pragmatically, this means that the man without 'place' is, in terms of the world of élite status and influence, a nobody, a nothing. On this negation of identity by placelessness, see Donne's 1608 letter to Goodyer: 'At most, the greatest persons are but great wens, and excrescences . . . but as moales for ornament, except they be so incorporated into the body of the world, that they contribute something to the sustenation of the whole . . . to this hour I am nothing, or so little, that I am scarse subject and argument enough for one of mine own letters.' The similarly disappointed Raleigh signs one of his letters

to Robert Cecil 'Yours not worthy any name or title, W.R.'. Both citations are from Marotti, *op.cit.*, p. 228 and p. 244.

17. Helgerson (1976), pp. 365–6.
18. Ibid., p. 39.
19. All references are to Golding (1965).
20. All references are to Apuleius (1967).
21. Moly is the magical herb which the god Hermes gives to Odysseus to defend him from and counteract Circe's metamorphic enchantments. For God as the perfect object of a specifically male desire, see p. 107–8 below.
22. For Guyon as allegorical reader, see below, pp. 269–73.
23. See above, pp. 42–3.
24. See Panofsky (1962), Chapter 5, 'The Neoplatonic Movement in Florence and North Italy', pp. 129–70.
25. Compare Elyot's recommendations for saturating the young student's environment with the signifying 'matter' of orthodoxy, above, pp. 61–2. Also, compare Philip Stubbes's technology of godliness in 'A Perfect Pathway to Felicitie', which, in the words of Peter Stallybrass 'collects meditations and prayers to transform every day into a spectacle of holiness . . . . In the *Pathway* the daily activities of sleeping, washing, eating become the ritualised occasions for the training of a godly body.' See also Helgerson (1976), pp. 27–8.
26. On the stripping away of all music, visual imagery and 'theatrical' gesture from the forms of worship in Zwingli's Zurich, see O'Connell (1986), pp. 295–7.
27. See, for example, Gascoigne, *op.cit.*, pp. 90ff. On the penitential works as texts saturated by the patriarchal discourses of the Word, see Helgerson, *op.cit.*, p. 49. By plagiarising the Christian Fathers, Gascoigne (conveniently and economically) enacts that conservation of the Word, the mnemonic fidelity, which 'Gascoigne's Goodnight' and other works enjoin.
28. See above, pp. 66–71.
29. Greene (1881–83), Vol. XII, pp. 153–88, *The Repentance of Robert Greene*; this reference, p. 162. For Greene's commodification of his own guilt, see Helgerson, *op.cit.*, pp. 79–105.
30. See above, pp. 69–70.
31. See Doran, (1954), p. 402.
32. See above, p. 71.
33. Cited in an editor's note in the Arden *Hamlet*, (Shakespeare, 1982), p. 497.
34. Cited in Doran (1954), p. 402.
35. Cited in Doran (1954), p. 402.
36. Fulke Greville, *op.cit.*, stanza 108.
37. Cited in Vinge (1967), p. 36.
38. Ibid., p. 36.
39. Cited in Braden (1978), p. 12.
40. Gordon (1949), pp. 156–7.
41. Compare the discussion of the *place*, below, p. 149.
42. For the proper hierarchical subordination of rhetorical embellishment,

see, for example, Richard Carew, *The Excellencie of the English Tongue* (?1595–6) in Smith (1904), Vol. II, p. 286.

43. See the Epistle Dedicatory to Rainolde (1945).
44. Puttenham (1970), p. 148.
45. Roger Ascham, *The Scholemaster*, in Smith, *op.cit.*, Vol. I; this reference, p. 5.
46. Compare Puttenham, *op.cit.*, p. 302. On the display of effortlessness as a signifier of 'natural' status, compare Whigham (*op.cit.*, p. 35), on 'Castiglione's *sprezzatura*, designed to imply the natural or given status of one's social status and to deny any earned character, any labor or arrival from a social elsewhere'.
47. Compare Bradbrook, *op.cit.*, pp. 91–2: '. . . the forward youth in search of honour, who employed lyrics as an adjunct to social manoeuvres in the ceremonious but chancy game for preferment, would have offended against decorum by publishing his "toys" . . . . These were but "the perfume and suppliance of a minute"; and *sprezzatura* or courtly nonchalance forbade the author to claim them even by a signature.'
48. George Pettie, *The Civile Conversation of M. Stephen Guazzo*, cited in Miller (1959), p. 24.
49. Henry Peacham, cited in Spingarn (1908), Vol. I, p. 48.
50. Richard Rich, cited in Miller, *op.cit.*, p. 74.
51. Dekker, in Miller, ibid., p. 86. Compare the discussion of the array of imported luxury goods in the *Discourse of the Common Weal*, above, pp. 74–5.
52. Rich, cited in Miller, ibid., p. 88.
53. For the following points, see Miller, *op.cit.*, pp. 207–13.
54. The turn to the public presses is a necessity, given what Bradbrook refers to as 'the chancy game for preferment'. On the inadequacy of the patronage system to the financial support of the writer, see Brennan (1988), Chapter 1, 'The Pursuit of Patronage', particularly pp. 13–18. See also Helgerson, *op.cit.*, pp. 23–6.
55. Marston (1966), p. 2.
56. Nashe (1958), Vol. II, 'Pierce Penilesse his Supplication to the Divell', p. 199.
57. Pettie (1908), p. 8.
58. Greene (1881–83), Vol. XII, pp. 95–150, *Greenes Groates-Worth of Witte*; this reference, p. 139.
59. Gascoigne, *op.cit.*, Vol. I, pp. 3–8. We should add to these strategies the autobiographical application of the prodigal son narrative, as discussed in Helgerson, *op.cit.* (1976).
60. Cited in Miller, *op.cit.*, p. 104.
61. Compare Hooker, above, p. 26.
62. Puttenham, *op.cit.*, p. 186.
63. Compare Greene, *op.cit.*, pp. 249 and 306.
64. Murrin (1969), p. 121.
65. The function of allegory as a mediator between different, and potentially contradictory, audiences is alluded to by Sir John Harington in his *A Briefe Apology for Poetry*, where he describes it as 'able with one kinde

of meate and one dish (as I may so call it) to feed divers tastes' (in Smith, *op.cit.*, Vol. II, p. 203). Compare Miller's discussion of Spenser's use of allegory as a means of negotiating the problem of multiple address (*op.cit.*, p. 85).

Chapter 4

1. Gascoigne (1910), p. 419; Nashe, *The Anatomy of Abuses*, in Nashe (1958), Vol. 1., p. 34.
2. All references are to Puttenham (1970).
3. The painting is far from being a simple celebration of Humanist achievements; see the brilliant analysis of its anamorphic death's head in Greenblatt (1980), pp. 17–21.
4. Fulke Greville (1973); *Life of Sidney*, p. 149.
5. In Smith (1904), Vol. II, p. 286.
6. Peacham (1971); Dedicatory Epistle, Aij.
7. In Smith, *op.cit.*, Vol. I, p. 335.
8. Peacham, *op.cit.*, p. 6.
9. References are to the King James Bible (1611): Genesis 1 and John 1.
10. Compare Louis Montrose (1983), p. 436: 'Having duly invoked the Divinity at the beginning of his work, Puttenham is thenceforth free to ignore metaphysical and theological perspectives. He can devote the rest of his substantial treatise to the place of poets and poetry in a pervasively secular world of human "experience and observation", a world shaped by human beings in their own images and in their own interests.' My own argument is that Puttenham's attachment to 'metaphysical and theological perspectives' is far more deeply entrenched than any formal invocation of the Deity suggests, in the structuring presuppositions of the 'official', logocentric, ideology of his text. While I share Montrose's emphasis on the secularity of Puttenham's 'world', I am accordingly more concerned than his position allows with the contradictory, and self-estranging nature of Puttenham's ideological negotiations with that world.
11. For an authoritative statement of this fundamental Humanist position, see Starkey (1948), pp. 164–6.
12. Cited in Hunter (1967), p. 17. On educational discourse and social mobility, see MacCaffrey (1961), and Ferguson (1965), p. 227; on courtesy literature as the educational genre most closely embroiled with the process of social mobility, see Whigham (1984).
13. See Whigham, ibid., pp. 32–3: 'For established and mobile Elizabethans alike, public life at court was governed by a rhetorical imperative of performance . . . . Elite status no longer rested on the absolute, given base of birth, the received ontology of social being; instead it had increasingly become a matter of doing, and so of *showing*' (Whigham's emphasis).
14. See above, p. 136.
15. See above, p. 137.

16. My account of the tension between paradigm and speech-act is parallel to Manley's description of a 'Horatian' poetic derived inductively from the 'contingencies of end, affect, time, place, circumstance and tradition', in tension with an enclosing 'naturalist poetics', in which 'All relations of fitness arise from the natural possibility of proportion'(p. 180). Manley's discussion focuses more exclusively on Puttenham's work as an art of *poetry* than I do here.

17. See the previous chapter, and Ramsey (1965), Chapter 5, 'The Role of Government', pp. 146–79.

18. For the development of a single, codified English, see Jones (1953).

19. As Manley notes, this characteristic of Puttenham's treatise was spotted by Sir John Harington, in a condescending passage in the *Briefe Apology for Poetry* (in Smith, *op.cit.*, Vol. II): '. . . though the poore gentlemen laboreth greatly to prove or rather to make Poetrie an art', he fails because he merely 'reciteth as you may see, in the plurall number, some pluralities of patterns, and parcels of . . . Poetrie'(p. 197).

20. Compare Whigham, *op.cit.*, pp. 5–6, on the contradictory address of the courtesy books, to both the upwardly aspirant, and the established elite.

21. See Erasmus (1973), pp. 157–72.

22. See More (1965), pp. 21–31; also Greenblatt's (1980) account of *Utopia*'s 'disquieting internal rupture', pp. 22–4.

23. Trousdale (1982), p. 50.

24. Compare Manley's discussion of 'the logocentric universe of the Renaissance' and its 'firm analogy between cosmic order and artistic principle'. He quotes (p. 16) John Hoskins *Directions for Speech and Style*; 'The Order of God's creatures in themselves is not only admirable and glorious, but eloquent; then he that should apprehend the consequence of things in their truth and utter his apprehensions as truly were a right orator.' This conflation of truth and utterance, or the categories of logic and rhetoric, is pursued at length in McNally (1969), Howell (1956) and Seigel (1968).

25. Jonathan Crewe (1986) gives this fall a more specific location in Puttenham's discourse, namely in the break which the emergence of drama introduces into Puttenham's 'history' of the poetic genres. See Crewe (1986), pp. 75–7.

Chapter 5

1. Fulke Greville, 'A Treatise of War'; Gabriel Harvey, *Marginalia*; both in Haydn (1946), pp. 129–30 and 235–6 respectively.

2. All references are to Castiglione (1928).

3. See Skinner (1978), Vol. 1; also Pocock (1975), Parts 1 and 2.

4. Pocock, ibid., p. viii.

5. For Guicciardini's historiographical practice and its political context, see Gilbert (1965), and Pocock, ibid., Chapter 5.

6. Pocock, ibid., p. 156.

7. See Erasmus (1973).

8. See More (1965), pp. 89–95; also the discussion in Greenblatt (1980), pp. 27–33, of More's dedication to a 'life lived as histrionic improvisation' in the 'theatrical' context of the Tudor court.

9. This quotation from the Ralph Robinson translation: see More (1910), p. 41.

10. On the problematic relationship of Book Four to the rest of *Il Cortegiano*, see Javitch (1978), p. 41, Rebhorn (1972), and Trafton (1972).

11. In a discussion of Puttenham's *Arte of English Poesie* as representing 'the failures of Renaissance humanism', Montrose (1983) traces this abdication of the Aristotelian civic orientation of humanistic counsel to the Neoplatonic and aestheticising stance of *Il Cortegiano*: 'The playworld of *Il Cortegiano* sublimates the political aspirations of the Italian social elite at a time when power was being consolidated in the hands of local princes and foreign kings. An analogous consolidation was undertaken by the Tudor dynasty' (p. 447). This 'sublimated' Castiglionian 'playworld' is seen as standing behind Puttenham's abandonment of any aspiration to the function of ethical or political counsellor in his vision of poet-courtiers as merely 'cunning princepleasers'. Montrose gives us a picture then of Castiglione and Puttenham at their analogous moments of proto-absolutist consolidation, declaring 'the impossible union between eloquence and virtue, the inevitable collusion between scholarship and power' (p. 438). A case can certainly be made for Puttenham's indifference to the higher aspirations of the Humanist courtier, but Montrose's account of Castiglione's treatise is seriously distorted. To begin with, it ignores Octavian's intervention in Book Four; presumably because it addresses precisely the question of the relationship between eloquence and virtue, the aesthetic accomplishments of the courtier and the political influence of the counsellor, which Montrose claims the treatise is obliged to 'sublimate'. Book Four is also the point at which the dialogical structure of the treatise matters most: far from the monological 'position' or 'message' which Montrose ascribes to it, here the treatise dramatises a variety of voices and positions, including the humanistic Octavian and the Neoplatonist Bembo, precisely as an invitation to assess different approaches to the questions of power and influence which Montrose invokes. That debate, around the humanistic agenda set by Octavian, shows Castiglione working not towards the 'sublimation' of political aspirations of which Montrose speaks (and in context, Montrose's 'sublimation' seems to mean 'abandonment'), but towards new strategies of counsel which will involve neither capitulation to princely power nor withdrawal from its corrupting environs. The currency of Castiglione's work in Elizabethan England thus represents an adaptation of the tradition of Humanist counsel to changed, and difficult, conditions, rather than its demise. Puttenham's work represents a different trajectory, derived from that tradition, but negating its ethical dimensions. Rather than assimilating both to the gloomy teleology of a putative 'death of Humanism', I think we should see the two Elizabethan texts (Puttenham and Hoby/Castiglione) as divergent responses to a domain of courtly politics where the centralisation of

power means that the strategies of counsel are obliged to become more indirect and 'theatrical', but are far from being wholly foreclosed.

12. Compare Manley (1980), p. 177: 'Like the psychagogic sweetness (*dulcia*) of the Horatian *Ars*, the "good grace [*sprezzatura*]" of the courtier's artless art is rhetorical in character.'

13. For this discussion of the constitution, and the choice between monarchy and democracy, see Castiglione, *op.cit.*, pp. 273–9.

Chapter 6

1. Thomas Elyot, *The Boke of the Governour*, Vol. 1, p. 6; Francis Bacon, *The Advancement of Learning*, Book 1, in Haydn (1946), p. 191.

2. All references are to Jonson, Vol. VII (1941), (the Masques), and Vol. IV (1932),(*Cynthia's Revels*).

3. For an authoritative overview of Ficino's work, see Kristeller (1943); also Cassirer (1963), pp. 64–74.

4. Kristeller, *op.cit.*, p. 166.

5. Ibid., p. 98.

6. See Wind (1968), pp. 90–5.

7. Cited in Wind, ibid., p. 219.

8. Ibid., p. 220.

9. For the trope of dismemberment in Neoplatonic discourse more generally, see Wind, ibid., p. 133.

10. Ficino, in Kristeller, *op.cit.*, p. 268.

11. Cited in Wind, *op.cit.*, p. 19.

12. Compare Gascoigne's regime of self-scrutiny, above, pp. 105–6.

13. All references are to Spenser (1933).

14. The education of Guyon in the disciplines of allegorical reading is also, of course, performed simultaneously upon the poem's reader. See Quilligan (1983), pp. 19–78 for Spenser's teaching of hero and reader to read 'typologically'.

15. All references are to Drayton (1961), Vol. 1, pp. 129–56.

16. For the concept of the *circuitus spiritualis*, see Panofsky (1962), p. 141.

17. For the development of the prince's role in the court masque and its predecessors, see Orgel (1965), Chapter 2, 'The Monarch as Masquer', pp. 19–35.

18. *The Vision of Delight*, ll. 176–8 and 201–4; in Jonson, *op.cit.*, Vol. X.

19. St Augustine, cited in Goldin (1967), p. 7; Derrida (1976), p. 36.

20. *Mercury Vindicated*, in Jonson, *op.cit.*, Vol. X; ll. 30–1.

21. 'It is a noble and iust aduantage, that the things subiected to *understanding* haue of those which are obiected to *sense*, that the one sort are but momentarie, and meerely taking; the other impressing, and lasting: Else the glorie of all these *solemnities* had perish'd like a blaze, and gone out, in the *beholders* eyes. So short-liu'd are the *bodies* of all things, in comparison of their *soules*. And, though *bodies* oft-times haue the ill luck to be sensually preferr'd, they find afterwards, the good fortune (when *soules* liue) to be utterly forgotten. This it is hath made the most

royall *Princes*, and greatest *persons* (who are commonly the *personators* of these *actions*) not onely studious of riches, and magnificence in the outward celebration, or shew; (which rightly becomes them) but curious after the most high, and heartie *inuentions*, to furnish the inward parts: (and those grounded vpon *antiquitie*, and solide *learnings*) which, though their *voyce* be taught to sound to present occasions, their *sense*, or doth, or should alwayes lay hold on more remou'd *mysteries*.' Jonson, *op.cit.*, Vol. X, p. 209.

22. See above, pp. 41–2.
23. All references are to Jonson (1981–82), Vol. II.
24. See above, pp. 86–90.
25. Castiglione (1928), pp. 276–7.
26. See above, pp. 166–9.
27. Erasmus (1973), p. 156. Compare Jerome Busleyden in a letter to Thomas More, November 1516: 'Your ideal state ... [in *Utopia*] ... devoted its energies not so much to forming laws as to training the most approved magistrates ... because after their likeness, the pattern of their virtue, the example of their conduct, the picture of their justice, the whole state and right course of any perfect commonwealth should be modelled.' Cited in Caspari, (1968), p. 91.
    See also the epigraph to this chapter from Elyot's *Boke of the Governour*.
28. It is interesting that the period also sees an increase in the use of mirrors; 'even men carried them at court, in their hats' (Neville Williams, cited in Whigham (1984), p. 224.)
29. See above, pp. 137–9.
30. On the original function of courtesy literature as a means of demarcating and reconfirming the circle of the 'authentic' courtier against the encroachments of the socially mobile 'imitators', see Whigham, *op.cit.*, p. 18.
31. See, for example, *Love Restored*, where Robin Goodfellow attempts to break through the throngs of the excluded and gain access to the masque itself (see above, p. 176). For the social and epistemological self-enclosure of the masque, see Barish (1960), pp. 244 and 245, and compare Montrose (1977): 'For those outside the Stuart court system, the court masque came to epitomise the cultural isolation, political tyranny, and spiritual corruption of the monarch and the aristocracy' (p. 35).
32. See Orgel (1975), p. 27.
33. See Gordon (1949), p. 159; also Orgel (1975), pp. 131–2.
34. Joseph Loewenstein (1988) sees *Cynthia's Revels* as Jonson's attempt to succeed Lyly as Master of the Revels, thereby effecting a career move from the increasing insecurities of the market-place to the relative security of royal patronage. Loewenstein accordingly sees Jonson confidently appropriating the Blackfriars as a theatrical location strategically 'straddling both spheres', and views the play's generic mix unproblematically as an 'attempt to fuse the techniques of public Humours comedy with those of the most immediately accessible model for a court dramaturgy, the mythological comedies of John

Lyly' (p. 270). My own argument stresses much more the problematic nature of Jonson's critical attitudes towards the Court even as he bids for its patronage, and of the contradictory coexistence of two different generic models at play within one dramatic frame. In short, where Loewenstein sees the authoritative management of a crucial career transition, I see a troubled hiatus within which resonate contradictions which will trouble Jonson throughout his years as a client of the Court.

35. According to Herford and Simpson (in Jonson, *op.cit.*, Vol. IV, p. 17), the Quarto is probably the text of the Court performance on 6 January 1601; the 1616 Folio adds passages in the fourth and fifth Acts which extend and sharpen the satire on the Court. As Herford and Simpson comment: ' "The knot of spiders", who filled the Court with their cobwebs, were handled trenchantly enough in the shortened version. But even Jonson had to put some curb on his censoriousness before such an audience: he not only suppressed a considerable portion of this satire at the Court performance of 1601, but he judged it politic not to print it in the text which appeared later in the year. He kept the manuscript, however, and drew upon it for the revision.'

36. Compare William Adlington's interpretation, in his 1566 translation of Apuleius' *The Golden Ass*, of the Actaeon story as what occurs 'when a man casteth his eyes upon the vaine and fading beauty of the world'. In the light of this conventional reading, Jonson's use of the Actaeon tale also assimilates Essex to the type of the man who mistakenly privileges the material entity over the Idea, or in Essex's case, I would suggest, the direct seizure of political power over the 'disinterestedness' of responsible counsel or service. The proximity of this reading of Actaeon to the dominant moralisations of Narcissus ties Jonson's use of Actaeon here more closely to the main body of the play. For more on Essex's violation of the complex code of amorous interaction between Elizabeth and her courtiers, see Montrose (1983), 'Of Gentlemen and Shepherds', pp. 441 and 444. Montrose (1977), 'Celebration and Insinuation', discusses Philip Sidney's 'Lady of May' and 'The Triumph of the Fortress of Perfect Beauty' as case studies in such erotic/political negotiation, centring upon a 'relationship between courtier-poets and queen . . . idealised as a love purified of physical desire'. It is precisely that erotic-political contract, so brilliantly analysed in this and Montrose's other studies, which Essex violates. See also Barkan (1980) for the full mythographic history of the Actaeon tale.

37. On the commodification of elite identity in courtesy books, see Whigham, *op.cit.*, especially p. 5.

38. See above, pp. 109–12.

39. Compare Whigham, *op.cit.*, p. 168: 'The spirals of extreme fashion and planned obsolescence emanated from the same center where the sumptuary prohibitions originated.'

40. The logical extreme of this refinement of vision within the empirical field of theatrical viewing is to be found in the invocation of a 'blind audience' in the Prologue to *The Staple of News* (1604):

> For your owne sakes, not his, he bad me say,
> Would you were come to heare, not see a Play.
> 　　　　. . . he'ld haue you wise,
> Much rather by your eares, then by your eyes:
> 　　　(Jonson, *op.cit.*, Vol. VI (1938), p. 282)

The tension between theatrical specularity and rational speculation persists throughout Jonson's career: O'Connell (1986), p. 300, sees the publication of the *Works* in 1616 as the logical outcome of Jonson's tendency to treat his plays as poems to be read rather than dramas to be seen. See also Barish (1973) and Murray (1983).

41. For the attacks on the boy's companies, see Jardine (1983), Chapter 1; and the anonymous pamphlet of 1569, attacking the children of the chapel Royal, cited in Furnivall's note to *Hamlet*, II.ii.327 (Shakespeare, 1963): 'Euen in her maiesties chapel do these pretty upstart youthes profane the Lordes day by the lasciuious writhing of their tender limbes, and gorgeous decking of their aparrell, in feigning bawdie fables gathered from the idolatrous heathen poets.'
42. See above, p. 85.
43. See above, p. 89.
44. Palinode, line 13.

Afterword

1. See above, pp. 1–2.
2. Extracts from Calendar of State Papers, Domestic, 1603–25, cited in *Eastward Hoe*, ed. Julia Hamlet Harris, (New Haven: Yale University Press, 1926). All subsequent citations are from this text unless otherwise stated.
3. H. M. Robertson, 'Sir Bevis Bulmer: a large-scale speculator of Elizabethan and Jacobean times', *Journal of Economic and Business History*, Vol. IV, 1931–32, pp. 99–120; this citation, pp. 110–11.

Bibliography

Allen, Don Cameron (1970), *Mysteriously Meant: The rediscovery of pagan symbolism and allegorical interpretation in the Renaissance* (Baltimore: Johns Hopkins Press).

Apuleius (1967), *The Golden Asse*, trans. William Adlington [1566], (New York: AMS Press).

Armstrong, A. Hillary (1967), *St.Augustine and Christian Platonism* (Villanova, Pa.: Villanova University Press).

Ascham, Roger (1967), *The Schoolmaster*, ed. Lawrence V. Ryan (New York: Cornell University Press).

Ashton, R. (1960), *The Crown and the Money Market, 1603–1640* (Oxford: Clarendon Press).

Bacon, Sir Francis (1985), *The essayes or Counsels, Civill and Morall*, ed. Michael Kiernan (Oxford: Clarendon Press).

Baker, Herschel (1952), *The Wars of Truth: Studies in the decay of Christian Humanism in the earlier seventeenth century* (New York: Staples Press).

Baldwin, Frances Elizabeth (1926), 'Sumptuary legislation and personal regulation in England', *Johns Hopkins University Studies in Historical and Political Science*, 44, no. 1, pp. 11–282.

Barish, J. A. (1960), *Ben Jonson and the Language of Prose Comedy* (Cambridge, Mass.: Norton).

Barish, J. A. (1973), 'Jonson and the loathed stage', in William Blissett, Julian Patrick and R. W. Van Fossen (eds.), *A Celebration of Ben Jonson* (Toronto: University of Toronto Press).

Barish, J. A. (1981), *The Antitheatrical Prejudice* (Berkeley and LA: University of California Press).

Barkan, Leonard (1980), 'Diana and Actaeon: the myth as synthesis', English Literary Renaissance, vol. 10, no. 3, pp. 317–59.

Barthes, Roland (1987), *Mythologies* (London: Paladin).

Baudrillard, Jean (1981), *For a Critique of the Political Economy of the Sign* (St Louis: Telos Press).

Beier, A. L. (1985), *Masterless Men: the vagrancy problem in England 1560–1640* (London: Routledge).

Boccaccio (1930), *The Genealogy of the Gods*, in *Boccaccio on Poetry*, ed. Charles G. Osgood (Princeton: Princeton University Press).

Bowlby, Rachel (1985), *Just Looking: Consumer culture in Dreiser, Gissing*

234   *Bibliography*

and Zola (New York: Routledge).

Bradbrook, Muriel (1960), ' "No room at the top": Spenser's pursuit of fame', in *Elizabethan Poetry*, Stratford upon Avon Studies 2 (London: Edward Arnold).

Braden, Gordon (1978), *The Classics and English Renaissance Poetry – Three case studies* (New Haven and London: Yale University Press).

Brennan, Michael (1988), *Literary Patronage in the Renaissance: The Pembroke family* (London: Routledge).

Buckley, G. T. (1965), *Atheism in the English Renaissance* (Chicago: University of Chicago Press).

Burke, Kenneth (1969), *A Rhetoric of Motives* (Berkeley, Los Angeles: University of California Press).

Callahan, John F. (1967), *Augustine and the Greek Philosophers* (Villanova, Pa.: Villanova University Press).

Campbell, L. B. (ed.) (1938), *The Mirror for Magistrates* (Cambridge: Cambridge University Press).

Campbell, L. B. (1947), *Shakespeare's Histories: Mirrors of Elizabethan policy* (Huntington Library, San Marino, California).

Caspari, Fritz (1968), *Humanism and the Social Order in Tudor England* (New York: Teachers College Press).

Cassirer, Ernst (1963), *The Individual and the Cosmos in Renaissance Philosophy*, trans. Mario Domandi (Oxford: Basil Blackwell).

Castiglione, Baldassare (1928), *The Book of the Courtier*, trans. Sir Thomas Hoby (London: Everyman).

Cave, Terence (1979), *The Cornucopian Text* (Oxford: Clarendon Press).

Certain Sermons or Homilies Appointed to be Read in Churches in the time of Queen Elizabeth of famous memory (1890), (Society for Promoting Christian Knowledge).

Chadwick, Henry (1986), *Augustine* (Oxford: Oxford University Press).

Cohen, Walter (1987), 'Political criticism of Shakespeare', in Jean E. Howard and Marion F. O'Connor (eds.), *Shakespeare Reproduced: The text in history and ideology* (New York and London: Methuen).

Colie, Rosalie, L. (1966), *Paradoxica Epidemica: The Renaissance tradition of paradox* (Princeton, NJ: Princeton University Press).

Collinson, P. (1967), *The Elizabethan Puritan Movement* (Oxford: Oxford University Press).

Copleston, F.C., *A History of Philosophy*: vol. 2 (1950) *Medieval Philosophy*; vol. 3 (1953) *Ockham to Suarez* (London: Burns, Oates and Washbourne).

Cressy, David (1976), 'Describing the social order of Elizabethan and Stuart England', *Literature and History*, no. 3, March, pp. 29–44.

Crewe, Jonathan (1986), 'The hegemonic theatre of George Puttenham', *ELR*, vol. 16, pp. 71–85.

Cross, Claire (ed.) (1969), *The Royal Supremacy in the Elizabethan Church* (London: Allen & Unwin).

Curtius, E. R. (1953), *European Literature and the Latin Middle Ages*, trans. W. R. Trask (New York: Princeton University Press).

Deloney, Thomas (1961), *The Novels of Thomas Deloney*, ed. Merritt E. Lawliss (Bloomington: Indiana University Press).

Derrida, Jacques (1976), *Of Grammatology*, trans. G. C. Spivak (Baltimore: Johns Hopkins University Press).

Dewar, M. (ed.) (1969), *A Discourse of the Common Weal of this Realm of England* (Charlottesville, Va: University Press of Virginia).

Dollimore, Jonathan (1984), *Radical Tragedy: Religion, ideology and power in the plays of Shakespeare and his contemporaries* (Brighton: Harvester Wheatsheaf).

Doran, Madeleine (1954), *Endeavours of Art* (Madison, Wisconsin: University of Wisconsin Press).

Drayton, Michael (1961), *The Works*, ed. J. W. Hebel (Oxford: Basil Blackwell).

Edwards, Philip (1979), *Threshold of a Nation: A study in English and Irish drama* (Cambridge: Cambridge University Press).

Einstein, Lewis (1902), *The Italian Renaissance in England* (New York and London: Columbia Press/Macmillan).

Eliot, John (1968 [1593]), *Ortho-Epia Gallica. Eliots Fruits for the French* (Menston: Scholars Press).

Elyot, Thomas (1967), *The Boke named the Gouernour*, ed. H. H. S. Croft (New York: B. Franklin).

Erasmus, Desiderius (1973), *The Education of a Christian Prince*, trans, Lester K. Born (New York: Columbia University Press).

Foxe, John (1965), *Foxe's Book of Martyrs* (abridged), ed. G. A. Williamson (London: Secker & Warburg).

Fulke Greville (1973), *Selected Writings*, ed. Joan Rees (London: Athlone Press).

Ferguson, Arthur B. (1965), *The Articulate Citizen and the English Renaissance* (Durham, NC: Duke University Press).

Fraser, Russell (1970), *The War Against Poetry* (Princeton: Princeton University Press).

Gascoigne, George (1907, 1910), *The Complete Works*, ed. J. W. Cunliffe, 2 Vols. (Cambridge: Cambridge University Press).

Gascoigne, George (1970 [1573]), *A hundreth sundrie flowres bounde up in one small posie: A hundred sundry flowers* (Menston: Scholars Press).

Gilbert, Felix (1965), *Machiavelli and Guicciardini: Politics and history in sixteenth century Florence* (Princeton, NJ: Princeton University Press).

Goldin, Frederick (1967), *The Mirror of Narcissus in the Courtly Love Lyric* (Ithaca, NY: Cornell University Press).

Golding, Arthur (1965), *Ovid's Metamorphoses*, ed. J. F. Nims (New York: Macmillan).

Gordon, D. J. (1949), 'Poet and architect: the intellectual context of the argument between Ben Jonson and Inigo Jones', *Journal of the Warburg and Courtauld Institutes*, vol. 12, pp. 152–78.

Gray, Hannah H. (1963), 'Renaissance Humanism: the pursuit of eloquence', *Journal of the History of Ideas*, 24, pp. 497–514.

Great Britain (1770), *The Statutes at Large, vol. 2: From the first year of King Edward IV to the end of the reign of Queen Elizabeth*.

Greenblatt, Stephen (1980), *Renaissance Self-Fashioning: from More to Shakespeare* (Chicago: University of Chicago Press).

Greenblatt, Stephen (1985), 'Invisible bullets: Renaissance authority and its subversion. *Henry IV* and *Henry V*', in J. Dollimore and A. Sinfield (eds.), *Political Shakespeare* (Manchester: Manchester University Press), pp. 18–47.

Greene, Robert (1881–83), *The Life and Complete Works*, ed. A. B. Grosart, 15 Vols (London: The Huth Library).

Greene, Robert (1966), *Greenes Groates-Worth of Witte and The Repentance of Robert Greene* (Edinburgh: Edinburgh University Press).

Haller, William (1963), *Foxe's Book of Martyrs and the Elect Nation* (London: Jonathan Cape).

Harrison, William (1897), *The Description of England*, reprinted as *The Description of England in Shakespeare's Youth*, ed. F. J. Furnivall (London: New Shakespeare Society).

Haydn, Hiram (ed.) (1946), *The Portable Elizabethan Reader* (New York: The Viking Press).

Hazard, Mary E. (1976), 'An essay to amplify "ornament": some Renaissance theory and practise', *Studies in English Literature*, xvi, 21, pp. 15–32..

Helgerson, R. (1976), *The Elizabethan Prodigals* (Berkeley and London: University of California Press).

Hexter, J. H. (1950), 'The education of the aristocracy in the Renaissance', *Journal of Modern History*, xxii, pp. 1–20.

Hill, Christopher (1979), *Reformation to Industrial Revolution: The Pelican economic history of Britain vol. 2, 1530–1780* (Harmondsworth: Penguin).

Histriomastix (1878), in Richard Simpson (ed.), *The School of Shakespeare*, 2 Vols. (London).

Holstun, James (1989), 'Ranting at the New Historicism', *ELR*, vol. 19, no. 2, Spring, pp. 189–225.

Hooker, Richard (1907), *Of the Laws of Ecclesiastical Polity*, 2 Vols., ed. Christopher Morris (London: Everyman).

Howard, Jean E. (1986), 'The New Historicism in Renaissance studies', *ELR*, vol. 16, pp. 13–43.

Howard, Jean E. and O'Connor, Marion F. (eds.) (1987), *Shakespeare Reproduced: The text in history and ideology* (New York and London: Routledge).

Howell, Wilbur H. (1956), *Logic and Rhetoric in England, 1500–1700* (Princeton, NJ: Princeton University Press).

Hunt, E. K. and Sherman, H. J. (1972), *Economics: An introduction to traditional and radical views* (New York: Harper Collins).

Hunter, G. K. (1967), 'Humanism and courtship', in *Elizabethan Poetry: Modern essays in criticism*, ed. Paul J. Alpers (Oxford: Oxford University Press).

Hurstfield, Joel (1973), *Freedom, Corruption and Government in Elizabethan England* (London: Jonathan Cape).

Jardine, Lisa (1983), *Still Harping on Daughters: Women and drama in the age of Shakespeare* (Brighton and Totowa, NJ: Harvester Wheatsheaf).

Javitch, Daniel (1978), *Poetry and Courtliness in Renaissance England*, (Princeton, NJ: Princeton University Press).

Jeffery, Violet M. (1928), *John Lyly and the Italian Renaissance* (Paris: H. Champion).

Jones, Richard Foster (1953), *The Triumph of the English Language* (Stanford: Stanford University Press).

Jonson, Ben, *The Works*, ed. C. H. Herford and P. and E. Simpson (Oxford: Oxford University Press). Dates as follows: Vol. IV (*Cynthia's Revels*), 1932. Vol. VI (*The Staple of News*), 1938. Vol. VII (The Masques), 1941. Vol. X (Commentary), 1950.

Jonson, Ben (1981–82), *The Complete Plays*, ed. G. A. Wilkes (Oxford: Clarendon Press); Vol. II, *Cynthia's Revels*.

Joseph, Sister Miriam (1947), *Shakespeare's Use of the Arts of Language* (New York: Columbia University Press).

Kelley, Donald R. (1970), *Foundations of Modern Historical Scholarship: Language, law, and history in the French Renaissance* (New York: Columbia University Press).

Knights, L. C. (1968), *Drama and Society in the age of Jonson* (London: Chatto & Windus).

Kristeller, P. O. (1943), *The Philosophy of Marsilio Ficino* (New York: Columbia University Press).

La Guardia, Eric (1966), *Nature Redeemed: The imitation of order in three Renaissance poems* (The Hague: Mouton).

Lake, Peter (1988), *Anglicans and Puritans? Presbyterianism and English conformist thought from Whitgift to Hooker* (London: Allen & Unwin).

Lanham, Richard (1976), *The Motives of Eloquence: Literary rhetoric in the Renaissance* (New Haven: Yale University Press).

Lewis, C. S. (1954), *English Literature in the Sixteenth Century, Excluding Drama* (Oxford: Oxford University Press).

Liu, Alan (1989), 'The power of Formalism: The New Historicism', *ELH*, vol. 56, no. 4, Winter, pp. 721–72.

Loewenstein, Joseph (1988), 'The script in the marketplace', in S. Greenblatt (ed.), *Representing the Renaissance* (Berkeley, LA: University of California Press), pp. 265–78.

Lovejoy, A. O. (1936), *The Great Chain of Being: A study in the history of an idea* (Cambridge, Mass.: Harvard University Press).

Lyly, John (1953), *The Complete Works*, 3 Vols., ed. R. Warwick Bond (Oxford: Clarendon Press).

Lytle, G. F. and Orgel, S. (eds.) (1981), *Patronage in the Renaissance* (Princeton, NJ: Princeton University Press).

MacCaffrey, Wallace T. (1961), 'Place and patronage in Elizabethan politics', in *Elizabethan Government and Society: Essays presented to Sir John Neale*, ed. S. T. Bindoff, J. Hurstfield and C. H. Williams (London: Athlone Press).

Major, J. Russell (1969), 'The Renaissance monarchy as seen by Erasmus, More, Seysell and Machiavelli', in T. K. Rabb and J. E. Siegel (eds.), *Action and Conviction in Early Modern Europe* (Princeton, NJ: Princeton University Press).

Manley, Lawrence (1980), *Convention 1500–1750* (Harvard: Harvard University Press).

Marston, John (1966), *The Scourge of Villanie*, ed. G. B. Harrison (Edinburgh: Edinburgh University Press).

Matthiesson, F. O. (1965), *Translation: An Elizabethan art* (New York: Octagon Books).

McNally, James R. (1969), 'Rector et dux Populi: Italian Humanists and the relationship between rhetoric and logic', *Modern Philology*, 67, pp. 168–76.

Miller, E. H. (1959), *The Professional Writer in Elizabethan England* (Cambridge, Mass.: Harvard University Press).

Montgomery, Robert L. (1979), *The Reader's Eye: Studies in didactic literary theory from Dante to Tasso* (University of California: University of California Press).

Montrose, Louis Adrian (1977), 'Celebration and insinuation: Sir Philip Sidney and the motives of Elizabethan courtship', in *Renaissance Drama*, New Series, Vol. VIII, ed. L. Barkan (Evanston: Northwestern University Press), pp. 3–35.

Montrose, Louis Adrian (1980), ' "Eliza, Queene of shepheardes", and the pastoral of power', *English Literary Renaissance*, 10, pp. 153–82.

Montrose, Louis Adrian (1983), 'Of gentlemen and shepherds: the politics of Elizabethan pastoral form', *ELH*, 50, pp. 415–19.

Montrose, Louis Adrian (1986a), 'Renaissance literary studies and the subject of history', *ELR*, vol. 16, pp. 5–12.

Montrose, Louis Adrian (1986b), 'The Elizabethan subject and the Spenserian text', in Patricia Parker and David Quint (eds.), *Literary Theory/Renaissance Texts* (Baltimore and London: Johns Hopkins University Press).

More, Thomas (1910), *Utopia*, trans. Ralph Robinson (London: Dent).

More, Thomas (1965), *Utopia*, ed. Edward Surtz S. J., and J. H. Hexter (New Haven and London: Yale University Press).

Mulcaster, Richard (1970), *Positions*, abridged and edited by Richard L. DeMolen (Columbia University, NY: Teachers College Press).

Murray, Tim (1983), 'From foul sheets to legitimate model: antitheater, text, Ben Jonson', *NLH*, 14, pp. 641–64.

Murrin, Michael (1989), *The Veil of Allegory: Some notes towards a theory of allegorical rhetoric in the English Renaissance* (Chicago and London: University of Chicago Press).

Nashe, Thomas (1958), *The Works*, ed. Ronald B. McKerrow and F. P. Wilson (Oxford: Basil Blackwell).

Nelson, William (1973), *Fact or Fiction: The dilemma of the Renaissance storyteller* (Cambridge, Mass.: Harvard University Press).

New, J. F. H. (1964), *Anglican and Puritan: The basis of their opposition, 1558–1640* (London: A. & C. Black).

Norbrook, David (1984), *Poetry and Politics in the English Renaissance* (London: Routledge).

O'Connell, Michael (1980), 'The idolatrous eye: iconoclasm, anti-theatricalism, and the image of the Elizabethan theatre', *ELH*, vol. 52, pp. 279–310.

Orgel, Stephen (1965), *The Jonsonian Masque* (Harvard: Columbia University Press).

Orgel, Stephen (1968), ' "To make boards speak": Inigo Jones's stage and Jonsonian Masque', in *Renaissance Drama: New series I*, ed. S. Schoenbaum (Evanston: Northwestern University Press).

Orgel, Stephen (1975), *The Illusion of Power: Political theatre in the English*

Renaissance (Berkeley: University of California Press).

Orgel, Stephen (1973) and Roy Strong, *Inigo Jones* (Berkeley: University of California Press).

Panofsky, E. (1962), *Studies in Iconology: Humanistic themes in the art of the renaissance* (New York: Harper Collins).

Peacham, Henry (1962), *The Complete Gentleman*, ed. V. B. Heltzel (New York: Folger Shakespeare Library, Columbia University Press).

Peacham, Henry (1971 [1577]), *The Garden of Eloquence* (Menston: Scholars Press).

Pettie, George (1908 [1576]), *A Petite Pallace of Pettie his Pleasures* ed. I. Gollancz (London: Chatto & Windus).

Pocock, J. G. A. (1975), *The Machiavellian Moment: Florentine political thought and the Atlantic republican tradition* (Princeton, NJ: Princeton University Press).

Popkin, R. H. (1960), *The History of Skepticism from Erasmus to Descartes* (Assen: Van Gorcum).

Prouty, C. T. (1966), *George Gascoigne: Elizabethan courtier, soldier and poet* (New York: Benjamin Bloom).

Public Record Office (1978), *Complete State Papers Domestic, Series 1: 1547–1625* (Hassocks).

Puttenham, George (1970), *The Arte of Englishe Poesie*, ed. G. D. Wilcock and A. Walker, (Cambridge: Cambridge University Press).

Quilligan, Maureen (1983), *Milton's Spenser: The politics of reading* (Ithaca, NY: Cornell University Press).

Rainolde, Richard (1945 [1563]), *The Foundacion of Rhetorike*, introduced by F. R. Johnson (New York: Scholars' Facsimiles and Reprints).

Ramsey, P. (1963), *Tudor Economic Problems* (London: Gollancz).

Ramsey, P. (ed.) (1971), *The Price Revolution in Sixteenth Century England* (London: Methuen).

Rebhorn, A. (1972), 'Octavian's interruption: Book IV and the problem of unity in Ii Libro del Cortegiano', *MLN*, 87, pp. 37–59.

Ricks, C. (1963), *Milton's Grand Style* (Oxford: Oxford University Press).

Robertson, D. W. (1962), *A Preface to Chaucer: studies in medieval perspectives* (Princeton, NJ: Princeton University Press).

Robertson, H. M. (1933), *Aspects of the Rise of Economic Individualism* (Cambridge: Cambridge University Press).

Rose, Mary Beth (1984), 'Women in men's clothing: apparel and social stability in *The Roaring Girl*', *ELR*, vol. 14, no. 3, Autumn, pp. 367–91.

Rosenberg, Eleanor (1976), *Leicester: Patron of letters* (New York: Octagon Books).

Saccone, Eduardo (1979), 'Grazia, sprezzatura, and affetazione in Castiglione's *Book of the Courtier*', *Glyph*, 5, (Baltimore:), pp. 34–54.

Salgado, G. (1972), *Cony-catchers and Bawdy Baskets: An anthology of Elizabethan low-life* (Harmondsworth: Penguin).

Saunders, J. W. (1951), 'The stigma of print. A note on the social basis of Tudor poetry', *Essays in Criticism*, I, pp. 139–64.

Seigel, Jerrold (1968), *Rhetoric and Philosophy in Renaissance Humanism: The union of eloquence and wisdom, Petrarch to Valla* (Princeton, NJ:

Princeton University Press).

Shakespeare, William (1963), *Hamlet*, A New Variorum Edition, ed. H. H. Furness, 2 Vols., revised reprint of the 1877 edition (New York: Dover).

Shakespeare, William (1982), *Hamlet*, the Arden edition, ed. Harold Jenkins (London: Methuen).

Shakespeare's England (1916), (Oxford: Clarendon Press).

Shapiro, Michael (1977), *Children of the Revels: The boy companies of Shakespeare's time and their plays* (New York: Columbia University Press).

Sheavyn, Phoebe (1909), *The Literary Profession in the Elizabethan Age* (Manchester: Manchester University Press).

Shell, M. (1982), *Money, Language and Thought: Literary and philosophical economies from the medieval to the modern era* (Berkeley: University of California Press).

Sinfield, Alan (1983), *Literature in Protestant England, 1560–1660* (London: Croom Helm).

Skinner, Quentin (1978), *The Foundations of Modern Political Thought*, 2 Vols. (Cambridge: Cambridge University Press).

Smith, G. Gregory (ed.) (1904), *Elizabethan Critical Essays*, 2 Vols. (London: Oxford University Press).

Smith, Hallett (1952), *Elizabethan Poetry. A study in conventions, meaning and expression* (Cambridge, Mass.: Harvard University Press).

Spenser, Edmund (1932–49), *The Works*, ed. E. Greenlaw, C. G. Osgood and F. M. Padelford (Baltimore: Johns Hopkins University Press).

Spingarn, Joel E. (1908–9), *A History of Literary Criticism in the Renaissance* (Oxford: Clarendon Press).

Stallybrass, Peter (1987), 'Reading the body: *The Revenger's Tragedy* and the Jacobean theater of consumption', *Renaissance Drama*, New Series, XVIII, ed. Mary Beth Rose (Evanston: Northwestern University Press and Newberry Library for Renaissance Studies), pp. 121–48.

Starkey, Thomas (1948), *A Dialogue between Cardinal Pole and Thomas Lupset*, ed. K. M. Burton (London: Chatto & Windus).

Stone, Lawrence (1964), 'The educational revolution in England, 1560–1640', *Past and Present*, 28, July, pp. 41–80.

Stone, Lawrence (1965), *The Crisis of the Aristocracy* (Oxford: Oxford University Press).

Stone, Lawrence (1966), 'Social mobility in England, 1500–1700', in *Past and Present*, 33, April, pp. 16–55.

Tawney, R. H. (1926), *Religion and the Rise of Capitalism* (London: Murray).

Tawney, R. H. and Power, E. (eds.) (1924), *Tudor Economic Documents*, 3 Vols. (London: Longman).

Taylor, Barry (1982), *Some Problems of Time and Desire in Renaissance Writing*, MA Dissertation, University of Sussex.

Tigerstedt, E. N. (1968), 'The poet as creator: origins of a metaphor', *Comparative Literature Studies*, 5, pp. 455–88.

Todorov, T. (1982), *Theories of the Symbol*, trans. Catherine Porter (Oxford: Basil Blackwell).

Trafton, Dain A. (1972), 'Structure and meaning in *The Courtier*', *ELN*, 2, pp. 283–97.

Trousdale, Marion (1982), *Shakespeare and the Rhetoricians* (London: Scholars Press).

Tuve, Rosamond (1966), *Allegorical Imagery* (Princeton, NJ: Princeton University Press).

Unwin, George (1904), *Industrial Organisation in the Sixteenth and Seventeenth Centuries* (Oxford: Clarendon).

Veeser, H. Aram (ed.) (1989), *The New Historicism* (London: Routledge).

Vinge, Louise (1967), *The Narcissus Theme in Western European Literature up to the Early Nineteenth Century* (Lund: Gleerups).

Wayne, Don E. (1987), 'Power, politics and the Shakespearean text', in Jean E. Howard and Marion F. O'Connor (eds.), *Shakespeare Reproduced: The text in history and ideology* (New York and London: Methuen).

Welsby, Paul. A. (ed.) (1970), *Sermons and Society: An Anglican anthology* (Harmondsworth: Penguin).

Welsford, Enid (1927), *The Court Masque* (Cambridge: Cambridge University Press).

Whigham, Frank (1984), *Ambition and Privilege: The social tropes of Elizabethan courtesy theory*, (Berkeley, Los Angeles and London: University of California Press).

Wilson, John Dover (ed.) (1944), *Life in Shakespeare's England: A book of Elizabethan prose* (Harmondsworth: Penguin).

Wind, Edgar (1968), *Pagan Mysteries in the Renaissance* (London: Faber & Faber).

Wilkes, G. A. (ed.) (1931), *The Complete Plays of Ben Jonson* (Oxford: Oxford University Press).

Wilson, Thomas (1925 [1572]), *A Discourse Upon Usury*, with an historical introduction by R. H. Tawney (London: G. Bell & Sons).

Woodhouse, J. R. (1978), *Baldesar Castiglione: A re-assessment of* The Courtier (Edinburgh: Edinburgh University Press).

Wright, Louis B. (1932), 'Translations for the Elizabethan middle class', *The Library*, 4th Series, vol. 13, no. 3, December, pp. 312–31.

Yates, Frances (1934), *John Florio: The life of an Italian in Shakespeare's England* (Cambridge: CUP).

Index